Wakefield Press

Imagining Home

Migrants and the search for a new belonging

Imagining Home

Migrants and the search for a new belonging

Edited by

Diana Glenn, Eric Bouvet and Sonia Floriani

Wakefield
Press

Wakefield Press
1 The Parade West
Kent Town
South Australia 5067
www.wakefieldpress.com.au

First published 2011

Cover illustration: rooftop mosaic by Antoni Gaudí for the Casa Batlló in Barcelona, photograph by Diana Glenn
Designed and typeset by Michael Deves, Wakefield Press
Printed in Australia by Griffin Digital, Adelaide

National Library of Australia Cataloguing-in-Publication entry

Title:	Imagining home: migrants and the search for a new belonging / edited by Diana Glenn, Eric Bouvet and Sonia Floriani.
ISBN:	978 1 74305 006 4 (pbk.).
Subjects:	Immigrants – Cultural assimilation – Australia. Emigration and immigration – Psychological aspects. Belonging (Social psychology) – Australia. Social integration – Australia.
Other Authors/ Contributors:	Glenn, Diana Cavuoto. Bouvet, Eric. Floriani, Sonia.
Dewey Number:	303.48200994

To our beloved children
Stephen, Sébastien and Selene

Contents

Migrants, home, belonging and self-identities

Diana Glenn, Sonia Floriani and Eric Bouvet

The peer-reviewed essays presented in this interdisciplinary volume explore the many facets of migration and the consequences of displacement on the biographies of those individuals who undertake the experience. As such, they provide an insight into the complexity of migration as an event and as an object of study. The core intent of the chapters is to analyse how migrants both experience and express the complex nature of migration, and how this biographical event of tremendous importance can affect and transform individual lives and community networks. The title of the volume – *Imagining Home. Migrants and the search for a new belonging* – is a synthesis of the key issue that is shared to varying degrees by all of the contributors in their analysis of the conflicting concepts of migration and home, and the many ways that the two notions can question and redefine each other. In other words, the assumption that the migrant's sense of disorientation about their home and their sense of belonging – which can be a consequence of the pluralisation of self-identities, languages, biographical plans and places that inevitably occurs in a migratory experience – turns out to be a more or less active search for a new home and a new sense of belonging.

As can be attested from the chapters of this volume, migration is above all experienced as a biographical 'trauma' through which migrants lose their sense of home and thus perceive themselves – metaphorically, at least – as homeless. The shift in the migrant's experience from *feeling at home* to *becoming homeless* lies at the core of most of the chapters. The authors assume that the migrant's homelessness is not a lasting condition as, even though all migrants sooner or later perceive themselves as homeless, most of them try in various ways to discover and construct a new sense of home. This recast sense of home may be transient or definitive, while the new home may be either a metaphorical space, a narrative construction or a physical place. The search and the recreated sense of home can be either in continuity with the pre-migratory life-experience, or inspired by both the pre-migratory past and the post-migratory present and future. The resulting homes might be re-elaborated according to the following three types: the *diasporic home*, a projection of the migrant's wish to feel at home more in the pre-migratory context than in the post-migratory one, and therefore still affected by the diaspora the migrant experienced; the *transnational home*, located beyond the borders of both the homeland and the adopted new land; and the *cross-cultural home*, which emerges from the negotiation between the home that was a long time ago and the home that could have been.

The migrant's sense of home and their perception of homelessness are interrelated with feelings of loss and the reconstruction of personal or cultural identity, a sense of belonging, and biographic continuity. The way migrants try to face and overcome their condition of being homeless is inevitably correlated to the ways that they try to reshape identity, recompose biographical disruptions, and redefine their sense of belonging. To some extent, the migrant's reconstruction of the sense of home is intended as a metaphor for their reconstruction of a sense of self, biography and belonging.

In discussing the migratory experience, the authors explore historical and contemporary, overseas and transnational, 'forced' and 'voluntary' migrations. All these types of migratory experience are analysed by adopting diverse methods and research instruments – from archival research to ethnography, from life-stories and semi-structured interviews to biographical, conversation and discourse analysis. Indeed, both the authors and their subjects of research come from or are located in different parts of the world. Moreover, the volume offers an interdisciplinary analysis of migrants and migration. The authors belong to many disciplines such as history, anthropology, sociology, political science, literature, linguistics, cinema and media studies. Active engagement with the conceptual frameworks and methods of other disciplines can provide a more complete exploration and understanding of a rich phenomenon such as migration. The range of interdisciplinary exchange is reflected in the volume's two-part division which deals firstly with the particular migration experiences of individuals and collectives, memory and self-identity, while in the second part the contributions offer a probing look at migration itself as a phenomenon explored in literature and the media.

In the opening chapter, Andreas Boldt analyses a particular migratory experience from a biographical-historical perspective. Clarissa Graves is a nineteenth-century Irish woman who moves from Dublin to Berlin as a consequence of her marriage in 1843 to the German historian, Leopold von Ranke. In managing her life experience as a transnational migrant, Clarissa never fully assimilates into the new city and the German culture, but tries to adjust herself to the new 'home' by creating a cosmopolitan 'world', in the form of a literary salon, that brings together a plurality of cultures, languages, intellectual activities and personalities. By spending her everyday life in a pluralised context, Clarissa avoids feeling like a stranger in her new country and continues to survey the world beyond the geographical borders of her new home. What is worthy of Boldt's analysis is his interpretation of this nineteenth-century migrant's 'solution' as a consequence of her biography. Although it was not common in her day, the young Clarissa was permitted by her parents to receive an education in several European countries. Thus, as a child, she lived in different places, spoke a variety of languages and grew accustomed to experiencing diverse cultures and life-styles. In a word, she became 'cosmopolitan' and chose to live her migration as a cosmopolitan experience. At the same time, she remained loyal to her first language, her home-country and her family who were still living in Ireland. As has been noted in the literature, migrants can easily lose themselves in a life experience that inevitably becomes pluralised. One common way of facing the problem is to try to recreate, in the new context, as many elements as possible of the pre-migratory life. As Boldt informs us through his meticulous study of archival sources, Clarissa always preferred to speak English while living in Berlin, and also chose to keep 'living' in Dublin through an almost daily correspondence with one of her brothers.

Migration is synonymous with exile in Wayde Brown's analysis of two historical cases of exile which are representative of North American diaspora: the mid-eighteenth-century exile of *l'Acadie*, a francophone community, established in Nova Scotia at the beginning of the seventeenth century, whose deportation was ordered by the British colonial authorities; and the early nineteenth-century exile of the Cherokee, an indigenous community removed by the United States' federal government. Taking a historical perspective which is indebted to other disciplines – chiefly, to architecture and archaeology – the author does not intend to deal with the consequences of these dislocations in the lands of exile. Rather, the focus of his analysis is on the 'left-behind' places of memory in the homeland and on the role they play in the 'return' of later generations of the diaspora, and in reconciling with the injustice of the exile. For this purpose, Brown compares the two sites now associated with the historical events, namely Gran-Pré in Canada and New Echota in the United States. Following historians such as Nora, Bevan and Samuel, the main assumption of Brown's analysis is the existence of complex interrelations among geographic sites, collective memory, 'official history' and the construction of a contemporary sense of nation and national identity. On this theoretical basis, the author analyses and explains how the two sites of Gran-Pré and New Echota have been constructed and identified as places of memory by the descendants of the exiled communities and of the post-exile settlement groups, and by the descendants of those who were responsible for the exile events. Brown also elucidates the role played by a 'left-behind' place of memory in reconstructing a sense of nation where the nation was subject to diaspora. The twentieth-century formal recognition of these geographical sites as places of memory by the respective federal governments might be interpreted as a formal attempt to include the diaspora events in the national history, thereby compensating for the forced exile and reaffirming a sense of national unity. In order to better pursue such aims, the involvement of the descendants of the diasporic communities is crucial.

In her exploration of the concepts of 'home' and 'homelessness' as seen by Palestinian women living in Lebanon, Maria Holt draws on interviews of women carried out in Lebanese refugee camps. In her discussion she examines how her informants have attempted to recreate home when home no longer exists. In doing so, Holt gauges the impact that exposure to violence and trauma has had on the formation of the women's identities. She argues that, at least for Palestinian refugee women who have been forcefully displaced, home is rarely synonymous with the familiar and the comfortable place/space where they belong. Rather, home and exile are experienced by the women on several levels, which include living on the margins, in a homeless and sometimes hostile environment, but where home may be redefined by some, not just as a glorified place of longing, but as a place where, in the words of L. Hammond, 'community identity, and political and cultural membership intersect'. In fact, one informant aptly makes a difference between 'home', where the family is, and 'homeland', the place of belonging. These interconnected levels are essential to the identity formation of the Palestinian refugee women. Holt concludes by drawing attention to the lack of acknowledgement of the central role of Palestinian women living in Lebanon – in a context where men have taken charge of telling the Palestine story – in preserving their nation's memories and maintaining a livable environment in exile.

Sonia Floriani gives an in-depth analysis of the transnational migratory experience of Calabrians who moved to Canada in the 1950s and 1960s. Presenting a case study of Calabrian men, women and children who migrated, Floriani's chapter strongly conveys theoretical notions about homelessness and its thematisation in the context of modern-day plurality. For the author, the migratory event and the diverse ways in which the experience has been lived and re-elaborated by the project informants, including their entrepreneurial activity, constitute the central core for examining the effect of the migration event on the shaping of individual biographies. Employing the Schutzian concept of 'here and now' in the interpretation of the oral narratives, Floriani decodes the biographical narratives of her Calabrian informants, interpreting the plurality and diversity of their self-identification in the time continuum by means of a micro-sociological perspective. Through a consideration of the spatial and temporal coordinates that of necessity are redefined by the dynamics of migration flows, Floriani delves into the strategies enacted by individuals whose oral narratives reveal the extent to which the calibration of their internal time continuum has been subjectively recast. Through the prism of the migratory experience, the informants' cultural dislocation has altered perceptions of space-time, such that dichotomies of here-elsewhere and then-now linear temporality present challenges, both real and metaphysical, for the migrant seeking to reconstruct their identity in the new location and rediscover a sense of home that has been irrevocably altered. Floriani's analysis evidences how the subjective experience of migration leads to a process of redefinition in the migrant's own spatial and temporal horizons that continues throughout their life.

Migration through a linguistic prism is the subject of the chapter by Colette Mrowa-Hopkins and Eric Bouvet. By means of a discourse analysis approach, they investigate how a group of French-born residents of Adelaide, who migrated to Australia in the 1950s and 1960s, have shaped their identity and sense of belonging in their country of adoption. Mrowa-Hopkins and Bouvet hypothesise that, at an individual level, the language used by migrants is likely to reveal the complexity of shifting identities, as well as a conflicting sense of socio-cultural belonging to a place that used to be 'foreign' to them. In order to elicit their data, the authors choose to focus on the analysis of pronouns and markers of modality (such as verbs of obligation, necessity and volition, for example) used by the informants. They argue that the choice of pronouns and modal expressions may indicate how the informants position themselves in relation to their home and adopted countries, thus revealing the extent to which the migrants are agents in constructing their identity. The study finds there is little evidence of a strong affiliation or disaffiliation to the French or Australian cultures among the French migrants interviewed. Furthermore, it suggests that the construction of identity is ambivalent and subject to tensions and shifts. While the reasons why the informants have adopted Adelaide as their 'home' remains unclear, the study shows the importance of discourse analysis as a tool for providing information as to how people perceive themselves in relation to their environment since their discourse reveals the personal, collective and imaginative dimensions of identity and sense of belonging. The merit of Mrowa-Hopkins' and Bouvet's study is that it adopts a methodological approach that could be extended to other migrant groups.

Michelle Barrett deals with migration focusing on how migrants can manage and redefine self-identity in everyday life. The chapter is based on empirical research whose case-study consists of Eurasian people – i.e. people of mixed European and Asian heritage – who migrated from South and South-East Asia to Australia. Through the migratory movement, Eurasian identities, that were already 'mixed', have inevitably increased in fluidity and ambiguity. The key hypothesis of this chapter is derived from the cultural geographer Divya Tolia-Kelly, who contends that in the migratory experience cultural artefacts, through the memory they are imbued with, are functional in (re)creating a sense of home and self-identity. More precisely, Barrett's intent is to explore the role played by the objects of home decoration chosen by Eurasian migrants in keeping memory alive, in (re)creating meaning and, thus, in (re)defining their sense of belonging and identity. As to the conceptions of Eurasian identity expressed by the objects of home decoration, which have emerged from the semi-structured interviews that the author held with these migrants in their houses, the chapter discusses three different approaches that have been adopted to anchor self-identity. More precisely, home decorations can represent either a Eurasian identity whose Asian component is felt to be more relevant, or a more situated Eurasian identity, or even a more hybrid Eurasian identity which also tries to come to terms with a new Australian identification. On the basis of this typology, it can be assumed that the correlation among the choice of home decorations, the memories and meanings they evoke and the post-migratory definition of ethnic identity are also affected by the migrant's pre-migratory biography. Among other conditions, the family background, the specific Eurasian ethnicity, the age of personal migration, the life-time mainly spent in Asia or also travelling in Europe resound through the varying openness, complexity and stability of the Eurasian identity in the Australian context of migration.

Diana Glenn explores connections between the metaphors of journeying found in a selection of celebrated classical literary texts and oral testimonies of the sea voyage undertaken by a group of first generation Campanians who migrated to Australia in the post-World War II period. By evoking the journeying typologies contained in works such as Homer's *Odyssey*, Virgil's *Aeneid* and Dante's *Comedy*, Glenn argues that the voyage undertaken by her informants some 50 to 60 years ago may remain the focal point of their migration experience; a moment often preserved almost intact in memory, which acts as a bridge between the familiar and the unknown, between pre- and post-migration. The sea voyage not only represents a special/physical relocation into an unfamiliar territory (horizontal voyage), but it also constitutes a redefinition of the self, a reconfiguration of identity, and, as a result, a negotiation of one's sense of belonging (vertical voyage in a metaphysical sense). In her analysis of the informants' narratives, Glenn highlights the dramatic impact that the sea crossing had on the migrants, which, for them, resulted in a sense of liminality. She quotes vivid recollections of the discomforts of travelling in crowded conditions, of the abundance of food on the ship, of people's expectations about the land that would change their lives, of disappointments and even despair on arrival. She also gives particular attention to the role of women migrants post-voyage, suggesting that by relocating to a new country, female informants acquired a new status as they became the custodians of familial and communal traditions, as well as the catalyst for adaptation and change, gaining agency and thus assuring the successful integration of the next generation.

Keith Jacobs argues that a close reading of literary texts can provide a rich medium for examining the complex nature and transformative power of the migratory experience. His presentation of selected fictional narratives, drawn from the Australian migrant literary genre, includes works such as Mary Rose Liverani's *The Winter Sparrows*; the autobiographical recount by Paul Kraus, *A New Australia, A New Australian*; Chandani Lokugé's *If the Moon Smiled*; *Café Scheherazade* by Arnold Zable; *The Sound of One Hand Clapping* by Richard Flanagan; and Graham Kershaw's novel *The Home Crowd*. According to Jacobs, a more active engagement with literary sources, far from constituting an unreliable scholarly enterprise, affords invaluable opportunities for an enhanced understanding of the migration experience. In his discussion and overview of the conceptual frameworks connected to migrant literature and its critical interpretation, Jacobs demonstrates how the endless variety of narration, whether autobiographical or fictional, provides fertile ground for exploring a sense of identity and emotional sensibility in the face of cultural and physical dislocation. As such, the variety, subjectivity and unrevealed aspects of the migration experience are evoked in profound and unexpected ways. The creation of what Jacobs terms 'discursive space' helps to diversify cultural practice, thereby encouraging new forms of commitment by means of a literary genre that complements the empirical study of the migratory experience. Through the literary medium, the destabilisation of selfhood and the reformulation of cultural identity resonate with a different focus. As a result, the critical reading of literary texts influences the reader's conceptualisation of how literature shapes our understanding of social phenomena and ways of being in the world.

Venus Tsang explores the transformative influence of storytelling and storytellers on identity formation and negotiation as evidenced in Maxine Hong Kingston's 1981 novel *The Woman Warrior*. Taking as its premise the concept of identity as a fluid and iterative process influenced by historical, cultural and individual viewpoints, Tsang's analysis of diverse storytelling modes highlights the interactive, multivalent nature of storytelling and postulates a four-fold typology of solicited, response, collaborative and performative storytelling. While the first of these conversational activities involves the creation of a narrative for a distinct purpose and with a particular audience in mind, the second is identified as a reaction to a story that has already been narrated. A dynamic approach characterises collaborative storytelling wherein two or more narrators contribute to the storytelling in spontaneous or deliberate ways and, lastly, the performative variety is the attempt by storytellers to engage their listeners in the narrative. In the exemplification of each type, the nature of the rapport and interactivity between storyteller and listener in the conversational mode is explored. Through a range of diverse characters whose stories are brought vividly to life, for example, Maxine, Brave Orchid, Moon Orchid, the no-name aunt, Fa Mu Lan and Ts'ai Yen, the author evokes ancestral patriarchal ideologies and strictures in order to demonstrate the exigencies of contemporary life in modern American society through the lens of Chinese migration and migrants to the United States. As they participate in the act of storytelling and the articulation of types, whether to achieve a specific goal or purpose, register a reaction, engage in the act of co-narration, or simply perform, the characters weave their tales and, in so doing, help the protagonist Maxine to realise and reaffirm her dual identity. Thus Tsang demonstrates how the act of storytelling fulfils a significant function in allowing the characters in *The Woman Warrior* to express and articulate their identity in a unique and multiform way.

Sukhmani Khorana discusses the cinematic traditions that have influenced the work of Indo-Canadian filmmaker Deepa Mehta, who is best known as the director of the elements film trilogy: 'Water', 'Earth' and 'Fire'. Since her first foray into feature film-making in the early 1990s, Mehta's work in cinema has attracted both praise and controversy, due to its reception by numbers of critics as a socio-political critique of her home country, India. Khorana maintains that by locating her screen output beyond the borders of both homeland and adopted home, Mehta is able to hone her diasporic practice. The resultant hybridity opens the door to greater artistic expression and allows access to a community of fellow practitioners whose creative output locates them within a wider and more fluid diasporic space. It is Khorana's contention that Mehta's bold crossover tropes produce work that traverses borders, culturally, politically and intellectually. In this respect, Mehta's diasporic and exilic films must be viewed in their situated contexts, whether that be transnational commercial cinemas such as B/Hollywood, the national cinema of the Canadian host society, South Asian diasporic cinema or transnational world cinema. Importantly, Khorana traces how Mehta has been influenced by film-makers of the calibre of Yasujiro Ozu, Ingmar Bergman and Satyajit Ray. An identifiable thread from this precursor influence is Mehta's use of local storytelling to explore cross-cultural themes. However, the author concludes that Mehta creates her own 'crossover cinema', as Khorana terms it; a description that encompasses the broad cultural reach of the director's personal and political deliberations on issues of identity and home.

The last chapter by Bruna Emanuela Manai and Franco Manai examines *Die Sprachen Moabits*, a radio feature, broadcast on Berlin's Offener Kanal in July 2007, as an acoustic representation not only of the linguistic and cultural situation of the neighbourhood of Moabit, but also in terms of its aesthetic and cognitive value. The authors retrace the history of Moabit, a neighbourhood situated in the heart of Berlin, from a marginal zone populated by French Huguenots, in the eighteenth century, to a place of settlement of a wide variety of ethnic populations in recent years. Because of its transient history, the authors qualify Moabit as a 'no-place', a place akin to a railway station, where individuals, groups, cultures and languages are in constant transit. Interestingly, they argue that, despite this lack of homogeneity, cultures are able to co-exist without being recast into a melting pot. Rather, they form a conglomerate of polymorphic nature, in the image of the 50 languages of Moabit collected for the radio program, described by the authors 'as intertwined, superimposed and entangled'. According to the authors, 'no-places' like Moabit may incarnate a new *aesthetic dimension* of living, where there is no common material or spiritual property to administer. What there is, however, is a restructuring of being-together within the rich and complex fabric of diversity and marginality.

PART 1

Migrants, memory and self-identity

Migration due to marriage: Clarissa von Ranke and the cosmopolitan cultural atmosphere of the new 'home'

Andreas Boldt

NATIONAL UNIVERSITY OF IRELAND, MAYNOOTH

Introduction

This chapter will examine Clarissa Helena Graves (1808–1871), who in 1843 married the German historian Leopold von Ranke (1795–1886), and her life spent away from her homeland, Ireland, in Berlin, Germany, where she lived from 1843 until her death. During this time Clarissa von Ranke built up a kind of socialising circle, known as 'Salon Ranke', where people of all professions and nationalities met to exchange their ideas and knowledge. Eminent people like the brothers Grimm and the scholar of philosophy Schelling, the Shakespearean translator Wilhelm von Schlegel, and English diplomats like Sir Andrew Buchanan and Lord Francis Napier met at Luisenstraße in Berlin, the home of the Rankes. In Clarissa's salon, Enlightenment thought and Romanticism were discussed, while the ideology of revolutionary movements was rejected. Even if the salon was dominated by conservative thought, several opinions that were 'revolutionary' at that time were discussed there: the position of women, cultural exchange and the nation-building of different states, like Ireland, Germany, Italy and America, and the role of religion in a changing society. With her poetry and traditions, Clarissa was a type of ambassador for her Anglo-Irish roots and British culture.

Family background

Mass migrations occurring in the last 200 years have seen people leave their homelands for a wide variety of reasons, whether forced or voluntary. Even today, thousands of people leave their homeland due to marriage – an often-neglected aspect when discussing migrations. Such a form of migration existed during the Middle Ages, mainly within royal families, and it has become gradually more common over the last 300 years within all classes of society. Clarissa Helena Graves is one example of such migration from the nineteenth century. While moving to her new home, she brought much of her cultural heritage with her, thus creating an international cultural atmosphere. Even if, over time, Clarissa felt increasingly like a Prussian woman, nevertheless she never forgot her home in Ireland.

Clarissa Helena Graves, born in Dublin in 1808, came from the well-known Graves family. The family was highly educated and was, in effect, an intellectual dynasty. The roots of the Graves family go back to 1647, when Colonel Graves of Mickleton in Gloucestershire, England, commanded a regiment of horses in the army of the Parliament,[1] volunteering for service in Ireland the same year. As a result of the Cromwellian Land Settlement, the Graves family acquired lands and later public office in Limerick. Clarissa's father, John Crosbie Graves, was Chief Police Magistrate in Dublin. In 1806, he married Helena Perceval from the equally long-established Perceval family who had lived in Ireland for centuries. From 1814 John Crosbie Graves lived at 12 FitzWilliam Square, Dublin. Helena Perceval supported her husband in his career and shortly after their marriage, Lord Redesdale, who was a patron of Helena Perceval, appointed John Crosbie Graves a Commissioner of Bankruptcy. Because of Helena's reputed 'royal descent' from several medieval kings of England, Ireland and France, the Perceval name was widely adopted by the children.[2]

Leopold Ranke and Clarissa Graves first encountered each other in Paris around July/August 1843 and subsequently met several times. Leopold von Ranke (the *von* was added to his surname when he was ennobled in 1865) was one of the most influential historians of the nineteenth century. He made important contributions to the emergence of history as a modern discipline and has been called the father of 'scientific' history. Due to his efforts, methodical principles of archival research and source criticism became commonplace in academic institutions, and he is generally credited with the professionalisation of the historian's craft. In September 1843 Leopold went to London, followed by Clarissa and her mother. On 1 October they became engaged and on 26 October 1843 Clarissa's brother, Robert Perceval Graves, officiated at the marriage in Bowness, Windermere, England.[3] On the same day as their marriage, Ranke left England with his bride and returned to Berlin. The news of Ranke's marriage quickly spread throughout Berlin. Most people in Berlin, including the royal family, were surprised 'as every one had been convinced that he would live and die a Bachelor'.[4] Clarissa was welcomed in the city, and it was easy for her to make her life in her new home.

The establishment of 'Salon Ranke' and Clarissa's activity

Notwithstanding their having several children during the early period of their marriage, the home of the Rankes became a preferred meeting place for several famous and educated personalities. The late 1840s marked the beginning of a cultural and intellectual meeting point that developed more and more into the famous 'Salon Ranke', which reached its full fruition after the revolutionary years of 1848/49, and continued, despite the worsening illness of Clarissa, to be an important salon for Berlin society during the 1850s and 1860s. The salon was famous for its musical parties, classes in poetry and literature (especially Shakespeare) and discussions of politics and history. Clarissa also gave classes in various languages including French, Italian and English. She fashioned this style of salon culture based on her experiences back in England and Ireland and adapted them to her new home in Berlin. Before the revolution of 1848, people of the calibre of the Court Preacher Strauss, the American Rev. John Lord, the Swedish soprano Jenny Lind, the families of Schelling, Puchta, Bellson, Heman and Napier, the historian and politician Raumer, Prof. Richter, Minister Eichhorn, the brothers Grimm and the Crown Prince of Bavaria, later King Maximilian II of Bavaria, were regular guests.

As the years went on and the increasingly ill Clarissa became more confined to her home, many people came to visit her rather than her husband. From the late 1850s onwards, she was the head of the salon. The number of famous names diminished, yet the intellectual and spiritual life continued. Friends of this period were Hertha von Manteuffel, the wife of Leopold's close friend Marshall Edwin von Manteuffel, the Prussian Ambassador in London Christian Karl Josias von Bunsen and his family, the writer Elfriede von Mühlenfels, whose nickname was 'the Boat' because she promoted the construction of a Prussian fleet, the nature researcher Christian Gottfried Ehrenberg and the Senior Court Preacher Wilhelm Hoffmann. British diplomats like Sir Andrew Buchanan and Lord Francis Napier were constant guests as well. Clarissa's closest friends were the writer Ida von Düringsfeld and the Prussian Prince Georg, general of cavalry, who was known as the Poet Prince, though he had little poetic success. Altogether the Ranke family was in contact with at least 400 people.[5]

The most important time when friends arrived in the salon of 'Madame Ranke' was the traditional English teatime in the early evening. It was possible to come along freely and without an invitation. In the morning young girls arrived and read letters aloud to Clarissa and wrote letters for her. Once a week Clarissa's Shakespeare class came together to read Shakespeare and other English authors, and they sang songs and ballads before and after class. From 1862, on Fridays, a so-called 'Open Evening' took place. The number of guests generally was around 70 or 80 and sometimes over 100. Drinking tea and having biscuits, followed by wine as the evening proceeded, guests discussed several topics in small groups. On occasion, piano concerts by ladies took place, followed by poetry presentations and society games. During Carnival, fancy dress balls were organised and several times large house concerts were held, the last one in 1869, being the presentation of an Italian comedy. As a result of these activities, Leopold's brother, Heinrich, called the house 'the happy island'.[6] It followed the example of the Anglo-Irish traditions with which Clarissa had grown up. A special circle developed to discuss religion and biblical knowledge. Clarissa continued to discuss the Bible with her brother Robert in Ireland until she died. After 1862 she managed to cope with her disability by writing letters, by singing and by religious devotion. During the 1850s and 1860s, English, Irish, American, French and Italian visitors became acquainted with Clarissa and her husband. Her salon was unique as the only internationally-minded one in Berlin at which artists, composers, and academics were welcome, as distinct simply from the salons that entertained nobility, diplomats and soldiers only. This is one of the reasons why her cosmopolitan salon is rarely recalled in German memory.[7]

Clarissa helped with her connections wherever she could. A large number of people were assisted in obtaining jobs or exchanges, and people from the Continent asked for her advice on what places to visit in Britain. Of course, London was mentioned as the most important place, followed by Dublin and the Irish countryside. Moreover she was involved in student exchange programs particularly after 1866, in which year Alexandra College in Dublin was founded for the education of young girls; Clarissa's brother, Robert, was one of the founders. Soon after, Clarissa became the head of an education circle for young English and Irish ladies in German schools and she was listed as one of eight referees on a leaflet. This education circle went hand in hand with the foundation and promotion of Alexandra College, as well as with girls' schools in England and Scotland. Clarissa's interest in promoting the education of young girls probably has its basis in her own upbringing. She left home at the age of seven, to be educated in England, Scotland, France and Belgium. Such an education was not unusual for upper-class Anglo-Irish boys, but very unusual for girls during the first half of the nineteenth century. Clarissa used her own experiences to foster a better education for young girls through exchange between her home country Ireland and her new home country, Germany.[8]

After Clarissa's death in 1871, all this ended. Ranke reverted to living his life as it had been before his marriage: he went to parties, but he never again organised one in his own house. Ranke's home remained quiet until his death. Much of the time during their marriage, Clarissa had been sick and suffered from a disease afflicting her spinal cord. From around 1850 onwards, Clarissa noticed the appearance of dysfunction and decline in her body. At first it had been single fingers, then the whole hand, followed by the feet and, as time passed, more and more parts of her body failed to function properly. Clarissa's letters to her brother Robert in Ireland show the different stages of this development in detail. She wrote of her disabled hands in her Christmas letters, of being unable to cut meat on the plate by herself, of weakness in her left leg and the necessity to rest longer and more often on her sofa. The writing of her letters got worse from month to month, and in 1862 she finally stopped writing. At this stage Clarissa could barely move her fingers and arms. This unimaginable suffering lasted for nearly two decades, from around 1850/1851 to 1871. It is difficult to imagine how Clarissa dealt with this situation, but she found a place in German society even if she was not able to leave the house during her last years of life. From 1860 onwards, Clarissa was wheelchair bound. Two methods she used to deal with her disease were her poems and her friendship circle, both of which served to disseminate aspects of her Anglo-Irish culture and attitude.

Apart from meeting people and being the head of her salon, writing poems was one of Clarissa's most beloved hobbies. Commencing in her childhood, her love of poetry came to be of great importance to her during her time in Berlin, not only in coping with her disease, but also as a means of dealing with the absence of her closest family relatives and home in Ireland. According to Clarissa, the collection 'Stars of my Life' had a central place for her, giving people whom she had met, or was impressed by, a lasting monument.[9] The original was carefully written, and the specially selected poems were marked with illustrations and photographs of the personalities she mentioned. The collection was divided into two major parts, one called 'Family' and the other 'Celebrities'. The first part was marked by her oldest memories of Dublin, like 'Childhood', 'Our old Home', 'The loss of my Father', poems about her brothers, Leopold, his brothers and Clarissa's own children. The section entitled 'Celebrities' covered English and Irish names as well as many celebrities from the continent such as King Maximilian II of Bavaria, the Countess of Stolberg-Werningerode and the composer Mendelssohn.[10] Altogether, the poems and visitors to her salon give one a fair idea of the number of people whom Clarissa met and knew, and those with whom she stayed in contact. Her poems are marked by a clear use of words, with a large infusion of romanticism. Her memories and depictions of Irish and English luminaries reached and influenced many people in Berlin and, by extension, Germany as a whole.

Clarissa left a further 24 books, mainly exercise books and note books, with more than 2600 pages of poems.[11] Two of them were called 'Continental Lore' and were translations of poems from different European countries.[12] There were also translations from Greek, Indian, Polish, Persian, Russian, Spanish, Swedish and Hungarian. Considering the wide variety of languages she was able to speak fluently, including English, German, Italian, French, Greek, Latin, Spanish and Flemish, she evidently felt embarrassed when she mentioned in a letter to her brothers in 1865 that her children could 'only' speak four languages fluently.[13] Nevertheless English remained the main language for her daily use: nearly all of her letters and poems were written in English, using a solemn tone.

The observation of German culture and general literature

In many other letters, Clarissa wrote about German culture. In 1846 she mentioned differences of habit for weddings in England and Germany, and had a major political discussion concerning German Catholics seeking a government led by the Church, which was seen by many as a threat. However, Clarissa's interests did not simply focus on Germany or Continental Europe, as through her family she still deeply shared in events in Ireland. The contents of her letters were discussed with Ranke and, consequently, it can be surmised that Ranke was well informed about what was going on in Ireland. In a letter to Robert that she wrote in October 1846, she states: 'Say what you think of the state of Ireland. Is it on the eve of famine as is reported here?'[14] In another letter, written a year, later Clarissa wrote:

> We have had the most extraordinary mild winter here, and the Spring is already wonderfully advanced, should a blight come, & winter return, (as some fear) the consequence might be awful. On the contrary if the early vegetation is unchecked what promise of plenty there is! God grant this may be the case in Ireland, & that abundance may succeed the present scarcity & misery there. Were the Potatoes diseased in your neighbourhood? I think great charity might be – evinced by the English supplying the poor Irish with some grain & potatoes for food.[15]

This concern for her country of origin shows that Clarissa thought not only about her brothers, but also the (Catholic) Irish population in general.

Clarissa was a critical observer. This can be seen particularly in the area of literature, especially English literature. She enthusiastically admired the poems of William Wordsworth and the works of Alfred Lord Tennyson. The books of Walter Scott she thought were well written, while the biography of *Frederick the Great* by Carlyle she deemed boring. Clarissa respected mostly the sermons of Cardinal Newman, besides other theological and pedagogical literature. She mentioned Newman critically to Robert, saying that she had:

> lately read 'Newman's answer to Kingsby' and was much interested in it although as a Roman Catholic Newman went beyond all my sympathies. Do you remember when I read his Sermons at Bowness and how they interested me?[16]

Clarissa also read several German books, including *Verlorene Handschrift* by Gustav Freytag, the geographical works of Raumer and the poetry of Eichendorff. Other works were read in the original, for example, Don Quixote in Spanish and Voltaire in French. Clarissa disagreed with the latter's way of writing, since in her opinion he entertained his readers with the 'lowest bestiality' (Bäcker-von Ranke 1967: 10–11). Other works from Italy, Portugal, Lower Germany and Frisia were read in the original.

Some conditions in Germany she found quite strange. The customs of German youth seemed to her rough and uncouth. Marriage, in her opinion, was guided too much by the mind and not enough by feeling. Engagements took place far too early, but the waiting time for marriage was too long and the necessity for the bride to obtain a dowry consisting of everyday clothes Clarissa found quite comical. She reacted similarly to the German custom of giving birthday presents consisting of everyday things, which would be necessary anyway, only enriched by sweets and flowers. On the other hand, Clarissa believed that socks, trousers and other such items should have a personal touch. The jubilee system of formal awards (given after a certain number of years) seemed to her simply exaggerated. She believed that the German officers and their educational system were the best in Europe and that the English military system was not of a similar calibre.

Clarissa's role and her contributions to war relief

Among all her letters, especially from the middle of the 1850s onwards, Clarissa mentioned daily politics, enriched with several other of her own and Leopold's personal comments. However, she had mainly one primary issue to comment on and to live for: the friendship between Ireland/England and Prussia/Germany. Especially during the 1860s and during the Franco-Prussian War, Clarissa became very worried. After the unsuccessful London conference to solve German-Danish disputes, Clarissa grew more troubled as public opinion in Prussia depicted England in a very bad light and with a great deal of hatred. She asked her brothers if the same was the case in England and Ireland. In her salon she disliked any comments that contained elements of hatred. Instead, she desired respect between the two countries. In her view the English should not behave arrogantly and should more readily acknowledge the help of Prussia as an ally at the battle of Waterloo.[17]

Since the late 1840s, Clarissa had developed a friendship with Florence Nightingale. In later years Nightingale became very famous and she was highly respected by Clarissa, who even wrote a poem about her, commenting on how she knew her before her rise to fame. Due to her keen interest in social affairs and education, Clarissa soon acquired pet names in Germany: one of them was 'the Nightingale' in 1860.[18] Furthermore, Clarissa changed her role more and more from that of suffering wife to an experienced person whose advice was widely sought. Clarissa's advice was highly respected – from the King of Prussia to friends back home in Ireland, such as her good friend, Fanny North:

> Whenever you are a little dispirited and weak, think of me, dear Fanny, and try to turn your thoughts away from yourself as much as possible; in this way only have I been able to bear my long imprisonment and to say 'Thy will be done'. I have grown into the habit of occupying others and fancying that I am occupied myself. Had I not been ill; I should never have known fully what a good kind world it is; since I have lost the use of my own hands; scarcely a day passes that some young friend does not offer to read or to write for me and when I do happen to be alone, still I try to employ myself making verses, or translating something that is put before me, but I am sure you will know much better than me to be always happy in every case and to be beloved.[19]

Unfortunately Clarissa soon faced a problem in the maintenance of a friendly relationship between Prussia and England, because of the war that broke out in 1866 between Prussia and Austria over Schleswig-Holstein.[20] In May 1866, prior to the outbreak of war, Clarissa wrote to her brother Robert, stating: 'I fear that you are right in saying it is now too late to avoid war, Leopold said you hit upon exactly the right point, Prussia's applying to Italy's example'.[21] Italy was mentioned because it achieved unification of the different Italian states in 1861, and both Leopold and Robert thought that the German states would try to follow the Italian example.

Although Ranke was very concerned with the historical and political outcome of the war in 1866, Clarissa continued to report on the conflict and the kind of effort the women left behind made to ease the suffering of wounded soldiers. Her own involvement became clear when she wrote to Robert in July 1866:

> The English are obliged to acknowledge the bravery of Prussia, but you have very little idea from the chary accounts in the *Times*, of all the glory our troops have been winning. They behave with the greatest dignity treating their enemies with respect and humanity, sharing their very food and comfort with them. Otto goes to a lazareth [hospital for soldiers], where Prussians, Austrians, Hungarians, Serbians, Swabians, Saxons, and every nation lie together, and talks and prays with the poor men as far as his knowledge of languages goes. He has a friend who talks Italian as well, and the dear hand who writes this can also write Hungarian and has already made some poor Hungarians happy by talking and writing for them in their own language. I have written a few lines on the Prussian banner, for which my young friend has drawn a pretty design which we mean to be published and sell for the benefit of the Prussian soldiers, every copy will cost 10 gr. that is 1 Schilling, could you sell some for me? And I would send you copies by Fanny Russell when she returns to London. The young friend of whom I just spoke is a Fräulein Elisabeth von Pape, who has lately lost her only brother in the battle of Königgrätz and I try to keep her occupied with something relating to the war, and it would make her so happy to make some money that she can herself dispose of. Everybody is trying to do something for the poor sufferers. Frl. v. Langen is occupied every day in [...?], cutting out, receiving packages in the Central-Committee and think! that yesterday 3000 woolen [*sic*] bandages were made there, to protect the troops against Cholera which is now getting very prevalent.[22]

The poems mentioned were sold in Berlin to 250 people. Clarissa fully backed the Prussians and encouraged several relations and friends to sell her poems. In another letter she described the general situation in Berlin, her own efforts for soldier's relief and her son Otto's involvement as well:

> I am very sorry, you all take so little interest in the success of Prussia, if you were here, I am sure you would greatly admire the liberality and kindness of all parties, I can give you no idea of it by letter. Almost all our ladies are either engaged in working for or in visiting the wounded soldiers, some of my friends have cut up most of their house-linen for bandages indeed there is nothing they have that they would not will-

> ingly give for the relief of the sufferers. Otto has gone very regularly to read and pray with the sick and dying, he is not now quite well, and I am afraid has got some fever-infection as he never avoided Cholera or Typhus patients. My friend, who writes this, has been very busy as her especial mission was to visit the Hungarians and to write letters for them home and interpret their wishes and wants in the hospitals. I was quite ashamed of sitting idle at home, but I have turned into a beggar and already Elisabeth von Pape and I have got above 30 rth. [*Reichsthaler*] in selling our banners. Some of my friends who are very abstemious in their families have given dozens of bottles of champagne for patients recovering from fever, and it is not only Prussian soldiers who are so well attended to, but all the wounded prisoners.[23]

Clarissa's diary survives for the year 1870. It is an octavo 'ladies' almanac' (*Damen-Almanach*) of over 250 pages, printed in Berlin by Haudesche and Spenersche. It records two days per page, and has set space for recording family birthdays and addresses. On the title page it states that it is the fourth annual edition, itself an indication that the maintenance of diaries and appointment books was increasingly viewed as a necessary activity of educated middle-class women. In it Clarissa provides a daily record of her visitors, of the events in her salon, of family activities, and of letters sent and received. Some of the daily entries are very brief – 'Visit from Miss Riley, Frl. v. Bita' (20 January 1870) – while others are larger: 'Otto preached for the queen-dowager at the Charlottenburg. Leopold went to the Ordensfest. The usual family party. The Mr Taquemot red [*sic*] a beautiful sermon, text: Our Father which art in heaven' (31 January 1870).[24] In all, over the course of the year, Clarissa mentions over 150 visitors, and the diary shows that, despite her illness, she kept up an active social schedule in the last sixteen months of her life.

France had a problem with Prussia's increasing power to arm and revitalise its own forces. Emperor Napoleon III had been preparing the French army since 1866. In 1870 the Spanish throne, vacant since a liberal revolution in 1868, was offered to a Prussian prince. The French refused to accept the Prussian king's word that the offer had been turned down as a sufficient reassurance; they demanded that the king declare the candidature would never be resumed. In 1870 the tensions between France and Prussia finally led to war.

Clarissa described in her letters the situation of families in Berlin facing the outbreak of the Franco-Prussian War in 1870.[25] She hoped that the English fleet would ensure the safety of the unsecured German coast. To stress her point, she wrote three anecdotes of the glory of three Prussian soldiers, and sent them to her friends and relatives. This hope was destroyed by the news that England had sent weapons to France. Clarissa was so angry that she described the 'Isles-Empire' as being served by Mammon and blinded by avarice. Clarissa quoted her husband and wrote that the reproaches against Germany and its bombing of Paris were not correct, and mentioned what Ranke had said: that if the English and French were talking of German cruelty they should better think of the numerous innocent victims of their own revolutions. At least nobody was hanged from lampposts in Berlin, nor were defenceless people tortured.

As in 1864 and 1866, Clarissa begged continuously for gifts for German soldiers. Many ladies of the upper classes did likewise, but only a few on such a large scale. On letter paper, at the top of which the new symbol of the Red Cross had been colourfully imprinted, Clarissa begged her friends and relatives in England and Ireland for monetary donations and material relief for soldiers. The military hospitals in Berlin welcomed everything Clarissa acquired from Ireland, and even the antiseptic towels, then unknown in Germany, were appreciated. Following the example of her English friend, Florence Nightingale, she tried to collect money, clothes and clinical material for the wounded soldiers and the soldiers at the front. Her two sons were involved as well: Otto looked after the wounded in hospitals in Berlin, while Friduhelm enrolled as a soldier and marched with the army to Paris. His letters to his mother and his uncle Robert give a good insight about the war and also an eyewitness account of the emergence for the first time of a new type of warfare which later produced the horrors of the First World War. When soldiers arrived in hospitals in Berlin from different nations like France, Germany, Austria, Italy and Hungary, Clarissa organised, with several friends, a service to write letters for the soldiers to their families at home.

In connection with this, the 'Iron Cross for Ladies' played an important role. The awarding of this honour for deserving and esteemed benefactors was entrusted to the 'Women's Committee for National War Relief', under the leadership of Princess Karl (Princess

Elisabeth of Prussia). These patriotic associations were formed by middle-class women as an outlet for their energies and as an expression of their image of solidarity with the war, and were based on an informal alliance between women volunteers and public authority. Clarissa reported that medallions were filled with the hair of girls and women who donated their hair for the fatherland, so much so that nobody knew what to do with it all. At first Clarissa was not quite sure if she should offer them to her relatives, but the sales went so well that she could only satisfy her British relations. It was important to Clarissa that all recipients should write a letter of thanks to the chairwoman of the Committee, Mrs von Ohlen und Adlerskron. Her sister-in-law, Helen, wrote such a moving letter that it was read in public and occasioned loud applause.

When the war came to an end in 1871, Clarissa looked forward to seeing the king-emperor, and she hoped that English-German relations would improve. Nevertheless, she was so weakened by her disease that she could not watch the return of the troops and gradually she stopped dictating letters. Clarissa died in Berlin in 1871.

Conclusion

Clarissa's migratory experience can be considered as extraordinary. Certain aspects of her experience, such as for international marriages within middle and upper classes (even though still limited), or the engagement in war relief in Germany, are an expression of her historical time. Nevertheless several aspects of her life remain unique. Her encouragement of more education for girls and the setting up of international exchange programs, as well as the establishment of her salon, reflect this aspect. Clarissa did not change her home experience of salons, but created a salon in Berlin following Anglo-Irish ideas, and therefore allowing even common people and foreigners to have a meeting point which did not exist in this form elsewhere in Berlin. Access to German salons was usually only allowed to the nobility, higher military ranks, and artists. Even though Clarissa never assimilated completely and understood herself, besides being Irish/English and Prussian, as a European woman, she was fully respected by the German society for whom she was a highly educated Anglo-Irish woman. Due to her knowledge of her homeland, German society developed, in the course of the nineteenth century, a positive and sympathetic view of Ireland, which was ruled by the 'big' neighbour England and where freedom should be granted to the Irish. From the perspective of Clarissa's relatives and friends in England and Ireland, the German states were highly respected due to high education standards, military improvements, and economic success.

Clarissa's role in Berlin was an important one. In her salon, the thoughts of the Enlightenment and Romanticism were discussed, and the ideology of revolutionary movements rejected. Even if the house of Ranke and the 'Salon Ranke' were dominated by conservative thoughts, several 'unconventional' opinions at that time were discussed: the position of women, cultural exchange and the nation-building of different states, like Ireland, Germany, Italy and America, and the role of religion in a changing society. Although Clarissa was fully integrated in the environment of her new home and she experienced no language or cultural problems, she nevertheless held on to a number of traditions and habits from her homeland. Some of these traditions, such as the salon culture, were grafted on to German traditions, which did not alienate Clarissa from her new home, but made her a more interesting person. Due to this, Clarissa introduced English culture to Germany and found admirers who translated, for example, the works of Shakespeare and Wordsworth into German for the first time. With her poetry and traditions, Clarissa was a kind of ambassador of her Anglo-Irish roots and English culture. The 'Salon Ranke' was the last important salon in Berlin of the nineteenth century, thus making it a meeting point for important personalities of Europe. As a forum for the exchange of opinions and culture, 'Salon Ranke' created something that we could call today an early version of a European cultural community.[26]

Notes

1 The Irish Rebellion against English rule started in 1641 which was defeated by Oliver Cromwell 1649–1652.

2 For further details see Boldt, A. (2007). *The role of Ireland in the Life of Leopold von Ranke (1795–1886): The historian and historical truth*. Lampeter: Edwin Mellen Press: 26–40. The main manuscript collection in relation to the family history of the Graves in Ireland is located in Trinity College Dublin (TCD), Ireland, Manuscript Department, Graves-Archive, MSS 10047. This collection contains about 3000 documents covering three centuries.

3 Further details can be found in Boldt, 2007: 43–49.

4 Letter of Starriett M. Owen to Helen Graves, 5 November 1844, Graves-Archive, TCD, MS 10047/20/52.

5 Particularly Gisbert Bäcker-von Ranke published several materials on Clarissa von Ranke. Noteworthy is Bäcker-von Ranke, G. (1967). *Rankes Ehefrau Clarissa geb. Graves Perceval*. Göttingen. However, he also finished a PhD thesis several years before which was never published and is nearly unknown to scholars: Bäcker-von Ranke, G. (1955). 'Leopold von Ranke und seine Familie: Kulturgeschichtliches Bild einer deutschen Gelehrtenfamilie im neunzehnten Jahrhundert'. Bonn: unpublished Diss. In his appendix (pp. 1–113) Bäcker-von Ranke presented a full list of friends, visitors and acquaintances.

6 Letter of Clarissa Ranke to Amalie Ranke, Wiehe, Clarissa von Ranke 8.

7 For further information see also Bäcker-von Ranke (1967) and Boldt (2007). The Ranke-Museum in Wiehe, Thuringia, Germany, holds over 600 letters of Clarissa von Ranke, giving good insight into the life and practice of Clarissa's salon. This collection once belonged to Dr Gisbert Bäcker-von Ranke, a direct descendant, who presented the museum with the papers in 1995. The letters afford valuable information on the private life of the Rankes as well as Clarissa's experience in a foreign country. I wish to thank the Ranke-Museum for the use of the archive and for permission to reproduce several letters.

8 For further information see Boldt 2007: 132–133, and the manuscript collection in TCD, MSS 10047, section Robert Perceval Graves.

9 A copy was made available to the author by Dr Graf von der Schulenburg, a descendent of Ranke.

10 Some English and Irish names included are: Bloomfield, Buchanan, Butler, Cobden, Coleridge, Drakes, Egmont, Hamilton, Hemans, Liston, Lowther, Napier, Nightingale, Owen, Scott, Sommerville, Swinburne, Todd, Twinning, Wilkinson and Wordsworth.

11 The blotter books were made available by Dr Bäcker-von Ranke as a gift to the Ranke-Museum, Wiehe, Germany, in 1995.

12 Amongst the German poems that Clarissa translated into English are those of the poets Geibel, Kinkel, Brentano, Herwegh, Heine, Tieck, Lenau; amongst the French ones those of Victor Hugo, Pierre-Jean de Béranger and Marie André de Chessier; amongst the Italian those of the humanist Poliziano; and among the Danish poems several by Andersen.

13 Letter of Clarissa Ranke to Robert and Helen Graves, Wiehe, Englische Briefe 69.

14 Letter of Clarissa Ranke to Robert Graves, 16 October 1846, Wiehe, Englische Briefe 32.

15 Letter of Clarissa Ranke to Robert and Helen Graves, Wiehe, Englische Briefe 254.

16 Letter of Clarissa Ranke to Robert Graves, Wiehe, Englische Briefe 257.

17 The battle of Waterloo was fought on 18 June 1815. The Imperial French army under the command of Napoleon was defeated by combined armies – an Anglo-Allied army under the command of Wellington and a Prussian army under the command of Bluecher.

18 Letter of Clarissa Ranke to Robert Graves, 31 January 1860, Wiehe, Englische Briefe 90.

19 Letter of Clarissa von Ranke to Fanny North, 13 January 1869, Wiehe, Clarissa von Ranke 46.

20 The wars of 1864 (Austria and Prussia against Denmark) and 1866 (Austria against Prussia) are also known as the German unification wars under the leadership of Bismarck.

21 Letter of Clarissa von Ranke to Robert and Helen Graves, 21 May 1866, Wiehe, Englische Briefe 167.

22 Letter of Clarissa von Ranke to Robert Graves, 24 July 1866, Wiehe, Clarissa von Ranke 36a.

23 Letter of Clarissa von Ranke to Robert and Helen Graves, 8 August 1866, Wiehe, Englische Briefe 262.

24 Staatsbibliothek Berlin, Germany, Manuscript Collection, Ms.germ.oct.644 (Tagebuch Clarissa von Ranke).

25 The Franco-Prussian War 1870/71 led to the unification of Germany.

26 For all the advice and help I received for this article and that I was able to attend the 'Moving cultures, shifting identities' conference in Adelaide in December 2007 I wish to thank my parents Liesbeth and Dieter Boldt, Níamh McGee, John Bradley, Tom Byrne and Marie Murphy.

References

Ranke-Museum, Wiehe, Germany.

Staatsbibliothek Berlin, Germany.

Trinity College Dublin, Manuscript Department, Graves-Archive, MSS 10047.

Bäcker-von Ranke, G. (1955). *Leopold von Ranke und seine Familie: Kulturgeschichtliches Bild einer deutschen Gelehrtenfamilie im neunzehnten Jahrhundert*. Bonn: unpublished Diss.

Bäcker-von Ranke, G. (1967). *Rankes Ehefrau Clarissa geb. Graves Perceval*. Göttingen.

Boldt, A. (2007). *The role of Ireland in the Life of Leopold von Ranke (1795–1886): The historian and historical truth*. Lampeter: Edwin Mellen Press.

'Left-behind' places of memory: The pattern of Grand Pré and New Echota

Wayde Brown
UNIVERSITY OF GEORGIA

Introduction

The work of Pierre Nora in defining late twentieth-century France provides a provocative perspective on the relationship between collective memory and the 'official history' or chronicle that describes the contemporary French nation.[1] Suggesting that the traditional and unconscious 'memory' (or experience of society) has been lost in the modern world, Nora explores *lieux de mémoire*, both physical and intangible sites within which such memory has been cached. He writes: '*lieux de mémoire* become important even as the vast fund of memories among which we used to live on terms of intimacy has been depleted, only to be replaced by a reconstructed history' (1996: 6). The British historian, Raphael Samuel, offers a very different perspective on the relationship between collective memory and official history, suggesting that the former remains a living aspect of British society, linked to the latter in a necessary and symbiotic relationship. Samuel observes: 'Like history, memory is inherently revisionist and never more chameleon than when it appears to stay the same' (1994: x). The work of Nora and Samuel are two important examples of a broad and interdisciplinary enquiry currently taking place into the roles of collective memory and 'place' in defining and explaining a contemporary sense of nation. However, this theory has primarily been used to consider nations that have remained within relatively established geographic boundaries or borders. But what of nations subject to diaspora? Given that physical evidence of the group's occupation of the homeland has often been erased by time, subsequent occupation, and even as part of the original exile event, it may be necessary to recreate such sites. Indeed, it may be necessary to undertake this process of recreation with a collective memory spanning generations of exile and often with an official history written by the very instrument or force responsible for the exile.

This paper considers the 'left-behind' places of memory of two nations subject to diaspora within North America. The first is *l'Acadie*, a francophone society established in present-day Nova Scotia in the early seventeenth century. *Le Grand Dérangement* refers to the forced dispersal of this population in 1755 to other colonies in North America by the British authorities. The place of memory considered is Grand Pré, one of the Acadian settlements used as a port of embarkation, popularised in Henry Wadsworth Longfellow's poem *Evangeline*, and the subject of a pending nomination for world heritage status. The second nation to be considered is the Cherokee Nation, a North American indigenous society, whose territory in the eighteenth century extended through the southern Appalachian Mountains, including north-western Georgia and western Tennessee. The exile event is the removal of the Cherokee people by the United States' federal government in 1838, from their homeland to what is now Oklahoma. Their forced journey is known as *Nunna daul Isunyi*, the 'Trail of Tears'. The site considered is New Echota, the Cherokee capitol where the Council and Supreme Court met, re-established as an historic park by the State of Georgia in the 1950s, and now a National Historic Landmark. In comparing the evolution of these sites, patterns emerge which reflect the role of collective memory in recovering places of memory, and the need for geographic *lieux de mémoire* in defining, and perhaps rediscovering, the nation.

Grand Pré

The French colony of *l'Acadie* dates from 1605. Importing technology from their home region of Poitou, seventeenth-century colonists built dykes along the tidal rivers, creating fertile meadow land, and leaving a distinctive modification of the landscape which remains today. Parish churches were another significant built element in the landscape, illustrating the role of religion in defining the Acadian society. A unique francophone culture evolved here, relatively removed from the more substantial French colony of Quebec. In 1713, however, the *Treaty of Utrecht* conferred British citizenship on the Acadians, after this region of North America was ceded to Britain, thus becoming the colony of Nova Scotia. Four decades of relative peace followed, during which time English-speaking settlers began to arrive. In 1755, for reasons that are still debated, the British colonial authority ordered the deportation of the entire Acadian population, and 8,000 to 10,000 people were exiled to other British colonies, an event referred to as *Le Grand Dérangement.* During the journey extended families, an important element of the agrarian Acadian society, were frequently separated, and significant numbers of Acadians died. Many of the refugees eventually found their way to other French-speaking regions, especially Louisiana, then a French colony, establishing the roots of today's 'Cajun' community. The deportation order also decreed the destruction of all Acadian buildings. The thoroughness of this act was recorded by one witness in his journal: 'Buildings burnt by Lieutenant-Colonel Winslow in District of Minas – 255 homes, 276 barns, 11 mills, and one mass house [church]' (Faragher 2005: 363). Within five years, the rich farmland of the Acadians was occupied by English-speaking planters from New England, whose descendants continue to occupy the land today.

The deportation order was lifted in 1763. Some Acadians returned to the colony, though not to the fertile meadows and orchards of the Annapolis Valley, but rather to the rocky coastal edges of Nova Scotia, in disparate, widely scattered pockets of settlement. The farmers became fishermen, and the Acadian Nation existed with little political voice, and a reduced sense of the collective, save memories of the exile and the years of wandering. A significant part of the exiled population established new homes in Louisiana, and in other coastal areas of Canada, especially in New Brunswick, a colony, now province, created in 1784. In the nineteenth century, a more political Acadian Nation began to evolve, signalled by a convention held in 1881 which five thousand Acadians attended and at which a national organisation, the *Societé nationale de l'Assomption*, was founded. Subsequently, symbols of nationality were adopted, including a flag, anthem and national holiday.

Grand Pré was only one of several villages from which Acadians were deported. In 1847, however, the American poet, Henry Wadsworth Longfellow, published *Evangeline*, asking: 'Where is the thatch-roofed village, the home of Acadian farmers … Naught but tradition remains of the beautiful village of Grand-Pré' (2000: 57). The poet's fictional heroine became the symbol of the virtues and travails of the Acadian people and, as discussed by Naomi Griffiths, the actual village of Grand Pré emerged as a symbol of the Acadian home, the 'Garden of Eden' (1982: 28). By the beginning of the twentieth century, the village site was an empty field, save for a few foundation walls, barely evident, and a row of ancient willow trees growing along one edge. As early as 1895, the Acadian press called for the erection of a monument at Grand Pré, '*à la mémoire des Acadiens de 1755*' [to the memory of the Acadians of 1755], claiming that the Acadian deportation was an event, '*qui surpasse en horreur les atrocités arméniennes de nos jours*' [that surpasses in horror the Armenian atrocities of our day] (d'Entrement 1895: 1). In 1907, John Frederic Herbin, a local businessman of Acadian heritage, lamented: 'The memory of the Acadians is kept only by scattered willows and apple trees, cellar excavations which have gaped under the sky for a century and a half, and disused dykes' (1907: 11). He noted traces of the church foundation and a row of willows dating from the French occupation, and called for the establishment of an 'Acadian and Longfellow Memorial Park' (1907: 12). Herbin eventually acquired the site, but seemed unable to interest the Acadian community in realising his dream of a memorial park. In 1917, he sold the site to a railway company that owned a line running along the southern boundary, with the understanding that a commemorative project be undertaken.

The next four decades saw the development of these fourteen acres into an historic park, through the curious partnership of the railway, the *Société nationale de l'Assomption*, and the government of Canada. In 1919, the railway commissioned a Montreal architect, Percy Nobbs, to create a landscape design for the site, initially to serve as a setting for a highly romanticised statue of Evangeline, Longfellow's heroine. The statue was eventually unveiled in 1920, but with no Acadians present at the ceremony: it was an event that both illustrated and sustained the strained relationship between descendants of the exiled Acadians and the heirs of the subsequent occupying group (LeBlanc 2003: 182). However, Nobbs' charge had been greatly expanded, and the statue became but one element in a larger landscape plan incorporating architecture, primarily a 'memorial church', but also a gatehouse and a well, formal axes and a meandering path, in addition to very specific landscape details such as new plantings of the willows that were highly symbolic for the Acadian Nation (Brown 2007: 32–33). The commission for the actual 'church' building, paid for by subscription from the Acadian community, was awarded to an architect of Acadian descent, R. A. Frechet. Though no description of the eighteenth-century village church survived, visual or textual, the Acadian press recorded: '*la société l'Assomption a reconstruit, d'après le plan original, la petite église de pierre de St-Charles, comme un monument à la mémoire des ancêtres malheureux*' [la société l'Assomption has reconstructed, following the original design, the small stone church of Saint Charles, as a monument to the memory of their unfortunate ancestors] (*L'Evangéline* 1923: 6). The building was designed in a vaguely French vernacular form, with a high-pitched gable roof and bell-cast eaves. A variety of additions was subsequently made to the site, including a bust of Longfellow. The government of Canada acquired the site in 1956. Since 1961, it has operated as a National Historic Park.

A crucial, if obvious, value of Grand Pré is its existence as a physical historical site. Though not the most important Acadian village, and with most physical evidence of Acadian occupation deliberately erased, Grand Pré remains, in Kapralski's terms, 'a territory with history' (2001: 35). At one level, Grand Pré reflects the agrarian, family-centred Acadian society, remembered by the contemporary collective as a 'golden age', as an Eden (Johnston 2004: 65–66). However, the site's history also incorporates direct connection with the diaspora event, as one of the villages documented as a point of departure during *Le Grand Dérangement*. Another aspect of 'site as real geography' is the possibility of identifying, even celebrating, the diaspora vector or route of exile, and the potential to consider it in reverse: Grand Pré as a pilgrimage destination for Louisianans of Acadian descent, for example. Significantly, in 1930, 6,000 Acadians came to Grand Pré to commemorate the 175th anniversary of the deportation, including, 'a delegation of forty Cajuns from Louisiana, including twenty-five maidens wearing Evangeline's traditional attire' (Chevalier 1990: 26).

Besides the identification of the site, a second theme is authenticity, in the sense both of the effort to authenticate the site's specific association with the pre-diaspora community and the diaspora event, and the effort to authenticate the value or legitimacy of these associations and *ergo*, the actual events. Herbin's descriptions of the site, and his interpretations of site features (for example, the well as a pre-diaspora feature), were the basis of the initial site development: 'In the field we can trace the site of the chapel where fathers and sons were imprisoned and the foundation of the priest's house' (Wood 1915: 120). More recently, archaeology has been used to authenticate 'scientifically', in this case, the location of the church and the graveyard. Indeed, the latest investigations form part of the current site presentation: trenches in the areas of the original church, the priest's house, and the graveyard, and thus located in the centre of the current park, have explanatory signs, and field staff are anxious to explain the value of their task. The site has been further 'authenticated' through formal recognition by the state through the establishment of a National Historic Park in 1961 by the Government of Canada. Moreover, in 2003, the placement of Grand Pré on Canada's list of tentative nominations for world heritage status suggests that the Acadian exile may be regarded as 'an event of outstanding universal significance' (Parks Canada 2005). Related to this recognition is the increasing role of professional museology on this site, especially with the opening in 2003 of a new visitor centre, incorporating sophisticated exhibitions and interpretative elements. This contrasts with the experience of visitors to the site in 1935, who noted on entering the memorial church: 'we found ourselves not in the memorial atmosphere of the Acadian maid, but in a souvenir establishment. Women, three deep, were pressing against a long counter buying memento' (Longstreth 1935: 148). A further effort to authenticate the site has been the gradual placement of physical, designed elements within the landscape. As noted, the 'memorial church' is not a replica of the original, nor is it presented as such in the contemporary interpretation. Nonetheless, it provides a tangible and recognisable demonstration of the site's association with history. A list of people resident in Grand Pré at the time of the exile is located in the 'apse' of the church and extends this authenticity. Evangeline's well and French willows, the two elements presented as pre-diaspora, are 'really' authentic.

A third theme emerging at Grand Pré is 'mythology', that is, the elaboration of the diaspora event in several, select ways that found resonance with the Acadian society, and which largely took place within the fictional realm. Most obvious is Longfellow's poem naming Grand Pré as the archetypical Acadian village, and creating the heroine, Evangeline. As noted, this helped create the image, the myth, of *l'Acadie* as Eden and *les Acadiens* as innocents. This romantic vision was extended, especially by the railway company, anxious to attract tourists, but also by the government in efforts to develop a tourist industry, as discussed by Ian McKay (1993: 102–138). The romance, especially as personified by Evangeline, was also evident in other aspects of popular culture, for example, *Evangeline*, shot in 1913 at Grand Pré, was the first widely-distributed feature film made in Canada (Morris 1978: 49–50).

The fourth theme linked to Grand Pré is reclamation. A century ago the site served to provoke a memory of the initial occupation and exile, while today it is a destination for returning exiles and a symbol of the reclamation of *l'Acadie*. The site as a place of pilgrimage – evident in the Acadian maidens visiting from Louisiana in the 1930s and in today's cultural tourists of Acadian descent – demonstrates this return, especially as visitors enter the memorial church and, amid the hushed atmosphere of the 'apse', find their family name on the list of Grand Pré residents exiled in 1755. Another indication of reclamation is management of the site. Today, management, including presentation of 'the story', incorporates a significant element of the Acadian community. Since 1998, a management agreement has formally incorporated a representative Acadian organisation in the management process. A corollary to reclamation has been reconciliation. In 2003, a Royal Proclamation acknowledged the suffering that resulted from the Crown's 1755 exile, though specifically admitting to no liability (*Canada Gazette* 2003).

New Echota

Recognition of New Echota as a historic site, and its evolution as a 'left-behind' place of memory, began a generation later than Grand Pré, but still provides an opportunity to investigate the generality of the themes observed at Grand Pré. The Cherokee Nation emerged as a distinct and permanent agricultural society at least a thousand years ago. As the nineteenth century dawned, the Cherokees maintained legal jurisdiction over much of north-west Georgia. In 1825, the Cherokee council established a new capitol, a venue for council and court proceedings. New Echota was a planned settlement, incorporating a grid pattern with one hundred one-acre lots and a two-acre town square, a two-storey Council house, a two-storey Supreme Court building and a print shop. A Cherokee syllabary, developed early in the century, enabled a bilingual newspaper, the *Cherokee Phoenix,* to be published in New Echota and be widely distributed as the first native American newspaper in the United States (McGinty 1955: 15).

As these Cherokee institutions were being built, other negative forces were working towards the erasure of a Cherokee presence in the North Georgia mountains. Principally driven by the westward expansion of white settlement, this force was exacerbated both by the discovery of gold in the region in 1829 and by the entrenched racism within American governmental institutions. In 1830, Congress passed the *Indian Removal Act*, calling for the relocation of Native Americans to western territories. In 1833 Elijah Hicks, writing in the *Cherokee Phoenix,* observed: 'The beautiful and beloved country of the Cherokees is now passing into the occupancy of the Georgians … settlers and droves of land hunters' (Carter 1976: 137). Though 'most of the Cherokee nation struggled to keep their mountainous homeland', in 1835 'they were betrayed by a minority faction who signed the Treaty of New Echota [forfeiting] Cherokee holdings in Georgia' (Scott 1995: 52). Seventeen thousand Cherokee (and 200 slaves) were gathered into internment camps by Federal forces, primarily located in Tennessee. The population was divided into sixteen 'detachments' of approximately 1,000 people each, and thereafter divided into groups each containing a few detachments, which were forcibly removed to what is now Oklahoma, at the time unoccupied land located 1,000 miles westward. The exile occurred over a period of several months in 1838 and involved three principal routes, two overland and one incorporating waterways. While some groups were escorted by the military, most were overseen by Cherokee appointed as 'conductors'. Estimates of total deaths from exposure, disease and other causes range widely, from 2,000 to 6,000 (Thornton 1984: 289). In Cherokee, the journey into exile is remembered by the evocative name *Nunna daul Isunyi*, 'the Trail of Tears'.

The Cherokee land was given over completely to white settlers. At New Echota, save for one house, no evidence of the Cherokee occupation survived. A visitor in 1902 observed: 'The scene of the former greatness of a once prosperous people is now a corn field' (Thornton 1902: D5). A monument was erected in 1931 by the Federal government, but with no official Cherokee presence at the ceremony. The local press reported: 'Today, the descendents of those who drove [the Cherokee] from his home assemble to mark the site of his last official town and to perpetuate ... the memory of one of the most pathetic pages in American history' (*The Calhoun Times* 1931: 2).

In 1952, the Georgia General Assembly authorised the public acquisition of the site for a 'new and useful memorial' commemorating 'forever the historic grounds of the foremost tribal family of America' (*Resolutions* 1952: 609). Archaeological investigations were undertaken by Clemens DeBaillou, who met Cherokee authorities in Oklahoma and corresponded with W. W. Keeler, Principal Chief, even sending him a piece of framing material excavated from one of the house sites. While a contemporary referred to DeBaillou as 'a trouble maker' (Cumming 1958), a 1970 assessment of the early efforts at the site suggested that DeBaillou was 'the only person involved who has attempted to see New Echota and the Cherokee Nation from the viewpoint of the Indian Society at that time' (Baker 1970: 19).

Development of the site included the restoration, reconstruction and relocation of historic resources. The Worcester House was restored by Henry Foreman, an expert on seventeenth-century American architecture. The Vann Tavern, a structure contemporary to New Echota, was moved from its original site in another county. DeBaillou supervised this structure's restoration, in the face of considerable criticism from preservation professionals (Little 1958). Thomas Goree Little, an architect who had worked at Colonial Williamsburg, supervised the construction of replicas of the Print Shop and the Court House, on their original sites, in 1958 and 1959, respectively. Indeed, the media referred to New Echota as 'Georgia's little Williamsburg' (Sparks 1960: 5).

Media coverage of the site's opening in 1962 illustrates a wide range of public response. The *Calhoun Times* warned that 'Anyone ... expecting to see an Indian wigwam ... is in for a big disappointment. New Echota wasn't that sort of town, and the Cherokees weren't that sort of Indians' (McGinty 1962: 1). A politician optimistically suggested: 'This dedication will make us better Americans, for Americans use their mistakes as stepping stones for something more worthwhile' (*Augusta Chronicle* 1962: 4a). In contrast to the 1931 ceremonies, there was a significant Cherokee presence, with one observer noting that 'Georgians and ... Cherokees heaped praise and admiration on each other' (*Augusta Chronicle* 1962: 4a). The scene was probably best captured by the earlier observations of Jess Wilbanks, the 77-year-old farmer who had owned the site: 'It's sure a show' (Sparks 1960: 5).

As noted, the development of New Echota began several decades later than Grand Pré and the figurative return of the Cherokee to this place is less developed. However, the process is evident and illustrates the four themes identified at Grand Pré. Though occupied for only a few years, New Echota's provenance, founded by the Cherokee Council, and its status as the capitol, offer an obvious geographical significance. Unlike Grand Pré, written descriptions of New Echota survive. Benjamin Gold, who visited in 1828, recorded that: 'New Echota is on a hansom [sic] spot of ground … with a Council House and Court House and two or three … stores, about half a dozen framed dwelling houses in sight which could be called respectable in … Connecticut' (cited in Malone 1955: 9). New Echota also lent its name to the later-repudiated treaty that symbolically began the exile. In this way it is a settlement more integrally involved with both people and events than Grand Pré. It shares with that French village, however, the sad memory of having served as one of many staging sites for the diaspora and, like Grand Pré, New Echota has more recently helped define the 'diaspora vector', as part of the 'Trail of Tears' route acknowledged by the U.S. Congress in 1987, and stretching 2,200 miles (3,540 kilometres) from Georgia to Oklahoma.

Authenticity at New Echota was, like Grand Pré, initially pursued through archaeology, with investigations in the 1950s regularly reported in the national journals. Archaeological evidence – for example, the foundation walls of the Boudinot house – remains a current element of the site interpretation and presentation. Historic reconstruction at New Echota was based on archaeological and archival evidence, with the intent to replicate the 'real thing'. Little's reconstructions of the Court House and the Print Shop were widely admired. Conversely, the relocation of the Vann Tavern was criticised by the preservation community, with its relevance to the site and the story of the Cherokee questioned (Gilmore 1975: 97). Because the design of the original Council House was disputed by professional and public officials, its reconstruction, first proposed in the 1950s, was realised only in the 1990s.

Recognition of the site by the state began with the erection of the noted granite monument in 1931 by the federal government, and continued with the development of the site in the 1950s under the auspices of the Georgia State Historical Commission. Federal Historic

Landmark status was conferred in 1976, and the site continues to be managed as a state park. From the initial development in the 1950s, professional museology has been a major site determinant at New Echota. Architect Little, for example, insisted on 'an accurate restoration' and a 'general ground rule' that 'the presentation ... shall be entirely educational and shall display a living type of display' (Little 1957). Construction of the visitor centre in 1966 was undertaken in a similar spirit, with the architects, Gunn and Meyerhoff of Savannah, proposing 'incorporating authentic Cherokee colours in the interior' (Gunn 1966).

The Cherokee exile, the Trail of Tears, has become a well known theme in American popular history, expressed in both film and literature and, in some measure, serving to represent a larger story in American history, that is, native Americans and the nineteenth-century expansion of the American state westward. In this way, the recorded details of the event are mythologised, as are other aspects of Cherokee history. For example, the story of the Cherokee intellectual, Sequoyah, and the development of a Cherokee syllabary and ensuing publication of the first Native American newspaper are often used to illustrate the Europeanisation of Cherokee society. In 1955, a report on the archaeological discovery of bits of printing type was entitled, 'Symbols of a Civilization that Perished in its Infancy' (McGinty 1955).

New Echota, the actual town site, has been conspicuously absent from this popularisation of Cherokee society and exile. In 1994, Barbara Little noted: 'There is little specific attention to New Echota as a place of importance in the Cherokee strategy for survival. But it is an essential place, especially for understanding the strategies of a culture that traditionally placed great emphasis on places in the landscape' (1994: 28). In part this may be due to the eponymous treaty signed at this place, which gave legitimacy to the event, and which was subsequently seen as an act of treason by the Cherokee. The site's role in the history-telling / mythology of the exile has increased with recent efforts, notably the designation of 'The Trail of Tears' as a National Historic Trail by the U.S. Congress.

A figurative reclamation by the Cherokee of their last capitol in Georgia has also been slow to develop. In the 1950s, the Principal Chief, resident in Oklahoma, expressed a desire to 'some day pay a visit to the land of my ancestors' (Keeler 1955). However, site development for the subsequent two decades demonstrated little Cherokee presence. In 1976, designation of the site as a National Historic Landmark provided an opportunity for a more obvious Cherokee participation, with members of the nation prominent on the ceremony's dais. Far more significant in signalling a gradual return of the Cherokee Nation to New Echota was the meeting of the Cherokee Council at New Echota in 1992, thus constituting the first meeting of the Council at this place since exile. In part it celebrated the sod-turning for a reconstruction of the Council House, a project which had been delayed for thirty years as the professionals worked towards an agreement on the plan and form of the nineteenth-century structure. The building was dedicated in 1996, when the Olympic Torch passed through New Echota enroute to Atlanta, with the participation of the Deputy Principal Chief of the Cherokee Nation. Visitors to New Echota today will see, at the entrance, flags of both the Cherokee Nation of Oklahoma and the Eastern Cherokee of Tennessee, as well as portraits of current principal chiefs: tangible evidence of a figurative return.

Conclusion

Both Grand Pré and New Echota, though at different stages of site evolution, demonstrate the discovery and recreation, by later diaspora generations, of 'left-behind' sites of memory. At each site four common elements are evident in this process. Central to this discussion is the identification of a physical, tangible location clearly associated with both the pre-exile occupation of the site, and the actual exile event. Grand Pré was a major Acadian village and a point of embarkation. New Echota was the site of the Cherokee capitol and the place where the *Treaty of New Echota* was signed.

A second element is physical evidence of the association between site and event. The initial destruction of such evidence at both places may be deemed very modern. Though writing of twentieth-century diaspora, Robert Bevan observes:

> systemic destruction of particular building types or architectural traditions … happens in conflicts where the erasure of memories, history and identity attached to architecture and place – forced forgetting – is the goal itself … [but] rebuilding can be as symbolic as the destruction that necessitates it … [and] can serve to mask the past; to erase the

> gaps, the voids, the ruinations that bear witness. And whoever builds does so in a situation of power relations reflecting the post-construction context. (2006: 8)

The fanciful reconstructions of the Memorial Church at Grand Pré and the Council House at New Echota demonstrate this requirement for literal representation of the story. Though these structures are obviously not original, the quest for authenticity is demonstrated at each place through the use of archaeological evidence in the interpretation and presentation programmes.

The reclamation of sites of memory in the 'homeland' cannot be explained merely by the tangible and, as Nora suggests:

> *Lieux de mémoire* are complex things. At once natural and artificial, simple and ambiguous, concrete and abstract ... if history – time and change – did not intervene, we would be dealing [with] simple memorials. (1996: 14–15)

Thus a third common element is the association of the sites with the specific exile events, using records, memories and myths, thereby providing a basis for the site to serve in the process of redefining the nation. Longfellow's fictional Evangeline, a resident of Grand Pré, and the Trail of Tears, associated with the *Treaty of New Echota*, illustrate this process.

A last common element, more obvious at Grand Pré than at New Echota, is the overt reclamation of the site by the exiled nation and the subsequent use of the site to reconcile and define. At Grand Pré, the site now incorporates a significant Acadian input in management decisions. Through the pending world heritage nomination, the significance of both the Acadian occupation of the place and the exile event are being acknowledged. At New Echota, the Cherokee Council has met for the first time since the exile, the flags of the Cherokee nations fly at the front entrance and the site is used for an increasing number of Cherokee activities. Reflecting on this process, Kapralski writes:

> the construction of a landscape and the construction of identity are inseparable parts of one process, as a result of which landscape becomes incorporated into the group's identity, being one of the symbolic representations of the latter. (2001: 35)

Ultimately these two sites reflect the dominance of geography over history or, as poet Elizabeth Bishop, who spent several childhood years in Nova Scotia not far from Grand Pré, and who was obsessed in both life and art by conflicting notions of migration and home, wrote: 'Topography displays no favorites; North as near as West. More delicate than the historians' are the map-makers' colors' (1983: 3).

Notes

1 The word 'nation' is used within this chapter to denote a group with shared history, and common customs and language, not necessarily organised as a sovereign state or country.

References

Baker, S. G. (1970). Report to the Georgia Historical Commission. 31 January. New Echota State Historic Site Archives.

Bevan, R. (2006). *The Destruction of Memory*. Chicago: University of Chicago Press.

Bodnar, J. (1992). *Remaking America*. Princeton, NJ: Princeton University Press.

Bishop, E. (1983). The Map. *Elizabeth Bishop, The Complete Poems*. New York: Farrar, Straus and Giroux.

Brown, W. (2007). Percy Nobbs and the Memorial Garden at Grand Pré. *Journal of the Society for the Study of Architecture in Canada* 32, 2: 29–38.

Carter, S. (1976). *Cherokee Sunset, A Nation Betrayed*. Garden City, New York: Doubleday.

Chevalier, J. (1990). *Semiotics, Romanticism and the Scripture*. New York: Mouton de Gruyter.

Cumming, J. (1958). Correspondence to Thomas Little, 25 March. New Echota State Historic Site Archives.

d'Entremont, H. L. (1895). *Un Monument à Grand Pré. Le Moniteur Acadien* 2 August: 1.

Faragher, J. M. (2005). *A Great and Noble Scheme*. New York: W. W. Norton.

Foreman, H. C. (1957). *Virginia Architecture in the Seventeenth Century*. Williamsburg: Virginia 350th Anniversary Celebration Corporation.

Gilmore, J. H. (1975). *The Georgia Historical Commission, Its History and Its Role in Historic Preservation*. PhD dissertation, University of Georgia.

Griffiths, N. (1982). Longfellow's Evangeline: The Birth and Acceptance of a Legend. *Acadiensis* 11, 2: 28–41.

Gunn, R. (1966). Correspondence to William Mitchell, 27 April. New Echota State Historic Site Archives.

Herbin, F. (1907). *The History of Grand Pré*. Toronto: William Briggs (third edition).

Johnston, A. J. B. (2004). The Call of the Archetype and the Challenge of Acadian History. *French Colonial History* 5: 63–92.

Kapralski, S. (2001). Battlefields of Memory. *History & Memory* 13, 2: 35–58.

Keeler, W. W. (1955). Correspondence to Clemens DeBaillou. 11 October. New Echota State Historic Site Archives.

LeBlanc, B. (2003). *Postcards from Acadie*. Kentville, NS: Gaspereau Press.

Little, B. J. (1994). People with History: An Update on Historical Archaeology in the United States. *Journal of Archaeological Method and Theory* 1, 1: 5–40.

Little, T. (1957). Correspondence to C. E. Gregory, 27 December. New Echota State Historic Site Archives.

Little, T. (1958). Correspondence to Joseph Cumming, 16 April. New Echota State Historic Site Archives.

Longfellow, H. W. (2000). Evangeline: A Tale of Acadie. In J. D. McClatchey (ed.), *Henry Wadsworth Longfellow, Poems and Other Writing*. New York: Library Classics.

Longstreth, T. M. (1935). *To Nova Scotia, the Sunrise Province of Canada*. Toronto: Ryerson Press.

Malone, H. T. (1955). New Echota – Capitol of the Cherokee Nation. *Early Georgia* 1, 4: 6–13.

McGinty, J. R. (1955). Symbols of a Civilization that Perished in its Infancy. *Early Georgia* 1, 4: 14–17.

McGinty, J. R. (1962). Echota Once Center of Cherokee World. *Calhoun Times* 10 May, 1.

McKay, I. (1993). History and the Tourist Gaze: The Politics of Commemoration in Nova Scotia, 1935–1964. *Acadiensis* 22, 2: 102–138.

Morris, P. (1978). *Embattled Shadows: A History of Canadian Cinema*. Montreal: McGill-Queens University Press.

Nora, P. (1996). *Realms of Memory: The Construction of the French Past,* 3 vols. New York: Columbia University Press.

Parks Canada. (2005). Press release. http://www.pc.gc.ca/progs/spm-whs/itm3-/site2/page2_E.asp [online, accessed 26 August, 2005]

Samuel, R. (1994). *Theatres of Memory*. London: Verso.

Scott, T. A. (ed.) (1995). *Cornerstones of Georgia History, Documents that Formed the State*. Athens, GA: University of Georgia Press.

Sparks, A. (1960). Indian Village Comes to Life Again. *Atlanta Journal Magazine* 4 September: 5.

Thornton, M. (1902). Tales of the Early Cherokee Civilization. *The Atlanta Constitution* 23 November: D5.

Thornton, R. (1984). Cherokee Population Losses during the Trail of Tears: A New Perspective and a New Estimate. *Ethnohistory* 31, 4: 289–300.

Wood, R. K. (1915). *The Tourist's Maritime Provinces*. New York: Dodd, Mead.

References with no authors identified:

—— (1931). *Atlanta Journal* 18 September: 2.

—— (1962). Georgians, Indians dedicate memorial. *Augusta Chronicle* 13 May: 4a.

—— (1931). *The Calhoun Times* 17 September.

—— (2003). *Canada Gazette* 137, no. 27, 31 December.

—— (1923). *Sanctuaires Historiques Canadiens. L'Evangéline* 26 July: 6.

—— (1952). New Echota State Memorial Park. *Resolutions of the General Assembly of the State of Georgia* 1: 609.

Keeping the memory alive: Palestinian women in Lebanon narrate home, homeland and homelessness

Maria Holt

UNIVERSITY OF WESTMINSTER, LONDON

Introduction

When the state of Israel was established in 1948, the majority of Palestinian Arabs fled to neighbouring countries. Today approximately 400,000 Palestinian refugees still reside in the camps of Lebanon. Their feelings of homelessness have frequently been reinforced by such events as the destruction of the Tal el-Zaatar refugee camp in Beirut in 1976, the massacre of Sabra and Shatila in 1982, and most recently in 2007, when battles between the Lebanese army and Islamist militants inside the Nahr al-Bared refugee camp near Tripoli caused hundreds of Palestinian refugees to flee from their homes in terror. These instances of abrupt and unexpected homelessness have confirmed for Palestinians the lack of safety and absence of belonging that have characterised their lives since 1948. In this chapter, I will argue that women experience home and homelessness in significantly different ways from men. Their close relationship with the home and their memories and imaginings of the Palestinian homeland have a profound impact on the transmission of identity to successive generations. The discussion is based on research I conducted in 2006 and 2007 with Palestinian women in the camps of Lebanon.

Um Fadi[1] is 52 years old. Her family is from Tulkarem, now in the West Bank. In February 2007, she told me the story of how her family left Palestine. Her father, who was unmarried, worked at Haifa Port. He was accused by the British of being a fighter and imprisoned for five years. Um Fadi's parents, along with the majority of Palestinian Arabs, were driven from their homes in 1948 by the violent process involved in the creation of the state of Israel, and forced to take refuge in neighbouring countries. Um Fadi's mother, who was from Haifa, was very young when she left Palestine. The family carried bread and cheese with them from home, and they travelled to Lebanon by ship. After her parents married, they lived in the Shatila refugee camp in Beirut. Um Fadi was born in Shatila and had two brothers who died in the war in Lebanon. She is a survivor of the 1982 Sabra and Shatila massacre. At that time, she said, her mother was taken from her home; she saw people being killed; a group of men and boys went out of the camp with a white flag to tell the Israelis that there were no fighters in the camp, but they did not return. Um Fadi now lives in Mieh Mieh camp in Sidon. Her most heartfelt desire is to return to Haifa.[2]

What does the concept of 'home' mean to women such as Um Fadi, for whom home, far from being a place of security, is associated with violence, loss and exile? Places and communities are created 'through a shared sense of history and shared practices and meanings' (Deeb 2006: 66). Yet if a woman's history evokes humiliation, if her 'shared practices and meanings' are associated with violence, homelessness and powerlessness, and if the conditions of her daily life do not permit the possibility of improvement, how can she raise her children with the dignity of a more tolerable future? Her marginalisation is further reinforced by the gendered nature of Palestinian national memory. The *nakbeh* ('catastrophe') of 1948, as a communal trauma, continues to resonate through the Palestinian diaspora, but it is, in Bresheeth's words, a 'suppressed story' (2007: 180). As he says, the 'narrative of Palestine in the cultural arena carved by Zionism is … a story of erasure, denial, and active silencing' (2007: 179). Events such as those described in Um Fadi's story emphasise the 'active silencing' that continues to this day.

In this chapter, I explore the themes of home and homelessness as a method of understanding the 'narrative of Palestine' and examine some of the ways in which refugee women in Lebanon have tried to re-create home in the absence of home. Their behaviour is linked to loss and pride: loss of their homeland and dignity, and pride in resisting the occupier or invader. My research interviews with Palestinian refugee women in Lebanon sought to capture how their memories of Palestine and their frequent exposure to violent conflict in Lebanon have buttressed their sense of identity, while challenging male ownership of the nationalist narrative. The particular question I pose is: what has been the impact of traumatic upheaval, humiliation and disempowerment, including the destruction of their homes, on women's identity-formation in the camps of Lebanon? The chapter discusses their experiences of 'living on the margins', firstly, by locating them within theoretical understandings of home and exile; secondly, from the perspective of memories and imaginings of the Palestinian homeland; thirdly, in terms of forced migration and the creation of a diaspora; fourthly, by considering women's relationships with the refugee camps in which they live; and finally, in light of their narratives of violence and resistance.

Theoretical understandings of living on the margins

Trauma has been described as 'an out-of-context experience that upsets expectations and unsettles one's very understanding of existing contexts' (LaCapra 2007: 206). Palestinians experienced the *nakbeh* of 1948 as a profound trauma which disrupted 'existing contexts' and shattered expectations. It was compounded by the actions of the newly created state of Israel, which not only destroyed many of the physical traces of Palestine, but also sought to suppress the legitimacy of Palestinian memory. This, in turn, produced what Hoffman describes as 'the transmission of traumatic experiences across generations' (2005: xii). As Thomson says, we compose our memories 'to make sense of our past and present lives' (1998: 300), but when the past has been colonised by an alternative version of history and the present allows no possibility of resolution or redemption, then refugees such as the Palestinian women are condemned to exist in 'a continuity of pain and trauma' (Bresheeth 2007: 161). While the pain of recollection is certainly strong for all refugees, it is balanced by more pleasant memories of 'an idyllic social structure where village relations are characterized by solidarity, unity, and generosity' (Davis 2007: 71), and of a landscape in harmony with local traditions and rhythms of life. These memories, too, have been handed down through generations, as exemplified in the following fictionalised account: 'We were living in Alama, in the country, amongst the plantations and the olive trees. There was bounty all around. Amongst the blossoms, the orange blossoms. Oh, how beautiful it was'.[3]

For Palestinians, 1948 is commemorated as the year when their world was turned upside down. It was the year in which 'Palestine ceased to exist. It lost its name, it lost its territory, and it lost many of its people' (Gilmour 1980: 19). Approximately 100,000 Palestinians fled north into Lebanon. Since that time, 'homelessness' has been a recurring theme for them. Given their history and the insecure nature of life for Palestinians in Lebanon, the concept of 'home' has developed particular, and sometimes contradictory, meanings. On the one hand, it is associated with homelessness in the sense of having lost or been forced out of the homeland and, on the other hand, it refers to homesickness, a longing to return. Home is located in the imagination and is also part of an unsatisfactory and frequently fearful present reality. Palestinian refugee women experience home and exile on several overlapping levels. The first level of meaning refers to life on the margins. As Edward Said observes:

> Every direct route to the interior, and consequently the interior itself, is either blocked or pre-empted. The most we can hope for is to find margins – normally neglected surfaces and relatively isolated, irregularly placed spots – on which to put ourselves. (1986: 63)

Buijs suggests that 'part of the process of crossing physical and metaphysical boundaries for migrants and refugees is an investment in an idealized perception of the society of origin or homeland' (1993: 3). The refugees experienced abrupt dislocation from the only homes they had ever known and a new condition of having nothing. They 'felt powerless in the wake of the sudden loss of control over their destiny and an intense frustration over the inability of any person, institution, or government to remedy their situation' (Peteet 1991: 24). This resulted in intense insecurity and bewilderment; a sense of loss and grieving. In response, women throughout the diaspora 'became caught up in family and communal survival' (Fleishmann 2003: 209). Those who remember Palestine with its villages and close-knit communities, and others who have only heard about it, have created 'an idealized perception' (Buijs 1993: 3), a place to which every Palestinian yearns to return. Thus 'home' is associated with safety and belonging.

The second level of meaning concerns the homelessness of life in an alien environment. Said has written about 'the loneliness of exile', the exile's 'broken history', 'the pathos of exile', 'the stigma of being an outsider' (1990: 359–62). Exile has been described as 'an affliction' (Nixon 1994: 117). It is characterised by marginality and lack of belonging. 'Dispossessed … of their social heritage, refugees lead a provisional life, drifting from camp to camp, disturbing local people's habits ... they are a burden on the community' (Minh-ha 1994: 12). Under such circumstances, the refugee can never feel 'at home'. The destruction of one's home is equated with an assault on identity and memory: for example, many of the older women I met described running away in 1948 'with nothing'. Palestinian families have tried to re-create homeliness, but their day-to-day reality remains precarious. Of the 16 camps set up after 1950 by the United Nations Relief and Works Agency for Palestine Refugees in the Near East (UNRWA), four have been destroyed altogether while others, such as Shatila camp in Beirut, Ain el-Hilwe camp in Sidon, Rashidiyya camp near Tyre and Nahr al-Bared camp in Tripoli, have been subjected to attacks and massacres.

The third meaning relates to Mohanty and Martin's argument that 'being home' supposedly 'refers to the place where one lives within familiar, safe, protected boundaries' (1986: 196). However, this version of home could be an illusion, a 'repressive space built on the surrendering of all responsibility' (Mohanty and Martin 1994: 198). The history of Palestinians in exile illustrates that 'home' can 'simultaneously be a place of safety and terror' (Brah 2003: 615). There are a number of reasons why home is rarely a place of safety. It is, first of all, a temporary remedy in the absence of return. Therefore, dwellings tend to be insubstantial, easily damaged but rarely repaired. High levels of poverty in the camps mean that residents are in no position to improve their houses. In addition, since the departure of the Palestine Liberation Organization (PLO) in 1982, the camps are largely defenceless and therefore unable to withstand attacks by enemies such as Israel and, on occasion, Lebanese militant groups. At the same time, they are also sites of significance and resilience for their inhabitants. In her novel, *The Eye of the Mirror*, Liana Badr wrote about the 1975–76 siege and massacre at the Tel al-Za'ter refugee camp in Beirut. Women of the camp emerge thus:

> triumphant and defiant. Despite the continuous bombardment of shells, they knead the dough and bake bread, under threat of sniper fire they fetch water, they feed their children, nurse the wounded and try to keep their families together. These simple and apolitical acts sustain the besieged camp for an entire year. They have no say in the political

> decisions made by men, but they dutifully pick up the pieces and try to normalize their lives. Survival becomes the ability to brew some tea and drink it with your friends and neighbours. (1994: vi)

A final level of meaning suggests the possibility of creating a new place to call home. Hammond argues that people who have been violently displaced may come to define 'home' 'not in geographic terms but as the conceptual and affective space in which community identity, and political and cultural membership intersect', and, in this sense, she adds, 'home is a variable term, one which can be transformed, newly invented, and developed in relation to the circumstances in which people find themselves' (2004: 10). There are differences among Palestinian camp-dwellers in Lebanon. While many women are adamant that 'home', for them, means a return to Palestine, others have formed significant relationships with the camps where they live, to the extent that, for some, they have come to replace the homeland. For example, Mona, an 18-year-old girl in Qasmiyye camp in southern Lebanon, said that their camp is a 'sweet place' because there are no strangers. It is not like other camps; it has trees and spaces.[4]

The Zionist/Israeli narrative of 'glorious rebirth' has caused its victims, the native Palestinians, to 'disappear from the scene' (Sa'di 2007: 286). Their story, as Bresheeth (2007) says, has been suppressed and this communal trauma has had a devastating effect on Palestinians' cultural identity as 'one people'. At the same time, as Hall argues, 'identities are the names we give to the different ways we are positioned by, and position ourselves within, the narratives of the past' (2006: 435). There is a tension between, on the one hand, the humiliation and disempowerment of the 'narrative of Palestine', as well as Palestinians' inability and the world's unwillingness to redress the wrong done to them and, on the other hand, points of significant difference between refugee communities in their various sites of exile which constitute, in Hall's words, 'what we have become' (2006: 435).

> **The 'narrative of Palestine'**
> My only hope in life
> Is to visit my homeland, Palestine
> Even if only once
> To breathe in its scent

And keep it in my memory
So I never forget it.
(Maysa Salloum, aged 13, Ain el-Hilwe refugee camp)[5]

Most Palestinian refugees have heard stories about their homeland from their parents and grandparents. They know about the villages that were left behind and about the rituals of everyday life. There are a few elderly survivors of the *nakbeh* living in the refugee camps of Lebanon who remember what life was like in Palestine before 1948. Um Marwan is 74 years old and was born in the city of Akka (Acre) in Palestine. Her father worked with the British army. They were living in a city, but there were parks for the children and orchards. She remembers going to the swings with her friends. Her uncles planted and harvested the land because her father was too busy; they were getting support from the land and this brought them money. When the war started, her brother came and told them they must leave. Her uncles, who were traders, said they should go to Lebanon. They were the last people to leave Akka; the city was empty. She was sure that, if she went back to Palestine, she would remember where her house was; it was 'like living in heaven', she said, a wonderful life.[6]

Um Farid, who is 78 years old, was married in Palestine at the age of 17. She has 11 children and 47 grandchildren. She is from the village of Kabri. Many Lebanese used to work in Palestine, she said, because it had a good economy and was an agricultural country. She went back to Palestine once, for a visit, but the Israelis had destroyed the village. It is now a park with pine trees.[7] Um Nabil, also from Kabri, recalls working in the fields and orchards of Palestine. Now in her 80s and living in extreme poverty in Bourj el-Barajne camp in Beirut, she recounted how her family used to own land; they grew grapes and olives and pressed the olives to make oil. Everything came from the land, she said. Her husband died soon after they left Palestine, when her daughter was only 15 days old. When Um Nabil arrived in Lebanon, she had to start working as she had no husband and needed to earn money. She had to leave her children alone in the tent where they lived.[8] As Rosemary Sayigh notes: 'The village – with its special arrangements of houses and orchards, its open meeting-places, its burial ground, its collective identity – was built into the personality of each individual villager to a degree that made separation like an obliteration of the self' (1979: 107). For all three narrators, the 'concept of deterritorialisation is understood as describing the displacement and dislocation of identities, persons and meanings' (Brah 2003: 627–628).

Peteet has written about the refugees' 'intense longing to return to their homes and their lands' (1995: 168). She observes: 'Place, or village, in the Palestinian consciousness, is what ties a person to the space of Palestine'. Moreover, Palestinians 'insist on a specific connection between space, place, culture, and identity' (1995: 170–171). In the 1980s and 1990s, Palestinian 'village memorial books' began to appear, produced by some of the elderly people who remembered life in pre-1948 Palestine. They include maps, photographs and descriptions of traditional practices. The memorial books, as Hammami remarks, are 'not simply about remembering a lost community – they are consciously nationalist narratives and their production is a conscious project of mapping the lost homeland – destroyed village by destroyed village' (2004: 35). However, as Hammami goes on to say, women 'are consistently located in the books in only two specific areas; under the 'social' in the form of descriptions of local dress and in weddings ... The only women's voices that consistently appear in the books are in the form of songs that women sung at weddings' (2004: 35). The authors of the books, Davis notes, are 'almost always older men' (2007: 56). The books aim to memorialise places that have been destroyed and the customs associated with those places. However, since women's voices have been almost entirely marginalised and thus the centrality of women to an imagined or remembered home obscured, the books merely reinforce the male-nationalist narrative of Palestine. In providing compelling personal recollections of the traditions of their homeland, several women in Bourj el-Barajne camp made clear the inadequacy of the memorial books as a comprehensive record of pre-1948 Palestine.

At the same time, there is another level of memory, associated with the trauma of flight in 1948. Amal, who left Palestine when she was a child, recalled her mother telling her that because of the bombs, people would have to leave for a week or two, so they left without clothing or even documents. Her older sister was engaged and had a pair of new shoes for her wedding, but her family said 'don't wear your new shoes or they will be ruined', so she left them, remembered Amal, for the Israelis.[9] According to Um Ossama: 'Living in Palestine, we were living in our home with our family ... It is different to live as a nomad, with no resources and no wealth' (Lynd *et al.* 1994: 106). Her words evoke the stark distinction between the security of one's own place/land and the danger and impermanence of exile. At the same time, 'the relationship of the first generation to the place of migration is different from that of subsequent generations, mediated as it is by memories of what was recently left behind' (Brah 2003: 625). Generational differences are also apparent in women's narratives. While older women speak from firsthand experience of the land, their daughters and granddaughters tend to focus on details of their lives in Lebanon. Yet all these memories, comprising recollections of the contentment of being 'at home', the trauma of upheaval and dispossession and the intense discomfort of an existence cut off an identity rooted in belonging, create a rich and densely woven tapestry and contribute to the complex 'narrative of Palestine'.

The Palestinian nation in exile

The question of how to conceptualise the Palestinian nation dispersed around the world and the ways in which attachment to the homeland has developed over generations has preoccupied theorists of 'diaspora'. Perceived as a 'rift between the location of residence and the location of belonging' (Gilroy 1994: 207), diaspora is a way of talking about Palestinians in exile. It is said to refer to 'the doubled relationship ... that migrants, exiles, and refugees have to places – their connections to the space they currently occupy and their continuing involvement with 'back home'' (Lavie and Swedenburg 1996: 14), while also evoking contradictory images. The notion of living on the margins or border positionality as 'a vantage point of privileged insight' (Brah 2007: 289) is unable to disguise the pain of exile that has 'torn millions of people from the nourishment of tradition, family and geography' (Said 1990: 358). Hanafi argues that 'the Palestinians abroad do not constitute a real diaspora, but rather a 'partially diasporized people'' (2005: 98). They have been 'diasporized' against their will and are perhaps better described, in Cohen's phrase, as a 'victim diaspora', caused by the formation of the state of Israel (1999: 272). The notion of 'diaspora' evokes the image of a journey, yet, as Brah says, 'diasporic journeys are essentially about settling down, about putting roots 'elsewhere'' (2003: 616). The concept of a transnational population at ease in 'a world of movement' (Rapport and Dawson 1998: 4) is at odds with the reality of forced migration and injustice. Nabulsi, for example, considers the notion of a cosmopolitan and mobile 'Palestinian Diaspora' to be 'largely a false image', since for her, 'the overwhelming character of the Palestinian people remains that of a landed people with a close bond to their homeland' (2002: 2). The ideas of journey and arrival sit uneasily with the experiences of Palestinian refugees whose claims for justice have still not been addressed and who remain, therefore, 'as a haunting diagnostic of the exclusionary nature of the Israeli state' (Peteet 2005: 23).

When they first arrived in Lebanon, the refugees did not imagine they would be staying long. While they did not want to be there and had no sense of permanence, they also saw the need to improve their living conditions. Wherever possible, they attempted to preserve some semblance of the village life they had left behind. Some of the refugee camps were established by people from one Palestinian village or a group of villages who knew each other and shared customs. This gave individual camps their specific characters. For example, Shatila camp in Beirut was originally founded by families from the village of Majd al-Kurum in the Galilee.[10] Even though their way of life had been taken from them, refugees sought to reassemble an orderly mode of living. Familiar surroundings provided protection, especially for women who were able to move safely within the boundaries of the camp. They could not hope to remake Palestine in the alien environment of Lebanon, but they could at least preserve some of the habits and traditions of home and, in this respect, women played a key role. Refugee narratives, as Farah says, 'show how women reproduce a sense of place while out of place in numerous ways', for example, by refusing to relocate outside camps and by fostering social networks that re-establish Palestinian belonging (2005: 210).

In conversations with refugee women in Lebanon, I asked them about the geographical location of family members. In almost every case, women reported that they had relatives in other parts of the world: Europe, North America, or other Arab countries. Um Marwan, for example, has a daughter living in the US and another in Australia. Um Farid's son married a Danish woman and is now living in the Gulf, while Um Fadi has brothers in Denmark, Sweden and Holland and sisters in Jordan, Syria and Denmark. In this sense, they are a highly transnational population.

The refugee camp as a site of significance

Despite their lack of belonging, Palestinians have become an integral part of Lebanon's 'geography of fear' (Khalaf 1993: 18). Since they have been home to several generations of refugees, the camps themselves have become sites of significance. In Peteet's view, they exist as 'a borderland of sorts, a remnant and a reterritorialization of Palestinian culture', although danger lurks on the margins of camps, a 'perilous territory of not-belonging' (1995: 175). After its destruction in 1976, Tel al-Za'ter camp became 'a symbol of tragedy, a repository of memory of defeat, massacre, and erasure ... it also symbolizes heroic resistance' (Peteet 2005: 142–143). After the 1982 massacre, Shatila camp 'became closely linked to heroic defence, steadfastness, and tragedy, a metaphor for defeat and trauma' (2005: 143). Refugees, as Peteet states, 'creatively imposed their own imprints on the space and meaning of the camps' (2005: 94).

Many refugee women display feelings of attachment to the camp where they live, but these are also ambivalent feelings and display a complex sense of belonging. In the words of Um Walid, a middle-aged woman with seven children, 'the camp is our society and culture'[11] and, for her children, it is also the only place they know and, as such, is a focus of loyalty and community. According to Rasmiyeh, 'Living in the camp is not that bad. You feel that you live among Palestinians like yourself. We are accustomed to camp life'.[12] For Latifeh there is a strong emotional attachment: 'I like living in the camp. I was born and raised here. I do not like to live outside because I feel my heart is in the camp'.[13] Um Munir, a woman in her early forties, observed that the camp is calm, better than living outside, and if anything happens, 'we are with our own people'.[14] Her neighbour, Jamila, agreed that the importance of the camp to her is that she is with her people as they endure the same suffering and it is important to be together.[15] Zahra, a woman in her fifties, said that there is a difference between 'home' and 'homeland'. For Zahra, home is equated with husband and children, the place where one lives, but homeland means belonging – everyone goes back to it: 'it is everything for us', she said.[16] Layoun refers to the 'place' of Palestinian women as 'inside' the home, as the nurturing sustainers of life (1992: 411). But this version of safe, familial life is thrown into doubt by the insecurity of the camps. There is a tension between the natural desire to feel comfortable and 'at home', on the one hand,

and, on the other, reluctance on the part of most refugees to become too settled. For example, a plan by UNRWA in 2007 to improve living conditions for camp dwellers was greeted with suspicion. While some argued in favour of greater comfort, others saw 'the use of concrete in construction ... as a threat to the Palestinians' struggle to return to their homeland' (Zaatari 2007: 2).

Even those who appreciate the symbolic value and the protection provided by the camp are critical of its many shortcomings, such as the inadequate structures, overcrowding and lack of amenities. Um Ghassan, aged 60, born in Palestine, declared it does not matter whether she lives inside or outside the camp. The problem in the camp, she added, is that no one has any privacy in their home; for example, if she wants to argue with her husband or children, everyone can hear and will gossip.[17] Um Nabil agreed that 'living in the camp is difficult', especially if a woman has no one to support her, and the houses are not healthy.[18] A younger woman, Reem, said that she has no choice but to live in the camp, but it 'is only a place'.[19] The theme of 'only a place' was echoed by several women. Um Aziz remarked that her place of residence is important because she was born there, got married and is raising her children. However, it is not the main place, but 'only a place, not a home'.[20] Fatme said that she has no choice and, although the camp 'is only a place', it also provides safety.[21] Other women echoed this sentiment. Layla, an illiterate 39-year-old woman, born in Sidon, said that she regards Lebanon as 'only a place to live'; she feels that everyone treats the Palestinians differently, does not feel comfortable and has no sense of belonging.[22]

Almost everyone agreed that 'home' means Palestine, but it sometimes became apparent in the interviews that it was meant in an abstract or symbolic sense. Although the right of Palestinian return is not negotiable, there are significant reasons why women might be unable or unwilling to go back; for example, they may believe the country is not safe, or have a husband or child buried in Lebanon. For some women, Lebanon itself has become 'home'. Um Samir, an elderly woman, born in Palestine, said that she considers Lebanon her homeland and is not hoping to return to Palestine. She does not want to leave the camp as it is like Palestine for her.[23] Um Tarik, a 52-year-old mother of six children said that her homeland is 'in her heart', in memories and imagination.[24]

In the summer of 2007, approximately 40,000 Palestinian refugees were forced to flee from their homes in the Nahr al-Bared camp in northern Lebanon. I had the opportunity to interview some of the women who had taken up temporary residence in other camps around the country. These women were devastated by the loss of their homes, their community and all their possessions. They felt unprotected and were uncertain about whether they would ever be able to return to their camp. Their experience confirmed their utter powerlessness and vulnerability. One of them, Um Khalid, a woman in her seventies, compared these events to the *nakbeh*.[25] The women also revealed another side to Palestinian imaginings of 'home'. According to Samira, a 35-year-old unmarried woman, Nahr al-Bared is 'completely different' from other camps in Lebanon. Residents had a lovely life, she said; they lived peacefully. The houses were bigger and more beautiful than those in Bourj el-Barajne, were tidier, with better furniture and gardens. The camp is equated, she said, with the homeland. The residents forgot Palestine because they were living happily.[26] Um Ahmad, also in her thirties, has lived in Nahr al-Bared since 1986. In her words, life in the camp was 'very beautiful'. She and her husband built their own house 15 years ago. Now they have lost everything. They left the camp with nothing; they even lost their shoes while running away.[27] The experience of the Nahr al-Bared residents is similar to those displaced from Tel al-Za'ter after the siege and massacre of 1976. Refugees forced to move to Shatila 'wistfully reminisced about the 'good days' … when the camp was like a big village … People used to know one another, know where they came from' (Peteet 2005: 101). This raises the question of when a location becomes home. What is the difference, as Brah asks, 'between 'feeling at home' and staking claim to a place of one's own?' (2003: 624)

Women, violence and resistance

Peteet argues that 'violence and suffering have been integral to the Palestinian national narrative of displacement and exile' (2005: 197). In the 1960s, a Palestinian resistance movement began to develop. The PLO and its commitment to an 'armed popular revolution', together with greater autonomy within the camps, provided an opportunity for some women to become politically active. During the period of the 'Palestinian revolution', women's status underwent considerable change. The 'meaning of work for women was transformed during this period ... Now to work was a national endeavour and a statement of women's increased autonomy and participation in public life' (Peteet 1991: 36). For many young women living in camps, the opportunity to contribute to the shared national project was a form of liberation.

During this period, there was a feeling of optimism and many people were confident that their efforts would enable them, in time, to return to Palestine. Abir, in Rashidiyya camp, described herself as 'a fighter for Palestine', ready to encourage her five children to join the fight and even herself to become a 'martyr'. She declared that she would never give up the struggle against Israel but would fight 'to the last woman'.[28] Although this revolutionary model of womanhood did not articulate itself in terms of 'feminism', it played a full part in the struggle for survival. However, as Fleischmann observes, women's 'very acts of participating publicly, sometimes even violently, in the major issues of their day, and transgressing gendered norms of behaviour constitute feminism' (2003: 209). At the same time, however, the transgression of boundaries remains difficult for women. Um Fawaz, a woman in her early fifties, told me how her husband, who had been a fighter, was killed in the first Israeli invasion of the south. Only 22 years old when her husband died and with a week-old baby, Um Fawaz found life very difficult. Society, she said, does not look kindly on widows and cannot accept that a woman might choose to live alone. She did not have the opportunity to remarry and was therefore prevented from having the large family she had wanted.[29] My research revealed that most women see themselves primarily in terms of marriage and childbearing. Without a husband, a woman's opportunities are limited.

Ain el-Hilweh in Sidon, with a population of more than 45,000 people, is the largest of the Palestinian camps in Lebanon. In 1982, as most of the men had been killed or imprisoned, for a time the camp became, in the words of one observer, a 'kingdom of women'.[30] Amina, an activist in the camp, told me that Palestinian women had an important role during the Israeli invasion; they became solely responsible for their families and society because all the men were in prison. Families sheltered in schools and hospitals. As most of the houses in the camp were destroyed, women started to clean the camp and rebuild the houses.[31] Visiting Shatila camp in Beirut shortly after the 1982 massacre, Rosemary Sayigh recalls: 'I was struck by the energy with which people – mainly women – were rebuilding their homes before the winter' (2001: 24).

Nadia, a 42-year-old woman in Bourj el-Barajne camp told me that during the Israeli invasion in 1982, her family moved from the south to Beirut. They lived in a Shi'a area but local hostility eventually forced them to leave. They returned to Rashidiyya camp but, by that time, the camp wars were taking place. Her mother was killed by a sniper.[32] Um Mahmoud, a woman in her early seventies who had given birth to 12 children, said that the Amal war was the most difficult time for women. She lost her son, her nephew, her brother's wife and her niece. During the war, she said, they were stuck in the camp. The Amal fighters would enter the camp, to kill and rape.[33] Here again, the danger of 'home' is emphasised, with its inability to provide adequate protection. Khaldat Hossein, a political activist, told me that, in her view, the greatest violence experienced by women refugees in Lebanon is that of being forced to live outside their own country, a sentiment echoed by many of the so-called 'ordinary' women of the camps.[34] Samira Salah, another politically active woman, said: 'Women have lost sons, husbands, and have been forced to become responsible, but they do not enjoy full rights because they are women'.[35] According to Amneh Jibril, head of the General Union of Palestinian Women in Lebanon, not being able to live on one's land creates feelings of permanent insecurity. Palestinians exist in a constant state of 'temporariness', which has persisted for over 50 years: 'They are condemned always to resist yet never to enjoy the fruits of resistance'.[36] Clearly, despite their exclusion from the male-nationalist narrative, many Palestinian women have participated in processes of resistance in courageous and innovative ways, from militant activism to the reconstruction of damaged camps and the protection of family life in conditions of extreme adversity.

Conclusion: the impact of homelessness on women's identities

For Palestinian refugee women in Lebanon, identity has been forged from a combination of factors. Firstly, the refugees' experience of 'living on the margins', neither a part of Lebanon nor acknowledged as victims of injustice, has nurtured a sense of embattledness. This has been reinforced by the repeated destruction of homes and locations, and the accompanying lack of safety for Palestinians. In this chapter I have attempted to show that women have suffered more profound marginalisation. As Hall argues, there are two sorts of identity for those who find themselves displaced, the first communal and celebrating the cultural assets of 'one people' and the other an acknowledgement of 'what we have become' (2006: 435). Even an acknowledgement by Palestinians of what they 'have become' fails to recognise the centrality of women in remembering the homeland and maintaining a tolerable environment in exile. Women's voices have been consistently marginalised or ignored in the belief that only men have 'the right to narrate', as we saw in the 'village memorial books'. Power 'is not only exercised over the land and its people, it also controls the story … and the meta-narrative of *truth* and *memory*' (Bresheeth 2007: 165, italics in original). This chapter has illustrated that Palestinian men continue to 'control the story', the 'narrative of Palestine', and thus obscure the vital role of women, as the preservers of their nation's memories and protectors of their families and camps who, as my research reveals, have made important contributions towards formulating an alternative practice of liberation.

Since the Palestinian-Israeli peace process seems to be failing and the armed struggle is no longer a realistic option, the Palestinian nation dispersed around the world is claiming the right to tell its own story. Although constrained by violence and threats of erasure, Um Fadi and other refugee women continue forcefully to articulate the 'narrative of Palestine' and, if their story-telling can affect the modalities of Palestinian-Israeli peace-making, they may one day enjoy the fruits of resistance.

Funding for this research was provided by the UK Arts & Humanities Research Council.

Notes

1 The identities of all the women interviewed for this chapter have been disguised.
2 'Um Fadi', interviewed in Ain el-Hilwe camp, Sidon, 3 February 2007.
3 The fictional character Um Hassan in Tal el-Zaatar camp, recalling her early life in Palestine, in the novel *The Eye of the Mirror* by Liana Badr, 108–109.
4 Meeting with groups of girls, aged 13–18 years, Palestinian Youth Centre, Qasmiyye camp, near Tyre, 31 January 2007.
5 Words and photographs by children from Lebanon's largest refugee camp, Ain el-Hilwe. This was part of the 'Eye to Eye' project (Save the Children UK), a multi-media project which enabled fourth-generation Palestinian refugee children in camps in Lebanon and the occupied Palestinian territories to express themselves through photographs and the web, Summer 1997.
6 'Um Marwan', interviewed in Bourj el-Barajne camp, Beirut, 1 February 2007.
7 'Um Farid', interviewed in Bourj el-Barajne camp, Beirut, 1 February 2007.
8 'Um Nabil', interviewed in Bourj el-Barajne camp, Beirut, 1 February 2007.
9 'Amal', interviewed in Bourj el-Barajne camp, Beirut, 4 February 2007.
10 For a description of how Shatila camp was created in the 1940s, see Rosemary Sayigh (1994).
11 'Um Walid', interviewed in Bourj el-Barajne camp, Beirut, 27 January 2007.
12 Rasmiyeh, from Bourj el-Barajne, quoted in Serhan and Tabari (2005), 48.
13 Latifeh, from Bourj el-Barajne, quoted in Serhan and Tabari (2005), 48.
14 'Um Munir', interviewed in Bourj el-Barajne camp, Beirut, 1 February 2007.
15 'Jamila'. Interviewed in Bourj el-Barajne camp, Beirut, 2 June 2006.
16 'Zahra', interviewed in Bourj el-Barajne camp, Beirut, 3 June 2006.
17 'Um Ghassan', interviewed in Bourj el-Barajne camp, Beirut, 1 February 2007.
18 'Um Nabil', interviewed in Bourj el-Barajne camp, Beirut, 1 February 2007.
19 'Reem', interviewed in Bourj el-Barajne camp, Beirut, 2 June 2006.
20 'Um Aziz', interviewed in Bourj el-Barajne camp, Beirut, 1 June 2006.
21 'Fatme', interviewed in Bourj el-Barajne camp, Beirut, 2 June 2006.
22 'Layla', interviewed in Bourj el-Barajne camp, Beirut, 2 June 2006.
23 'Um Samir' interviewed in Bourj el-Barajne camp, Beirut, 3 June 2006.
24 'Um Tariq', interviewed in Bourj el-Barajne camp, Beirut, 2 June 2006.
25 'Um Khalid', interviewed in Bourj el-Barajne camp, Beirut, 24 July 2007.
26 'Samira' interviewed in Bourj el-Barajne camp, Beirut, 24 July 2007.
27 'Um Ahmad', interviewed in Bourj el-Barajne camp, Beirut, 24 July 2007.
28 'Abir', interviewed in Rashidiyya camp, Tyre, 5 June 2003.

29 'Um Fawaz', interviewed in Bourj el-Barajne camp, Beirut, 4 June 2003.
30 'Raafat Morra', interviewed in Beirut, June 2006.
31 'Amina', interviewed in Ain el-Hilweh camp, Sidon, 7 June 2003.
32 'Nadia', interviewed in Bourj el-Barajne camp, Beirut, 27 January 2007.
33 'Um Mahmoud', interviewed in Bourj el-Barajne camp, Beirut, 3 June 2006.
34 Khaldat Hossain, Democratic Palestinian Women's Organization, interviewed in Mar Elias Camp, Beirut, 18 September 2002.
35 Samira Salah, Arab Union Women's League, interviewed in Beirut, 29 May 2003.
36 Amneh Jibril, head of the General Union of Palestinian Women in Lebanon, interviewed in Ain el-Hilweh camp, Sidon, 7 June 2003.

References

Badr, L., translated by S. Kawar (1994, original text 1991). *Eye of the Mirror*. Reading: Garnet Publishing.

Brah, A. (2003). Diaspora, Border and Transnational Identities. In R. Lewis & S. Mills (eds), *Feminist Postcolonial Theory: A Reader*. Edinburgh: Edinburgh University Press, 613–634.

Brah, A. (2007). Cartographies of Diaspora: Contesting Identities. In M. Rossington & A. Whitehead (eds), *Theories of Memory: A Reader*. Edinburgh University Press, 286–289.

Bresheeth, H. (2007). The Continuity of Trauma and Struggle: Recent Cinematic Representations of the Nakba. In A. H. Sa'di & L. Abu-Lughod (eds), *Nakba: Palestine, 1948, and the Claims of Memory*. New York: Columbia University Press, 161–187.

Buijs, G. (1993). Introduction. In G. Buijs (ed.), *Migrant Women: Crossing Boundaries and Changing Identities*. Oxford: Berg.

Cohen, R. (1999). Diasporas and the Nation-State: From Victims to Challengers. In S. Vertovec & R. Cohen (eds), *Migration, Diasporas and Transnationalism*. Cheltenham: Edward Elgar Publishing, 266–279.

Davis, R. (2007). Mapping the Past, Re-creating the Homeland: Memories of Village Places in pre-1948 Palestine. In A. H. Sa'di & L. Abu-Lughod (eds), *Nakba: Palestine, 1948, and the Claims of Memory*. New York: Columbia University Press, 53–75.

Deeb, L. (2006). *An Enchanted Modern: Gender and Public Piety in Shi'i Lebanon*. Princeton & Oxford: Princeton University Press.

Farah, R. (2005). Out of the Shadows: Listening to Place-Based Narratives of Palestinian Women. In W. Harcourt & A. Escobar (eds), *Women and the Politics of Place*. Bloomfield, CT: Kumarian Press, 206–220.

Fleischmann, E. (2003). *The Nation and its 'New' Women: The Palestinian Women's Movement 1920–1948*. Berkeley: University of California Press.

Gilmour, D. (1980). *Dispossessed: The Ordeal of the Palestinians.* London: Sphere Books.

Gilroy, P. (1994). Diaspora. *Paragraph* 17.3: 207–12.

Hall, S. (2006). Cultural Identity and Diaspora. In B. Ashcroft, G. Griffiths & H. Tiffin (eds), *The Post-Colonial Studies Reader.* London & New York: Routledge, 435–38.

Hammami, R. (2004). Gender, Nakbe and Nation: Palestinian Women's Presence and Absence in the Narration of 1948 Memories. *Review of Women's Studies.* Birzeit University: Institute of Women's Studies. 2: 26–41.

Hammond, L. (2004). *This Place Will Become Home: Refugee Repatriation to Ethiopia.* Ithaca & London: Cornell University Press.

Hanafi, S. (2005). Rethinking the Palestinians Abroad as a Diaspora: The Relationship Between the Diaspora and the Palestinian Territories. In A. Levy & A. Weingrod (eds), *Homelands and Diasporas: Holy Lands and Other Places.* Stanford, California: Stanford University Press, 97–122.

Hoffman, E. (2005). *After Such Knowledge: A Meditation on the Aftermath of the Holocaust.* London: Vintage.

Khalaf, S. (1993). *Beirut Reclaimed: Reflections on Urban Design and the Restoration of Civility.* Beirut: Dar an-Nahar.

LaCapra, D. (2007). From History in Transit: Experience, Identity, Critical Theory. In M. Rossington & A. Whitehead (eds), *Theories of Memory.* Edinburgh: Edinburgh University Press, 206–211.

Lavie, S. & Swedenburg, T. (1996). Introduction: Displacement, Diaspora, and Geographies of Identity. In S. Lavie & T. Swedenburg (eds), *Displacement, Diaspora, and Geographies of Identity.* Durham & London: Duke University Press, 1–26.

Layoun, M. (1992). Telling Spaces: Palestinian Women and the Engendering of National Narratives. In A. Parker, M. Russo, D. Sommer & P. Yaeger (eds), *Nationalisms and Sexualities.* New York & London: Routledge, 407–423.

Lynd, S., Bahour, S. & Lynd, A. (eds). (1994). *Homeland: Oral Histories of Palestine and Palestinians.* New York: Olive Branch Press.

Minh-ha, T. T. (1994). Other Than Myself/My Other Self. In G. Robertson, M. Mash, L. Tickner, J. Bird, B. Curtis & T. Putnam (eds), *Travellers' Tales: Narratives of Home and Displacement.* London & New York: Routledge, 8–26.

Mohanty, C. T. & Martin, B. (1986). Feminist Politics: What's Home Got To Do With It? In T. de Lauretis (ed.), *Feminist Studies, Critical Studies.* Bloomington: Indiana University Press, 191–212.

Nabulsi, K. *Being Palestinian* (2002).

http://www.ucl.ac.uk/~uctytho?Being_Palestinian.html [accessed 08/06/2005]

Nixon, R. (1994). Refugees and Homecomings: Bessie Head and the End of Exile. In G. Robertson, M. Mash, L. Tickner, J. Bird, B. Curtis & T.

Putnam (eds), *Travellers' Tales: Narratives of Home and Displacement.* London & New York: Routledge, 111–127.

Peteet, J. M. (1991). *Gender in Crisis: Women and the Palestinian Resistance Movement.* New York: Columbia University Press.

Peteet, J. M. (1995). Transforming Trust: Dispossession and Empowerment among Palestinian Refugees. In E. V. Daniel & J. C. Knudsen (eds), *Mistrusting Refugees.* Berkeley, Los Angeles & London: University of California Press, 168–186.

Peteet, J. (2005). *Landscape of Hope and Despair: Palestinian Refugee Camps.* Philadelphia: University of Pennsylvania Press.

Rapport, N. & Dawson, A. (eds). (1998). *Migrants of Identity: Perceptions of Home in a World of Movement.* Oxford & New York: Berg.

Sa'di, A. H. (2007). Afterword: Reflections on Representation, History and Moral Accountability. In A. Sa'di & L. Abu-Lughod (eds), *Nakba: Palestine, 1948, and the Claims of Memory.* New York: Columbia University Press, 285–314.

Said, E. (1986). *After the Last Sky: Palestinian Lives.* New York: Pantheon.

Said, E. W. (1990). Reflections on Exile. In R. Ferguson, M. Gever, T. T. Minh-ha & C. West (eds), *Out There: Marginalization and Contemporary Cultures.* New York: New Museum of Contemporary Art, & Cambridge, Mass: MIT Press, 357–366.

Sayigh, R. (1979). *Palestinians from Peasants to Revolutionaries: A People's History.* London: Zed Press.

Sayigh, R. (1994). *Too Many Enemies: The Palestinian Experience in Lebanon.* London: Zed Books.

Sayigh, R. (2001). Sabra and Shatila Revisited. *Middle East International.* 13 July, 21–24.

Serhan, B. & Tabari, S. (2005). Palestinian Refugee Children and Caregivers in Lebanon. In D. Chatty & G. L Hundt (eds), *Children of Palestine: Experiencing Forced Migration in the Middle East.* New York & Oxford: Berghahn Books, 35–57.

Thomson, A. (1998). Anzac Memories: Putting Popular Memory Theory into Practice in Australia. In R. Perks & A. Thomson (eds), *The Oral History Reader*. London & New York: Routledge, 300–310.

Zaatari, M. (2007). UN Aims to Raise Living Conditions in Ain al-Hilwah. *Daily Star.* 4 May, 2.

The Homeless Self: Migrants, space-time and biographical strategies

Sonia Floriani

UNIVERSITY OF CALABRIA

Introduction: migratory experience and space-time

This chapter deals with the socio-historical phenomenon of Italian migration to Canada in the 1950s and 1960s. As a result of the large numbers involved, which had no equal in other phases,[1] and which, according to the historian Bruno Ramirez, made Italy 'the second only to Great Britain as the source of Canadian immigration' (1989: 7), the sociologist Clifford J. Jansen (1988: 15) named this wave the 'postwar boom'. In the two decades, almost 18% of Italian migrants to Canada came from the Calabria region in the south of the country (Jansen 1988: 60). This component of the migratory wave has constituted the empirical case study of my sociological research, whose most relevant findings I discuss in the following pages.

In my study, which privileges a micro-sociological perspective, emphasis has been placed on Calabrian migration as a *subjective experience of migrants*. The focus of the analysis will be on the migratory experience, and the main purpose will be that of dealing with the ways the subject has been experiencing and re-elaborating the migratory event, and the extent to which the migratory experience has been shaping her/his biography. The analytical intent is in tune with the conceptual distinction, proposed by the Italian sociologist Paolo Jedlowski (2008), between 'doing' and 'having' experience, whose distinction finds its inspiration in the dichotomy between the two German terms for experience, namely *Erlebnis* and *Erfahrung*. While the first of the two terms – *Erlebnis* – denotes the immediate experience, its vivid being, the other – *Erfahrung* – is meant as the experience the subject not only comes across, but also what they reflect on, and, in so doing, gain. According to Jedlowski, 'experience' should be intended as a whole, consisting of what the subject lives and understands, and who they become. As the author states, it is ineluctable to experience day after day, mainly in a state of unconsciousness that does not allow sedimentation. Meanwhile, it is inevitable that the latent flow of experience is sometimes interrupted by the questions posed by the subject about what the sense of their individual experience is. The experience that the subject gains and has is made up of the answers they are able to give to those questions, the meanings discovered in their life experience, and the answers and meanings on which the subject can found new biographical orientations and self-identities.[2]

As to the subjective migratory experience, my analysis is concerned with a specific dimension of it. More precisely, the emphasis will be on the ways that Calabrian migrants have subjectively experienced the change and/or the loss of their space-time coordinates, and on how they have been rethinking and redefining the coordinates, and relocating themselves in the space-time. The assumption that underlies my intent is that the subjective experience of migration is – among other things – *a redefining process of the migrant's space-time horizons*. This assumption is indebted to the definition of migration by French ethnologist Jean-Pierre Raison (1980). According to Raison, while migration in its broadest sense is to be intended as a temporary or permanent physical movement, overseas migration – such as Calabrian migration to Canada – is a long-distance and long-term space movement; two of whose main consequences are the migrant's subjective perception of space as fragmented, and their lifelong aspiration to rearrange the fragments in a new whole. As Raison (1980) also argues, this kind of migration inevitably implies a time movement, through which a biographical phase comes to an end, and a new one starts. The main consequence is the migrant's lasting aspiration to overcome the subjective perception of temporal interruption and to construct a new line of continuity. Following Raison, I regard the migratory experience as *a subjective experience of space-time caesura*, through which space is perceived as split into *the here and the elsewhere*, time as split into *the time before and the time after*, and biography is experienced as *an interrupted project*. As a consequence, the redefinition of space-time and biography is one of the migrant's lifelong concerns.

A historical outline and the case study

The migration movement from Italy to Canada began at the end of the nineteenth century and became quite a strong phenomenon in the 1920s as a consequence of the 'Quota Act', the immigration policy enacted by the United States in 1921–24 in order to greatly limit the admittance of new immigrants to that country (De Clementi 2007).[3] As a result of the 'Great Depression' of the 1930s, the advent of Fascism in Europe, and World War II, the migratory stream from Italy to Canada ceased. The reactivation of its flow in the second post-war period, and its expansion into a major movement, were especially favoured by:

> the policy of sponsorship enacted by the Canadian government: prospective immigrants could be admitted to Canada as long as residing relatives agreed to act as sponsors and assume the financial responsibility for the newcomers during the period of their settlement. (Ramirez 1989: 9)

Because of this sponsorship system and Italian post-war culture, which revolved around the primacy of familial values (Alba 1985), the movement took the shape of 'migration chains' linking Italian villages with Canadian locations, and based on kinship and relationships among co-villagers (Sturino 1989; Ramella 2001).

By contrast, the new immigration policy passed by the Canadian Government in 1967 was quite unfavourable to Italian migrants. Since this policy based the selection of new entrants on work skills and qualifications, it actually limited admittance to qualified workers only (Ramirez 2002). As a consequence of their being mostly unskilled workers, the influx of Italians into the country drastically declined in the 1970s. As Ramirez (1989: 9) has pointed out, 'by 1972 they made up only 3.8 per cent of the total immigrant entries into Canada'. Calabrian entrepreneurs, who represent the most relevant component of my interviewee sample, benefited from the last immigration policy. They are men who migrated to Canada as young adults, that is, they came of age up until their thirties. They all had an artisan background, were themselves trained in a craft and, before migrating, attempted to start and carry out their own activity in the home-village. The rest of the interviewee sample benefited, instead, from the sponsorship policy. They are men who migrated in their teens; all of them are of peasant origin, and were themselves involved in agriculture before migration. The interviewee sample also consists of men who migrated as adults together with wives and children; women who migrated either before or after marriage; and professionals, both men and women, who left Italy in their preschool years.[4]

All my interviewees moved from Calabria to Canada, from small villages to 'large' cities, namely Montreal and Ottawa, respectively in Quebec and Ontario, the two Canadian regions towards which most of Italian post-war migration was directed.[5] I collected semi-structured interviews with these migrants in their cities of residence in Canada. Except for those who migrated as preschoolers, and so felt more comfortable speaking in English, the language used was Italian. The core question I asked each of them was about the story of their migration, and the kind of biographical experience they now think it has been.

Calabrian migrants' choices, projects and achievements

The choice to migrate from Calabria to Canada was made exclusively by adult men. Women, teenagers and children did not have a voice in this decision. According to their self-narratives, men who migrated as young or middle-aged adults were not forced to do so, but decided to leave of their own free will. Nevertheless, they have been re-elaborating this decision not as a personal, conscious and willing choice, but as *a forced choice*, a sort of fatality, or a surrender to destiny. As to this migratory experience, then, the terms 'decision' and 'choice' should always be written between quotation marks, which should be used in particular for those interviewees who migrated during childhood or adolescence because they were not asked at all to express their feelings and thoughts about a decision taken mainly by their fathers or older brothers. Thus, these interviewees could not comprehend the purposes and coordinates of the migratory event, and were forced to go on 'a journey started by others' (Favaro 2003: 89 – translation mine) in order to guarantee them more opportunities and a better future. Migrant women could not give their opinion either (which in most cases would have been negative) because men did not ask them; neither could the interviewees who left during adulthood, already wives and mothers, who had always dedicated themselves to domestic and family care; nor those who migrated in their late teens, and became housewives when they got married and had babies. All women had then to surrender and submit to a decision which husbands, fathers or older brothers and sons had already taken on their behalf.

Since migration was a 'choice' taken by adult men, only they were carrying a migratory project, whose time-line was affected above all by their age, intent and working identity. The entrepreneurs who migrated as young adults – after having been trained in a craft and having tried to start their own activities in the home-village – were carrying a short-term project. These interviewees' intention in migrating was that of a temporary relocation in Canada in order to realise the economic capital to use, back in the homeland, to build a house and to start a new and more ambitious business. Given that various circumstances made the project not realisable, their migration had to become *a definitive 'choice'*.

All of the adult migrants were unskilled workers and did not have their own project. Nevertheless, their migratory intent was that of *a definitive movement* because they were followed by wives and children. Above all, they wanted to guarantee their offspring opportunities not available in Calabria. These men – like all the women – personally would not gain good positions in Canada and, in a sense denying themselves, would eventually be gratified by their children's and grandchildren's socioeconomic mobility. Craftsmen, teenagers and children would, in fact, have successful careers. All of the artisans and most of the adolescent migrants made the entrepreneurial choice (Franzina: 2007), that is, the ones who took over factories that were in continuity with the crafts they had been trained in; and the others, who were of peasant origin and who were themselves involved in agriculture, food factories or restaurants before migrating had success. In all cases, however, entrepreneurship was undertaken by chance, many years after their arrival in Canada, and was mostly encouraged by the previous owners for whom these migrants had worked for a long time as production or business managers.

In contrast with the correlation between being a migrant and becoming an entrepreneur (assumed in much of the literature: Sombart: 1916; Light and Bhachau: 1993; Kwo Bun and Jin Hui: 1995), the interviewees believe that their migrant condition hindered the entrepreneurial 'choice'. As migrants, they are aware that their cultural background was not adequate to decode and take the socioeconomic *stimuli* offered by the host context. However, in their case, there were two aggravating circumstances. Firstly, Calabrian migrants came from an undeveloped, static, peasant region (Piselli and Arrighi: 1985), whose unpredictability encouraged a pessimistic attitude rather than a positive approach to planning, and whose cultural orientations to fatalism and resignation were extraneous to the rational 'spirit' of those who become entrepreneurs (Weber: 1904–05). Secondly, they moved to Canada, which was a modern country, already pluralised in ethnocultural terms, and whose demographic, social and economic dynamics were enormous (Jansen: 1988).

Although the interviewed migrants can account for their late, casual entrepreneurial 'choice', they all express poignant regret because of the awareness of how much more it would have been possible to achieve if the choice had been made earlier, and if the time spent working for others had been invested in their own business. Men and women who migrated as preschoolers could attend school and were awarded diplomas and university degrees and, thus, obtained prestigious jobs mostly as professionals.

The subjectification of the space-time coordinates

This section aims to analyse, through an interplay between theoretical assumptions and biographical narratives, how migration has upset the Calabrian migrants' *space-time* coordinates, and in which ways and to what extent they have relocated the *here* and the *elsewhere*, and redefined the *past*, the *present* and the *future*.

The Schutzian notion of 'here and now' is adopted as a key to read and interpret the migrants' self-narratives. This concept defines the core of everyone's everyday life, 'that sector of the world of his every day life which is within his scope and which is centered in time and space around himself' (Schutz 1945a: 545). Quoting Alfred Schutz more extensively:

> The place which my body occupies within the world, my actual Here, is the starting point from which I take my bearing in space. It is, so to speak, the center *0* of my system of coordinates. Relatively to my body I group the elements of my surroundings under the categories of right and left, before and behind, above and below, near and far, and so on. And in a similar way my actual Now is the origin of all the time perspectives under which I organize the events within the world such as

> the categories of fore and aft, past and future, simultaneity and succession, etc. (Schutz 1945a: 545)

According to self-narratives, the premigratory perception of the here and the elsewhere was a dichotomy which, setting up the one against the other, put all emphasis on the here. The migrant's idea of the elsewhere, to which they were going to move, was very elusive, a sort of opposite projection of the here. The home-village, which the migrant was going to leave, was the only here of the whole premigratory biographical experience and, as such, included all temporal dimensions of their life: here the past occurred – both the personal one and the past handed down from generation to generation; here the present, which was a transition time, was occurring; and, although they were going to migrate, here the future would have liked to be spent. But the last statement should not be read as a paradox. Since the elsewhere was unknown, Calabrians, who were mostly carrying a short-term migratory project and perceiving migration as a fatality, could not think of their future there.

Before migration, then, the interviewees could clearly perceive *the objectiveness of the here-elsewhere dichotomy:* the here was the native village, the immediate, physical, tangible space where they had spent the past, were spending the present, would have liked to spend the future; the elsewhere was the host country, the far away and strange land to which they were going to move, but in which they could not even imagine spending their future.

Once in Canada, the migrant's immediate perception of the elsewhere was just as they feared before migrating: the host context was perceived as a space other than her/himself, than what was familiar, as a space which was unknown and, thus, difficult to decode. Even though the present was occurring in this space, it could not be thematised because the 'thinking as usual', which was obvious for the host community, could not be taken for granted by the migrant, whose historical-cultural tradition and common sense horizons were different. Like the Schutzian figure of 'stranger', in the beginning at least, the Calabrian migrant had to deal with what was obvious for the Canadian community as if it had been an obscure, incomprehensible, incoherent form of thought, which not only made ordinary, everyday actions and interactions uncertain, but also made it impossible to elaborate the present through the re-elaboration of her/his own experience. The migrant's common sense, which had been handed down from elsewhere and, thus, was inadequate to the host context, would have, instead, made it possible to keep constructing the present in the native 'here'.

Since they had just arrived, in the 'elsewhere' the migrant could not have a past. In fact, their personal and transmitted past had been stored in the native 'here'. As Schutz writes:

> Only the ways in which his fathers and grandfathers lived become for everyone elements of his own way of living. Graves and reminiscences can neither be transferred nor conquered. The stranger, therefore, ... may be willing and able to share the present and the future with the approached group in vivid and immediate experience; under all circumstances, however, he remains excluded from such experiences of its past. Seen from the point of view of the approached group, he is a man without a history. (Schutz 1944: 502)

The future, rather than being 'vivid and immediate', was becoming 'here', while 'elsewhere' was becoming more and more faint. Although everyone was imagining that they would go back home and stay 'here' in the future, nobody could construct a project out of imagination. In the 'elsewhere', which was now the immediate life context, the poor command of both French and English made it really difficult to think and carry out a biographical project. *Through migration*, then, the interviewees could *no longer* take for granted *the objectiveness of the here-elsewhere dichotomy* and *of their past-present-future perceptions.* According to self-narratives, proximity and tangibility could not actually be the criteria in order to distinguish the here and the elsewhere, and immediacy and remoteness those criteria to establish when the present, the past and the future would be.

The migrant's perception of the native 'here' changed the first time they went back 'home'. All interviewees had the chance to do so many years after migration. Since during these years they had neither kept in touch with relatives and friends, nor had they received other sources of information, nobody could imagine how dramatically the home-village had changed. As a consequence, its impact on the returning migrant was shattering. Like the Schutzian figure of 'homecomer', the Calabrian migrant felt the native village to have 'at least in the beginning – an unaccustomed face. He believes himself to be in a strange country, a stranger among strangers' (Schutz 1945: 369). The returned migrant was expecting to be familiar with the physical space, the social life and the 'organized pattern of routine' which they used to share with the community before migrating, but, upon returning, felt that they no longer belonged to the place, whose physical layout, atmosphere and habits, values and common sense had been radically altered. As a consequence, the migrant had to accept that neither the premigratory, crystallised past, nor the present and the future 'in immediacy', could now be shared with their former co-villagers, and thus, they had to stop perceiving the native village as their biographical 'here', and to make it become the elsewhere, in which the premigratory past could finally be stored.

Meanwhile, the migrant did not start thinking of Canada as their new biographical 'here and now', although it was the immediate and tangible context in which they had actually spent the most recent past, were spending the present, and would spend the future, and even though they had been increasingly taking for granted the Canadian everyday life. *By coming back 'home'*, then, Calabrian migrants experienced *the doubling of the biographical 'elsewhere'* and *the dichotomisation of the temporal coordinates*. In other words, they experienced every space as the 'elsewhere', and the past as split into a far past already crystallised and a near past not yet re-elaborated, of a present and a future no longer possible, and, on the other hand, of a present not yet thematised and a future not yet planned.

The migrants' perception that every space is the 'elsewhere' has been lasting and has gradually turned into the sensation of always being on a metaphorical journey from one elsewhere to another, or, more precisely, always halfway there because the departure and the arrival points have become more and more confused. Thus, time has been mainly perceived as journey-time; as a time which is unreal, suspended, unmoving but very rapid. However, Calabrian migrants have not long surrendered to this space-time perception. They all quite soon started to search for the space-time in which to relocate the biographical 'here and now' as opposed to the 'elsewhere and then'.[6] The criteria on which they have most based their space-time redefinition are *not* the *objective* criteria of tangibility and immediacy that are the founding criteria for the Schutzian concept of 'here and now'. These criteria are *subjective* and related to the experience that they have been undergoing and the ways in which they have been re-elaborating it. In other words, they are *experiential* criteria. Therefore, the migrant's 'here' is *not necessarily* the visible and tangible space where they enact 'immediate and vivid' experience, and is *not inevitably* correlated to the present time. More precisely, the space the migrant comes to perceive as 'here' is *every space* that is *relevant to her/his biographical experience*, and 'elsewhere' is otherwise *every space* which has become *irrelevant* to the life experience, which is *other* than her/himself and her/his biography. Being the founding criterion, the *experiential relevance*, the 'here' might even be either *a crystallised space* correlated to *a presentified past* or *a coming space* which is *an anticipation of the future*. As a consequence, the migrant no longer perceives time as *a linear sequence*, according to which present follows past and is followed by the future. In the migrant's experience, time has indeed become *a circular continuum*.

In search of the lost home

It can be concluded from the previous discussion that Calabrian migration has been an experience of subjectification of the space-time coordinates, which multiply and become contingent and, so, cannot be objectively defined. It means that *plurality* comes to be a constituent trait of the migrant's 'here and now'. Peter L. Berger has hypothesised that plurality is a key feature of modernity. According to his theory, modern pluralisation is to be assumed as a set of processes of multiplication and differentiation of structures, institutions and shared meaning systems, whose effects on the subjective experience make it an experience of plurality, diversity and discrepancy, which is deprived of its obviousness and, thus, can no longer be taken for granted (Berger, Berger and Kellner: 1973). As such, modern experience implies a 'movement from fate to choice' (Berger 1979: 11): everything that in traditional society was supposed to depend on destiny, in modern, pluralised times comes to be a matter of choice. Because of the many and different possibilities that modern society offers, everything is not really given, but can be chosen. Yet, as the author points out, *an unlimited chance of choice*, which is typical of modernity, together with the lack of shared and taken for granted horizons, can easily become *an impossibility of choosing*, which would be symbolic of the modern subject's experience.

The main consequence of the Calabrian migrants' experience of subjectification and pluralisation of the 'here and now' has been the impossibility of choosing *where and when it is their home.* According to their self-narratives, the loss of an 'objective' sense of the 'here and now' has been experienced and re-elaborated as *a loss of the sense of home.* Through migration, in fact, all interviewees end up by perceiving that the 'here and now' is *actually nowhere*, but could be *everywhere.* Thus, they feel that they have become *homeless.*[7] In this regard, there is a clear correspondence between the Calabrian migrant's experience and the Bergerian hypothesis on the consequence of modern plurality. We might comment on this migratory experience by quoting the authors:

> The final consequence of all this can be put very simply (though the simplicity is deceptive): *modern man has suffered from a deepening condition of 'homelessness'.* The correlate of the migratory character of his experience of society and of self has been what might be called a metaphysical loss of 'home'. It goes without saying that this condition is psychologically hard to bear. It has therefore engendered its own nostalgias – nostalgias, that is, for a condition of 'being at home' in society, with oneself and, ultimately, in the universe. (Berger, Berger and Kellner 1973: 82)

However, Calabrian migrants have not intended to surrender to the loss and the nostalgia. As their biographies tell us, after having experienced and thematised the sense of homelessness, most of them have been continuously searching for the space, the time, the life-sphere where they could *again* feel at home. In other words, their constant effort has been to individuate the space-time in which to relocate the 'here and now' and get a *new* sense of home.[8]

The migrants' ways of searching have been many and different. The degree of awareness of being homeless and of the related suffering has directly affected the migrant's way of searching and the new sense of home they have acquired, together with the relevance of their pre-migratory life experience, the kind of migratory choice and project, and the postmigratory career and social integration. On this basis, I have elaborated *a typology of migrants' biographical strategies*, which consists of *three typified ways of overcoming the sense of homelessness.* In this aim, I have referred to some figures with which classical sociology has conceptualised the condition of *otherness.*

The first type is termed *the surrender to the condition of being homeless*, and cannot actually be intended as a biographical strategy. In its most typical form, it is a *passive* surrender to a *quite unconscious* sense of homelessness. Women are the main carriers of this type, especially those who migrated in adulthood. As discussed earlier, these women were not allowed by men to take part in the migratory decision nor, either before and after migrating, to enjoy extradomestic life-spheres. As a consequence, they experienced migration as a movement from one house to another, from the family home in the native village to the conjugal house in a Canadian city. Moreover, the Canadian house always being located in an Italian neighbourhood, and settled mostly by migrants coming from the same village or region, they could keep speaking their native dialect and maintain crystallised, premigratory habits, atmospheres, uses and rituals.[9]

This way of living has preserved the women not only from 'contamination' by the Canadian culture and society, but also from the awareness of not belonging to the context in which they have been spending their life day after day. However, they could not endlessly avoid becoming aware of their strangeness. The first time they painfully felt not able to decode and penetrate most of the meaning universes of their children who were born and grew up in Canada, these migrants felt homeless and then desired to face and overcome this condition. But by what means? Actually, Calabrian women have more or less consciously surrendered to inhabiting a home located in the space-time that was the premigratory here and now and, even though it has objectively become the elsewhere and then, continues as such. But this 'new' sense of home is quite unstable because it cannot be confirmed outside the domestic walls, in the Canadian, immediate and tangible context.[10]

If passiveness and unconsciousness are key features of the first way of dealing with homelessness, the other two types are instead permeated by a lucid and strategic creativeness. In both cases, in fact, it is to be assumed that there is a correspondence between the Calabrian migrant and the Simmelian figure of 'stranger'. The stranger – as sociological 'form' elaborated by Georg Simmel – is a person who moves to a place in which he intends to stay, 'who comes today and stays to morrow', and, since 'he has not belonged to it from the beginning', whose position is connoted by:

> the unity of nearness and remoteness ... in the relationship to him, distance means that he, who is close by, is far, and strangeness means that he, who is also far, is actually near. (Simmel 1908: 402)

Moreover:

> that synthesis of nearness and distance ... constitutes the formal position of the stranger ... Another expression of this constellation lies in the objectivity of the stranger. ... But objectivity does not simply involve passivity and detachment; it is a particular structure composed of distance and nearness, indifference and involvement. (Simmel 1908: 404)

This objectivity is nourished further by the freedom he can enjoy from whatever has been transmitted from the past, from habits, prejudices and traditions, and from the need to follow and reproduce them.

The second biographical strategy is *the identification with the par excellence home*. It is typical of migrants who are aware of and deeply suffer as a result of their sense of homelessness and, thus, have been long and restlessly searching for a new home. This search is very hard because the migratory experience has deprived them of the chance of having only one home. In order not to become disoriented because of the plurality of their experiences, migrants *strategically* choose to look for the *par excellence* home, which can be either the most desired, or the one that is more easily accessible. The *par excellence* home, whatever it might be, is always located in the space-time that is more relevant to the migrant's biography. As a consequence, they have to surrender to feeling a stranger to the rest of the space-time coordinates.

Entrepreneurs who migrated as young adults, after having become artisans and having tried to start their own business, are the main carriers of this strategy. The native village and the premigratory time were really meaningful in their biographies. More precisely, 'there' and 'then' they felt the craft to be their home; here and now the entrepreneurial activity, based on the premigratory craft, is still the biographical space-time that can give their life the strongest sense of home. It means that home is still in the premigratory 'here and now' which has been revitalising, day after day, through the postmigratory entrepreneurial activity.[11] Outside the walls of the factory and in the rest of their life-spheres, the condition of being homeless is longing, but according to their self-narratives, it is quite irrelevant.[12]

The coexistence of homes is the last typified strategy. It is carried by the migrant who is not so afflicted with the awareness of his homelessness, and tries to overcome it by constructing *a complex sense of home* that can connect his biographical spaces and times. This migrant aims to double the here and now of his life, and reassess the elsewhere and then. Therefore, home is not only here and now in the Canadian city of residence, but also 'here' and 'now' in the Calabrian native village – the last being *an interstice* of his most relevant here and now. This type of migrant ends up performing the figure of 'marginal man' elaborated by Robert E. Park. According to Park, the marginal man is:

> a cultural hybrid, a man living and sharing intimately in the cultural life and traditions of two distinct peoples; never quite willing to break, even if he were permitted to do so, with his past and his traditions, and not quite accepted, because of racial prejudice, in the new society in which he now sought to find a place. He was a man on the margin of two cultures and two societies, which never completely interpenetrated and fused. ... historically and typically, the marginal man [is] the first cosmopolite and citizen of the world. (Park 1928: 892)

The condition, which Park assumes as permanent, is complex and delicate: the marginal man, as cultural hybrid, is not only enriched with suggestions, curiosities, and perceptive, critical and creative capabilities, but is also characterised by restlessness, tensions and inner conflicts. This kind of biographical strategy might be a solution to the risks deriving from doubleness. The typified migrant is, in fact, a 'marginal man' who is aware of his discrepancies and nostalgias, and *strategically* chooses not to renounce any of his homes, but to make them coexistent by establishing the relevance of the space-time coordinate of each home. As a result, one space is more and the other less relevant, and one time is prevailing and another interstitial.

Among the interviewees, this type of migrant is best embodied by entrepreneurs who migrated as teenagers, whose premigratory life experience was not so relevant as to produce mystifications which have obscured the postmigratory ambitions. The postmigratory space-time is more meaningful because here and now biography has been planned, here and now this project has been a state of pursuing and realising through private and working choices, and, thus, here and now the migrant can feel at home *again*. However, it does not imply giving up the *other* home which, although still relevant, is interstitial and so cannot hinder the space-time of the Canadian home.[13]

Notes

1 In the 1950s, almost 251,000 Italians migrated to Canada, which is almost 16% of all migrants to the country in the decade. In the 1960s, about 191,000 migrated, which amounts to 13.5% of all immigrants in this decade. In the first half of the century, the overall number of Italian migrants to Canada was almost 172,000 (Ramirez 1989; 7; see also Martellini 2001).

2 Jedlowski's theory of experience is elaborated within his sociology of everyday life. As to the concepts of everyday life and common sense, he states: '*Everyday life* is the set of activities we daily carry out ... despite its banality, everyday life is endowed with enormous richness ... After all, everyday life is *the* life we have ... *Common sense* is the form of thought and sensitivity according to which things are taken for granted: what we do and run into seems so familiar as to become *obvious*' (Jedlowski 2000: 165, translation mine).

3 Because of its enormous industrial expansion and, thus, of its need for unskilled and semiskilled labour, between 1880 and 1920 the United States attracted about 4 million Italian migrants. In these decades, the Italian migration stream towards Canada, although increasing, remained quite limited. In fact, in the last decade of the nineteenth century an average of 360 Italians per year entered Canada, and in the first three decades of the twentieth century the overall number of Italian migrants was almost 147,000 (Ramirez 1989: 6). These migrants were especially occupied in large construction projects, and were mostly temporary, coming and going according to the fluctuations of the labour market (Jansen 1988: 17).

4 The interviewee sample consists of 34 men and 16 women. Among the men, 15 migrated in their youth, 10 during adolescence, 7 in preschool age, and 5 as middle-aged adults. Among the women, 9 migrated in adulthood or late teens, and 7 as preschoolers.

5 According to the 1981 population census – i.e. the census which was published soon after the decline of Italian migration to Canada – in Quebec the overall number of Italians by origin was almost 164,000, and in Ontario about 488,000 (Ramirez 1989: 10).

6 Roland, an entrepreneur who migrated in his youth, gives us a good example of this perception when he speaks of the migrant's identity dilemma: 'Migrants are always put in a dilemma, which can last till death. ... A big dilemma, because we were born – like I was born – in Italy. So, when I'm here, I'm considered an Italian; when I go back to Italy, an American. Therefore, I feel very often to be neither Italian nor Canadian... So, who do you think I am? The answer is not easy. I might say: whoever

I am, I feel comfortable in my shoes. When I go back to Italy, since I was born there, I still feel Italian; when I'm here, since I work hard and behave honestly, I'm Canadian. This is me, I can't change, and I don't want others to make me change … I can say: I'm a Canadian entrepreneur, Calabrian by origin, and I'm glad to be Calabrian-Canadian'.

7 According to Nicholas, a carpenter who is now the owner of a big furniture factory, being a migrant is synonymous with becoming homeless: 'Once you migrate, you'll be an emigrant forever and everywhere. At least, I do feel so. I feel that I'm an emigrant here and there. Although we have been living here for a very long time, and we are now well-adjusted to this culture and lifestyle, we are nothing but emigrants … I'm proud of being Calabrian, but, when I go back to my home-village, I feel an emigrant there also. I have a house there, but I'm not at home because I don't belong to them anymore. They also think of me as a stranger'.

8 The positiveness of this search is best expressed by Cosimo, an entrepreneur who migrated as a teenager: 'I believe in a race which is peculiar: there is the emigrant. The emigrant, from whatever part of the world, when he goes to another country, he goes to build, not just for a change of air. If I came here and I think that I have to stay here, I don't want to stay anyway, to live it doesn't matter what life. So, I have to live well'.

9 Talking about Calabrian women's lifestyle, Joe, who migrated as a preschooler and is now a bank manager, asks himself: 'They have gone out only to attend wedding parties … but, given by whom? Of course, by their co-villagers'.

10 Quoting again from the interview with Joe, Calabrian women's surrender can be described as follows: 'Even though they are aware that culture has been dramatically changing in the home-village, these migrants are still sharing the ancient mentality they took here when they came'. This 'strategy' is also carried by men who migrated as middle-aged adults. However, as workers they have had to deal with Canadian society, and to be conscious of their strangeness. Thus, their surrender has been less passive than women's.

11 For example, Nicholas also told me: 'When I was a little boy, I had a dream. I was already dreaming of having a factory which would have employed thirty workers. While I was growing up, I tried my best in order to make this dream come true. And it happened here … First of all, I'm a craftsman. I'm sure of it. When I bought the factory, I was not thinking of money, of making profits, of becoming rich. I just wanted to realise my dream. Just to make you understand: if I had had a house, I would have sold it in order to make money to invest in my factory … I have always had my heart and my soul in my factory. In my factory and in my family. Wherever I would have had my factory – here or elsewhere, in my home-village or in whatever world city – I would have worked with the same

passion. Because this is the dream I have long had inside me. Because my factory is what I am. Who I am'. The sense of this strategy can be also expressed by quoting again Roland's self-narrative: 'My roots are still there, in my home-village, in my culture, where I come from. Because, if you ask me: 'who is your mum?', I can't answer: 'my neighbour' ... My mum is the woman who gave me birth'.

12 This strategy is also of professionals who migrated as preschoolers. In fact, they have been *intentionally* locating their *most authentic home* in the Canadian here and now, which is the only space-time of their whole biographical experience, and, thus, where objectiveness and subjective perceptions can meet. In order to avoid or recompose generation conflicts, they have also been *strategically* mediating with their parents' crystallised space-time coordinates. As Nick, a bank consultant who grew up in Canada, has told me: 'Although Italian migrants are integrated into this society and their children feel Canadian, they don't want to renounce their cultural heritage ... In the heart and soul of all Italian parents there is a wish, which turns out to be a priority for their children, a sort of obligation. Parents want them to speak Italian, and to preserve Italian culture'.

13 According to Theodor, an entrepreneur who migrated during adolescence: 'We were born in Italy, and we still love the country where we come from. But, we grew up here, and this makes us Canadian. Canada is the country that we now love and respect the most. Actually, we feel the strongest loyalty to this country ... We are Italian by origin, but, above all, we are Canadian. Italy is our first homeland, which we had to leave; Canada is our new homeland, where I'm happy to live, where I now belong the most ... Since I grew up here, my way of thinking is Northern American, and I feel more comfortable to live here than elsewhere. I don't know much about the Italian way of living; so, when I go back, I always get a little disorientated'. Maybe, as Cosimo has pointed out, 'if I didn't have my family house there, an old house which I have restored, I wouldn't feel at home'.

References

Alba, R. D. (1985). *Italian Americans: into the Twilight of Ethnicity*. Englewood Cliffs: Prentice-Hall.

Berger, P. L. (1979). *The Heretical Imperative. Contemporary Possibilities of Religious Affirmation*. New York: Doubleday.

Berger, P. L., Berger, B. & Kellner, H. (1973). *The Homeless Mind. Modernization and Consciousness*. New York: Random House.

De Clementi, A. (2007). Caratteri storico-antropologici dell'emigrazione italiana. In O. De Rosa & D. Verrastro (eds), *Appunti di viaggio. L'emigrazione italiana tra attualità e memoria*. Bologna: il Mulino, 27–34.

Favaro, G. (2003). Migrare. Sguardi ed esperienze di bambini e adolescenti. *OU. Riflessioni e Provocazioni* XIV, 1: 87–91.

Franzina, E. (2007). L'emigrazione nella storia d'Italia fra intraprendenza e imprenditorialità. In O. De Rosa & D. Verrastro (eds), *Appunti di viaggio. L'emigrazione italiana tra attualità e memoria*. Bologna: il Mulino, 51–68.

Jansen, C. J. (1988). *Italians in a Multicultural Canada*. Lewiston-Queenston: The Edwin Mellen Press.

Jedlowski, P. (2000). *Storie comuni. La narrazione nella vita quotidiana*. Milan: Bruno Mondadori.

Jedlowski, P. (2008). *Il sapere dell'esperienza. Fra l'abitudine e il dubbio*. Rome: Carocci.

Kwo Bun, C. & Jin Hui, O. (1995). The many faces of immigrant entrepreneurship. In R. Cohen (ed.), *The Cambridge Survey of World Migration*. Cambridge: Cambridge University Press, 523–531.

Light, I. & Bhachau, P. (eds), (1993). *Immigration and Entrepreneurship. Culture, Capital and Ethnic Networks*. New Brunswick: Transaction.

Martellini, A. (2001). L'emigrazione transoceanica fra gli anni quaranta e sessanta. In P. Bevilacqua, A. De Clementi & E. Franzina (eds), *Storia dell'emigrazione italiana. Partenze*. Rome: Donzelli, 369–384.

Park, R. E. (1928). Human migration and the marginal man. *American Journal of Sociology* XXXIII, 6: 881–893.

Piselli, F. & Arrighi, G. (1985). Parentela, clientela e comunità. In P. Bevilacqua & A. Placanica (eds), *La Calabria*. Turin: Einaudi, 365–492.

Raison, J.-P. (1980). Migrazione. In R. Romano (ed.), *Enciclopedia Einaudi* 9. Turin: Einaudi [series 1977–1982], 285–311.

Ramella, F. (2001). Reti sociali, famiglie e strategie migratorie. In P. Bevilacqua, A. De Clementi & E. Franzina (eds), *Storia dell'emigrazione italiana. Partenze*. Rome: Donzelli, 143–160.

Ramirez, B. (1989). *The Italians in Canada*. Ottawa: Canadian Historical Association.

Ramirez, B. (2002). In Canada. In P. Bevilacqua, A. De Clementi & E. Franzina (eds), *Storia dell'emigrazione italiana. Arrivi*. Rome: Donzelli, 89–96.

Schutz, A. (1944). The stranger: an essay in social psychology. *The American Journal of Sociology* XLIX, 6: 499–507.

Schutz, A. (1945). The homecomer. *The American Journal of Sociology* L, 5: 369–376.

Schutz, A. (1945a). On multiple realities. *Philosophy and Phenomenological Research* V, 4: 533–576.

Simmel, G. (1908). The stranger. In K. Wolff (ed.), *The Sociology of Georg Simmel*. New York: Free Press, 1950, 402–408.

Sombart, W. (1916). *Der Moderne Kapitalismus*. München-Leipzig: Duncker & Humblot.

Sturino, F. (1989). Italian Emigration. Reconsidering the Links in Chain Migration. In R. Perin & F. Sturino (eds), *Arrangiarsi. The Italian Immigrant Experience in Canada*. Montreal: Guernica, 63–90.

Weber, M. (1904–05). *The Protestant Ethic and the Spirit of Capitalism* (translated by T. Parsons). New York: Scribner, 1930.

Can they call Adelaide home? Identity and the sense of belonging in French migrants' discourse narratives

Colette Mrowa-Hopkins and Eric Bouvet
FLINDERS UNIVERSITY

Introduction

Using a discourse analytic approach, this chapter investigates how a group of French-born residents of Adelaide (Australia) construct their identity and develop 'a sense of belonging' (Meinhof and Galasiński 2005) for the place in which they settle. The approach is based upon the key theoretical assumption that our identity is not static but fluid (Bauman 2000), and shifts as a result of cultural contacts and migration. Within this premise, fragments of multiple identities and tensions between cultural belongings are likely to become apparent through the language used by the migrants, particularly the pronominal forms they select and the lexico-grammatical repertoire they use, as they recount their life experiences. The data for the present study consist of seven interviews with French-born Adelaide residents who migrated to Australia from the early 1950s to the early 1970s. The interviews reveal the strains that exist between past experiences, present situations and future aspirations. This aspect, when examined through the lens of linguistic analysis, highlights how the French migrants who were interviewed construct their sense of belonging around the seemingly opposite notions of stability and change that are present throughout their narratives. The findings could be significant in gaining an insight into the way some French migrants in Australia position themselves in relation to the concepts of 'home' and 'belonging'. Even though our study draws on a small number of interviews conducted in one Australian city, we believe that it provides an important contribution to the understanding of the value of the concept of 'home', as it extends beyond the usual association of place and identity, commonly understood as an attachment to physical settings.

Who are the French in Australia?

Little is known about the experience of French migrants to Australia in the 1950s and 1960s. The few studies that have been carried out on this group of migrants suggest that the French tend to blend well socially and culturally into Australian society (see, for example, Stuer 1982; Van Maanen 2004; Bouvet and Boudet-Griffin 2005). It is therefore not surprising to find that, according to recent interview data collected during our research, the French migrants who have spent the last 40 to 50 years in Adelaide are willing to call their place of adoption 'home'. Although French migrants to Australia tell stories and anecdotes about successful settlement, the interviews also reveal a degree of tension between the socio-economic success story of settlement and the longing for a reconstructed past through future projections. In other words, the informants' narratives display a sense of identity that is derived from both their individual engagement with their physical/material contexts (the *situational* sense of belonging) and an imaginative reconstruction of a place that arouses feelings of who they claim to be (the *emotional* sense of belonging). In the face of such tension, a question arises about the extent to which the French migrants we interviewed identify with this particular place called Adelaide, located far away from their original geographical 'home'. This is the broad question that we will examine in this study.

In order to probe the nature of the tension between the *situational* sense of belonging and the *emotional* one, we propose to investigate the sense of belonging experienced by a group of French-born residents of Adelaide, by analysing the discursive forms they use while narrating their migration story. Rather than analysing the thematic content of their narratives, in this chapter we prefer to focus on the language that migrants use, in order to interpret the seemingly contradictory statements they make about themselves. When, for example, an interviewee says '*non je* ***veux pas*** *rester en France. En Australie, je suis bien*' ('I **don't want** to stay in France. In Australia, I feel good'), the use of the modal verb underlines both the existence of a tension about having to choose a place to settle, France or Australia, and the active role of the speaker in making such a decision. Similarly, when another interviewee asserts '*Je suis maintenant plus australienne que française*' ('I am now more Australian than French'), her identity claim is marked by the temporal adverb *maintenant* (now) as the key element of her identity shift, suggesting the awareness of a strain between two cultural allegiances that she cannot endorse to the same extent. In this way, our approach follows other studies of migration narratives (such as Meinhof and Galasiński 2005), suggesting that identity should not be thought of in terms of bound categories that only tend to underscore differences, but rather 'as a process which reveals itself through our ways of speaking' (2005: 1). Along with these authors, we also find that this discursive approach is particularly useful in understanding the tensions that are at the heart of the migrants' identity claim.

Thus, relying on a close analysis of linguistic data, we wish to account for the way that migrants encode their positions through, in particular, their choice of pronouns and the use of modality. We believe that these phenomena contribute significantly to the construction of a complex set of multilayered identifications and may provide a deeper understanding of the sense of belonging for the French migrants we have interviewed for the present study. Our discourse analytical approach is therefore articulated on theoretical assumptions that focus on the central role of language in identity construction, and cuts across multiple disciplines, as will be discussed in the next section.

Theoretical and methodological framework

The attempt to define what contributes to a particular identity can be viewed from many different perspectives. Most socio-linguistic and discourse analytic studies that have focused on migrants' discourse and identity in recent years (De Fina 2000, 2007; Meinhof and Galasiński 2005; Pavlenko and Blackledge 2004; Rampton 1999, 2001; Riley 2007) adopt a 'constructivist' paradigm that views the sense of belonging as negotiated through language rather than an 'essentialist' notion of identity. In other words, rather than interpreting talk as a reflection of thoughts, motivations and memories of an inner self, constructivists focus on how selves and identities are constituted through talk. They examine how identities are claimed and negotiated in discourse or personal narratives (Benwell and Stokoe 2006: 9–10). This paradigm also views identity as the result of a dynamic interplay involving the individual self-representation in interaction with others, as a 'dynamic and shifting nexus of multiple positions, or identity options' (Pavlenko and Blackledge 2004: 35). In other words, our sense of self is connected to the cultural and emotional contexts in which we interact with others in particular situations through talk. From this perspective, identity is not static, but rather changing and ambivalent as people adjust to different contexts and other speakers.

Another aspect of contemporary discourse in relation to identity research is relevant here, as it focuses on the link between the notion of place (understood as a geographical location or particular physical setting) and identity construction (Benwell and Stokoe 2006). Within this view, it is argued that through their personal stories, migrants make a claim on *who* they are in relation to *where* they are, have been or are going. However, according to Benwell and Stokoe (2006: 210), the physical setting 'is not 'real' beyond the practices that produce it'. Acknowledging the locally negotiated discourse constraints casts doubt on the extent of individual agency with respect to the multiple identity options available, which are likely to be constrained by both the physical and the social situation as well. In other words, to what extent are people really 'free to construct their identity in any way they wish' (Benwell and Stokoe 2006: 10), and to what extent are their multiple identity options shaped by various external forces? As is argued by Floriani in this volume, the migration experience is '*a subjective experience of space-time caesura*, through which space is perceived as split into *the here and the elsewhere*'.[1] Accordingly, *home* may be conceived not so much as a physical location but rather as an ongoing series of adjustments realised through the language of self-(re)presentation, allowing for multiple identities to coexist or overlap within the immediate context of talk, as well as the larger social and historical context.

What all of these theoretical approaches suggest is that identity is made up of the ways we perceive ourselves and how we are perceived by others, as revealed through talk-in-interaction. If it is assumed that the subjective views, feelings and attitudes of individuals (the *emotional* sense of *belonging*) are at once context-bound and socially constructed, then it is possible that the repertoire of identity options seen as 'imaginable' or 'negotiable' within a *situational* sense of *being* is limited by the socio-historical context of the migrants' lived experience and shaped by the linguistic resources available to them in a given situation. The extent to which migrants, cast as imaginative and individualistic agents, are able to create a sense of attachment and sustain a coherent sense of self through their appropriation of a new physical space in Adelaide is therefore likely to be the result of a 'forced choice', as pointed out by Floriani in Chapter 4.

In attempting to interpret our data in the light of these theoretical assumptions, we need to acknowledge that the discursive construction of identity, as it is enacted in the context of the French migrant narratives, encourages certain self and social positioning, exposing tensions between multiple affiliations and revealing ambivalence within the discourse of *belonging*. As the preceding discussion has made clear, the option to choose who we are is not entirely dependent upon free agency as much as it is constrained by situational experiences. This calls for a brief overview of the socio-historical context in which French migration to Australia occurred after World War II, particularly in terms of the socio-demographic characteristics of French migrants, before proceeding with a detailed analysis of the interview data.

But who exactly are the French migrants? The socio-historical context of post-World War II French migration to Australia

Although the presence of French migrants in Australia has been recorded since the early colonial days, it is in the post-World War II era that the greatest number of French migrants arrived in Australia, due to a migrant recruitment campaign by Australia and the availability of assisted passage schemes. The French-born interviewees who produced the data used in this study migrated to Australia between the 1950s and the early 1970s.

A study by Bouvet and Boudet-Griffin (2005), based on data collected from Alien Registration documents available at the National Archives of Australia, attempted to determine the socio-demographic characteristics of the French migrants who settled in South Australia. According to this study, which examined 677 cases of French-born migrants who established residence in South Australia in the 1950s and 1960s, the French migrant population was young and arrived in Australia either as single men and women or as nuclear families (unlike southern European migrant groups that are often characterised by chain migration and community networks). Although a large number of the migrants were born in metropolitan France, some originated from North Africa, from where they had been displaced after the former French colonies had gained independence at the end of the 1950s and in the early 1960s.

According to Bouvet and Boudet-Griffin's data, 71% of French migrants benefited from the two assisted passage schemes available during that period. The General Assisted Passage Scheme (GAPS) was made available to the French in late 1960 (Bouvet 2007). Approved applicants were eligible to receive assistance with accommodation and employment on arrival in Australia. A subsequent scheme, the Special Passage Assistance Programme (SPAP), took effect on 1 July 1966, replacing the GAPS The SPAP was specifically intended to attract skilled and semi-skilled workers and it is under the latter programme that the greatest number of French migrants arrived in Australia.

It has been argued that, besides incentives such as sponsored passages and the certainty of employment in Australia, two major socio-political events affecting the French from the mid-1950s to the late 1960s could have played a part in enticing a number of French people to consider emigration (Stuer 1982). The first event was the independence gained by several former French colonies in North Africa, which resulted in the forced repatriation to France of hundreds of thousands of French settlers. Some of those French repatriates from North Africa found their way to Australia, as attested by Bouvet and Boudet-Griffin's quantitative study of migrant registration documents (2005), which shows that 16.2% of French nationals who settled in South Australia during the early to mid-1960s were born in northern Africa. The other important event was the protests of May 1968. Political instability in France and violent social unrest may have increased the desire of some to emigrate. Indeed, between 1969 and 1970, the number of arrivals in Australia from France was 2,215, more than double the figure of 1,018 arrivals for the 1967–1968 period (Stuer 1982).

Research on the French in Australia points to the individualistic nature of the French migration movement, in which people migrate independently from each other. It is important to note that, unlike many other migrant groups, the French did not form clear community clusters in terms of geographical settlement, although a notable proportion of the French population was found within or close to Adelaide's manufacturing areas. Probably more than any other period in the history of French migration to Australia, the 1950s and 1960s were essentially a time of working class migration. For over two decades, thousands of skilled and semi-skilled men and women, supported by assisted migration, came to Australia. The majority of the working population arrived in Australia equipped with a variety of professional skills. This allowed them to be employed across professional sectors, even though a shift towards less highly qualified occupations in Australia was generally observed when comparing pre- and post-migration employments (Bouvet and Boudet-Griffin 2005). It is more likely that the majority of these young migrants were motivated by wanting to start a new life in a new country, rather than having been forced to migrate for economic reasons.

The study of Adelaide-based French migrants recounting their migration journey

The data analysed for this study consist of seven semi-structured interviews of French-born migrants who arrived and settled in Australia from the early 1950s to the early 1970s. The interviews were collected as part of a larger project aiming to document the motives and processes of post-World War II French migration to Australia. The interviews were conducted in French by native-speaker interviewers. The participants included two couples in their sixties and seventies, an 80-year-old mother and her son, three single females and a male married to a Dutch-born Australian resident. One of the two couples (both of whom were small business owners in France) migrated in their early thirties; the other couple migrated in their late teens. Several of the interviewees were involved in food and hospitality businesses. Questions were asked about the motives for migrating to Australia, the migrants' experience with bureaucracies, family relationships, adaptation to new environments, cultural attitudes, friendship networks, language issues, and regrets and aspirations. Each conversation lasted between one and two hours. All interviews were audio-recorded and transcribed. During the transcribing process, no particular attention was paid to the prosodic features of speech, such as pauses, stress and intonation. Our analysis focuses, instead, on pronominal reference and the expression of modality, which, according to Meinhof and Galasiński (2005), represent a particularly rich source of data for examining identity construction and self-positioning. Along with these authors, we agree that we cannot rely on a generic list of identity markers or linguistic resources with which the speakers construct their identities.[2] Specifically, personal pronouns and the expression of modality were selected for analysis, since it is believed that these grammatical features of discourse are more likely to carry the speakers' expressive values.

In order to identify the forms likely to contribute to the construction of identities and self-positioning, the entire body of transcripts was read and instances of personal pronouns at the grammatical level, referring to the self and others, were marked for analysis. These are thought to be potentially salient for encoding position and revealing the speakers' stance[3] as indicators of the clarity of agency of the interviewees, following Meinhof and Galasiński (2005) who advocate this approach. These pronouns included the subjective markers (*je/moi*, *nous/nous, on – I/me/myself, we/us*) together with their emphatic forms (*moi je, nous on*, etc. – *I, we*, etc.), as opposed to objective markers (*on*, *c'* or *ça, ils – one, it, they*). Besides pronominal choice, expression of modality (obligation, necessity, and volition)[4] was also taken into consideration as a marker of the speaker's attitude towards the content of their utterance, and towards others, in terms of the extent of their engagement with them. Such items included modal verbs (*vouloir*, *pouvoir*, *devoir*, *il faut/il fallait – will, can, ought to, it is/was necessary*), as well as a close set of lexical verbs (*croire/penser – to believe/think*), modal adjectives (*certain – certain*) and adverbs (*peut-être – perhaps/maybe*) indicating possibility or uncertainty. According to Meinhof and Galasiński (2005), these elements reveal interesting patterns in the process of migrants' social integration, either as affiliation with, or distance from, their own and other social, ethnic, or cultural groups.

Initial findings and discussion

The analysis of discourse markers as indicators of emotional and situational attachments reveals tensions between stability and change, between belonging and resistance to belonging. Our discussion first focuses on the functions of the non-agentive markers *on* (one), *ils* (they) and *il fallait* (one had to), which invoke collective identities, and compares them to the agentive markers: *je/nous*; *je voulais* (I wanted); *je crois* (I believe). Of notable interest were shifts occurring between the collective nature of the group identity and their relation with others, and singularity, that is, speakers' self-representations as individual agents in control of their life choices.

Non-agentive markers are used to express various kinds of obligations where the individual feels powerless, thus lending the individual a 'migrant identity' shaped principally by external forces, rather than by one's own agency. The typical non-agentive marker in French is the indefinite third person pronoun *on* that was found to account for 45% of all occurrences of pronouns. In *on dit,* meaning 'one says', 'people say', or 'it is said', the identification of the agent remains unclear, referring to a larger group 'out there', or suggesting universality and taken-for-granted opinions. However, in spoken French, the pronoun *on* is also used very commonly to refer to collective referents normally expressed by 'we' or 'they'. When referring to 'we', it can be categorised as inclusive, and when referring to 'they' it can be considered as exclusive. A particular difficulty relates to assigning the exact referent of the *on* forms that are being used, specifically the differentiated uses of 'they' and 'we'. We would like to suggest that this distinction is crucial in determining the distance created by the speakers as they move between their different selves and other social groupings ('us' *vs.* 'them').

Contrary to expectation, we found that the most frequent use of the pronoun *on* referred to the emphatic form of 'we', as in '*nous, on*', which we included with the subjective markers. The typical non-agentive use of the pronoun *on*, as in '***on** nous a montré des films*' (ML),[5] which may be translated as 'they showed us some films', or in the passive voice 'we were shown some films' (implying people at the Australian embassy, or migration authorities), does not feature prominently in our interview data. Due to the lack of clarity of referent, we found that the pronoun *on* was not a reliable indicator of the non-agentive or collective identity, in spite of the fact that it figures most prominently in our data.

Occurrences of the collective pronoun *ils*, meaning 'they', on the other hand, were mostly found to occur without explicit mention of its referent (non-anaphoric use). However, there were also many occurrences of 'they' with clear references to agentive identifiable groups, which we did not include in this part of our analysis. Thus, in addition to the non-agentive use of *on*, the non-anaphoric pronoun *ils* reinforces the powerlessness of the speakers as agents of their own actions. This is moreover confirmed by the syntactic juxtaposition of *ils*, the agents of the process, with the first person pronouns *nous* or *me,* or second-person pronoun *vous,* the subjects acted upon. Surprisingly, this pronominal structure features largely in the migrants' narratives, either as '*on nous*', or '*ils nous*', establishing a distance between the

French speakers as a group and 'them', the authorities. In addition, the occurrences of framing referents, such as the mention of '*le bateau*' ('the ship') in the example below, gave us a clue to the type of referent that was implied, in this instance vaguely implicating the Australian officials:

1 *... mais on a eu des ennuis à Fremantle parce qu'* ***ils*** *ne* ***nous*** *ont pas dit qu'il fallait apporter les radios. Non,* ***ils nous*** *ont rien dit, alors on ne les a pas apportées, alors le bateau, je sais pas,* ***ils*** *ont téléphoné quelque part et puis après* ***ils*** *ont dit oui, ça va ... (AS)*

... but we were in trouble in Fremantle because **they had not told us** *that we needed to bring X-rays.* **No, they had told us nothing** *so we did not bring them, so the boat, I don't know,* **they** *rang somewhere and then* **they** *said yes, that's OK ... (AS)*

A focus on markers of modality expressing necessity or obligation further highlights this lack of agency in the French migration discourse that has been revealed so far by the use of non-anaphoric reference in pronominal choice. By investigating the use of modal verbs such as *falloir* and *devoir* as non-agentive markers, we found the most predominant use to be '*il fallait*' ('it was necessary'), occurring in the context of the red tape associated with the migration process:

2 ***Il fallait*** *refaire les papiers, alors on a ... (AS)*

It was necessary *to redo the papers, so we ...*

3 *On m'a répondu qu'il* ***fallait*** *que j'aie un travail sous contrat. (ML)*

I was told that **I had to have** *a work contract.*

Other uses of *il fallait* occur in the context of work obligations, as in '***Il fallait*** *que j'aie la nationalité australienne*' ('I needed to have Australian nationality') (MB).

Such a use indicates that it was not a matter of choice but an obligation, as in the following: '*Il* ***fallait*** *pointer*' ('One had to clock in') (ML). Overall, these examples suggest a lack of choice, or reflect a fatalistic view of the migration process, as in the following: '***fallait*** *en rire*' ('one had to laugh about it') (DB).

To a certain extent, other expressions of modality, such as the negative form of *pouvoir*, in the sense of 'not being able to', and *être obligé de* (to be obliged to/to have to), further consolidated our interpretation of the French migrants' lack of agency or powerlessness. Finally, *il fallait* was occasionally found to express an individual urge, almost beyond the subject's control, as in '*Il* ***fallait*** *que je retourne en Australie*' ('I felt the need to return to Australia') (ML).

By contrast to non-agentive markers, we now focus on the use of the agentive markers signalling the migrants' own engagement, or stance in the process of their own identity construction, and explicit self-positioning. We found that the first person statements with *je* (I), or its emphatic form *moi, je*, were being used for:

1. narrating one's actions as the singular agent of the action:

   4 '*J'ai visité, … j'ai été, j'ai eu*' ('I visited, … I was, I had') (AL)

2. enunciating self-reflective comments:

   5 ***moi, j'ai*** *vraiment eu un grand grand coup de cafard quand* ***je suis*** *arrivée à Bonegilla.* ***J'ai*** *mis un moment à m'en remettre. (MB)*

   (I got very depressed when I arrived at Bonegilla. It took me a long time to get over it)

   6 ***Je*** *me suis trompée (I made a mistake) (EL)*

3. stating facts about oneself, or an opinion:

   7 ***Moi,… j'ai*** *pas de frère pas de sœur …* (**I** … **I** don't have any brothers or sisters)

4. and expressing likes and dislikes:

   8 ***Je*** *ne cherchais pas la grande ville.* ***J'aime bien*** *La Colle-sur-Loup, les environs de Nice, mais* ***j'aime pas,*** *disons, la grande ville. (AL)*

   I was not looking for a big city. **I quite like** La Colle-sur-Loup, the surroundings of Nice, but, let's say, **I don't like** big cities.

In combination with the plural *nous* (we), as an extension of *je* (I), expressing the same functions, the first-person category accounted for the majority of all occurrences of all pronouns, including *on* and *ils*. These were most often associated with modal verbs expressing volition as in '*je voulais*' (I wanted), and lexical verbs expressing beliefs as in '*je crois*' or '*je pense*' (I believe, I think).

The modal verb *vouloir* (to want/wish) combined with the first-person pronoun as in *je voulais* (I wanted) was most often associated with the idea of moving, or changing places and figured most prominently in the interviews. Examples of this include: '***je voulais*** *partir,* ***je voulais*** *partir*' (I really wanted to leave) (DB); '***je voulais*** *voir du pays*' ('I wanted to see some country', or rather 'I wanted to travel around') (ML); '*non,* ***on voulait*** *aller à Perth*' ('no, **we wanted** to go to Perth') (EL); '***Moi, je voulais, je voulais*** *voir l'Australie*' ('I wanted to see Australia') (ML). This usage emphasises the need to position oneself in space, but also uncertainty as one cannot find a place to settle.

The modality expressing personal opinion as in '*Je crois*' (I believe) was found to indicate doubt, rather than certainty, as it was accompanied by repetitions, reformulations, or even negations, as in the following:

9 ***Je crois que ... je crois que ... je ne sais même pas.*** *(ML)*

I think that ... I think that ... I don't even know.

10 *ah je dirais* ***... je crois que ... je crois que. Je ne pense pas ...*** *(JR)*

I would say ... I believe that ... I believe that. I don't think ...

11 ***je crois, oui, oui, certainement,*** *je ne me rappelle pas mais certainement. (ML)*

I think, yes yes, certainly, I can't remember but certainly.

Overwhelmingly, the choice of pronouns and modality used in self-(re)presentations suggest that the French migrants we interviewed in this study exercised a fair degree of control over their own lives. Even though the motives for migrating may have been influenced by certain socio-historical factors, such as the events of May '68 and the availability of assisted passage to Australia, on the whole, these French migrants appear to retain clarity of agency. Undoubtedly, extending this analysis to a larger group of interviewees in Australia would contribute a more definitive conclusion with regard to the pre-eminence of agency by this group of migrants. Furthermore, a comparative study between the French and other migrant groups in relation to this would no doubt corroborate distinctive positioning associated with different ethnic groups.

Tensions revealed through shifts of agency

Having chosen Australia, and specifically Adelaide, as a place to settle does not preclude a longing for the country of origin. This is brought to light when the migrants are faced with the difficulty of adapting to the constraints of the new place; hence the tensions evident between stability and change in the migrants' discourse narratives. Of particular interest in relation to this were noticeable shifts occurring within the discourse between singularity, or personal agency, and collective identities, including relations with other social groups. The shifts were realised through pronoun switches within a single utterance, indicating, as in the examples given below, that once the individual has left France, they are relinquishing some part of their personal identity:

> 12 ***Je** suis parti de – je me rappelle plus si c'est Charles de Gaulle ou quoi – et puis **nous** sommes partis de l'Angleterre. (DB)*
>
> **I left** from – I can't remember if it was Charles de Gaulle (airport) or what – and then **we** left from England.

> 13 ***J'ai appris** l'italien avant d'apprendre l'anglais ... au fur et à mesure **on** a appris l'anglais. (DB)*
>
> **I learnt** Italian before I learnt English ... as **we** went on **we learnt** English.

These shifts between agencies representing individual vs. group identities were most often conveyed through markers of modality indicating, at the same time, singularity of purpose (*je voulais/I wanted*), where the individual attempts to regulate their environment, and uncertainty (*je crois/I believe*), where individual options for belonging remain open to change. By highlighting the tensions created by these shifts in agency, the point we wish to emphasise here has to do with the pull between the migrant's personal agency on the one hand, and on the other the wider context involving relations with others and settings, which restricts the available options for the positioning of self. It could be said that, rather than having to choose between the situational sense of *belonging* and the emotional sense of (be) *longing*, the French interviewees prefer their options for belonging to remain open to change. What our study reveals, moreover, is that a sense of attachment to a place emerges *per force*, not as the result of personal agency but as the outcome of locally negotiated discourse, itself influenced by wider contextual constraints. These include the circumstances in which the interviews were conducted; the individual speech styles of the interviewees; the role relationships between the speakers in positioning themselves vis-à-vis other groups; and the influence of the other groups' perception of them.

These locally negotiated contextual constraints at the discourse level can be clearly illustrated in the following examples taken from the data. In one instance, at the beginning of the interview, a speaker selects the past historic tense (a literary tense in French), which he later drops from his narrative. This is revealing of the personal discourse constraint that compels this informant to adopt the social stance of an educated speaker facing the interviewer, who was a French university lecturer. In another instance relating to the larger social context, a speaker endorsing the Anglo-stereotypical view that 'the French are arrogant' is not free to make any kind of identity claim. This instance, which shows the influence of the prevailing ethnocentric public discourse, constrains the available options for identity positioning. Yet, rather than adopting an oppositional stance to the French, it could be said that the speaker's positioning perhaps reflects how well she has 'made Australia home'. This instance of self-positioning also highlights our understanding of categorical identity statements that other interviewees seem explicitly to endorse, as in '*Je suis maintenant plus australienne que française*' (ML) ('I am now more Australian than French').

Following Meinhof and Galasiński (2005), we have explored how the (re)construction of personal as well as social and cultural attachments to a place contributes to a group of French migrants' identity and sense of belonging. Our study uses the analysis and the interpretation of linguistic data to examine the ways in which identities are socially constructed through discourse within a socio-cultural and historical context. While at the grammatical level pronominal choice and use of modality reveal the extent to which the French migrants we interviewed project themselves as passive subjects or active agents in shaping their own identity, it should be noted that the analysis of the migrants' personal identification and affiliation or disaffiliation with others presented in this chapter is necessarily selective. A focus on the expressions of the French migrants' personal stance and on how they position themselves in relation to others would convey a more complete picture of how they construct their own personal spaces and social groupings, from which a sense of belonging could be more strongly established. However, a linguistic analysis of the migrant discourse narrative such as the one we have adopted can, even succinctly, yield interesting insights into the process of identity (re)construction, and thus enhance our understanding of how French migrants position themselves in relation to their adopted country.

Conclusion

Our study suggests that the analysis of pronominal choice and modality markers drawn from French migrant interviews can be related meaningfully to personal and social stances or positioning. Pronoun use can show how speakers position themselves in relation to others and has implications for the way French migrants align themselves with others. Modal expression denotes the speaker's attitude or judgment and has implications for evaluating others' positioning. The analysis of such micro-linguistic phenomena in the data we have collected corroborates the view that identity is first and foremost constituted through language by speakers representing themselves as individual agents. The notion of agency when applied to our data helps identify the construction of the self in opposition to the authorities, but not necessarily in contrast to other groups. Apart from a few categorical statements made by some interviewees, we did not find the expression of a strong affiliation or disaffiliation either with the Australian or the French host culture and its values. What we found, instead, was the construction of an identity that is ambivalent; that is to say, speakers displayed both resistance when facing the constraints of categorisation or having to choose between 'here' and 'there', and expression of volition, as in 'I wanted to'. Furthermore, this ambivalence was also evident in the use of the pronoun *on* which is sometimes inclusive – meaning 'we', and at other times exclusive – meaning 'they'. The shifting pronoun use could mean an ambiguity about a conscious representation of the self and an 'idealised' one, claiming attachment for a place that is only imagined. It is worth noting that the importance of being neither French nor Australian was stressed by several interviewees.

The extent of the French migrants' willingness to adopt Australia, and particularly Adelaide, as *home* remains unclear. What does seem clearer, however, is that place-identity construction – how one remembers, feels about, and generally thinks about a specific place – appears to be shaped by personal life events that are used to justify the choice of one place over another. Besides the linguistic features analysed, the macro socio-historical context has particular relevance in clarifying the construction of this positioning. In the final analysis, the sense of belonging, as displayed through the discourse of the French migrants' narratives, is affirmed through the speakers' acceptance of the coexistence of multiple identities and openness of choices rather than sustained through strong identity markers of agency versus non-agency. Our analytical approach shows that language is crucial to understanding the way people depict their world and the positioning they assume within it, shifting between the personal, imaginative, and the collective nature of the sense of belonging. This discourse analysis approach, applied in the context of a small sample of French migrants in this study, could be extended not only to larger samples, but also to other groups of migrants, thus allowing comparisons across ethnic groups in terms of identity construction and sense of belonging.

Notes

1 See Floriani, Chapter 4 in this volume.

2 'Constructive of identity in one context, a certain expression does not have to be constructive of identity in another' (Meinhof & Galasiński, 2005: 65).

3 *Stance* in this paper is defined as 'the lexical and grammatical expression of attitudes, feelings, judgments, or commitment concerning the propositional content of a message' (Biber & Finegan 1989: 93).

4 '(...) modality can be broadly defined as the expression of the speaker's stance towards the propositional content of an utterance' (Koester 2006: 64). Expressions of modality include 'ways in which language is used in communication to express personal beliefs and adopt positions, to express agreement and disagreement with others, to make personal and social allegiances, contracts and commitments, or alternatively to dissociate the speaker from points of view, and to remain vague or uncommitted' (Stubbs 1986: 1).

5 The notations in brackets refer to the initials of the speaker's name.

References

Bauman, R. (2000). Language, identity, performance. *Pragmatics*, 10: 1–5.

Benwell, B. & Stokoe, E. H. (2006). *Discourse and Identity*. Edinburgh: Edinburgh University Press.

Biber, D. & Finegan, E. (1989). Styles of stance in English: Lexical and grammatical marking of evidentiality and affect. *Text*, 9: 93–125.

Bouvet, E. J. (2007). French migration to Australia in the post WWII period: Benevolent tolerance and cautious collaboration. *FULGOR*, 3, 2: 15–37. http://ehlt.flinders.edu.au/deptlang/fulgor. (online, accessed 3 February 2009)

Bouvet, E. J. & Boudet-Griffin, E. (2005). French migration to South Australia (1955–1971): What Alien Registration documents can tell us. *FULGOR*, 2, 2: 1–20 http://ehlt.flinders.edu.au/deptlang/fulgor. (online, accessed 2 February 2009)

De Fina, A, (2000). Orientation in immigrant narratives: The role of ethnicity in the identification of characters. *Discourse Studies*, 2, 2: 131–157.

De Fina, A. (2007). Code-switching and the construction of ethnic identity in a community of practice. *Language in Society*, 36, 3: 371–392.

Koester, A. J. (2006). *Investigating Workplace Discourse*. London: Routledge.

Meinhof, U. H. & Galasiński, D. (2005). *The Language of Belonging*. New York: Palgrave Macmillan.

Pavlenko, A. & Blackledge, A. (eds) (2004). *Negotiation of Identity in Multilingual Contexts*. Clevedon: Multilingual Matters.

Rampton, B. (1995). *Crossings*. London: Longman.

Rampton, B. (1999). Sociolinguistics and cultural studies: New ethnicities, liminality and interaction. *Social Semiotics*, 9, 3: 355–374.

Rampton, B. 2001, Ethnicity and the crossing of ethnic boundaries. In R. Mesthrie & R. Asher (eds), *Concise Encyclopaedia of Sociolinguistics*. Oxford: Elsevier Science, 321–324.

Riley, P. (2007). *Language, Culture and Identity*. London: Continuum.

Stubbs, M. (1986). A matter of prolonged field work: Notes towards a modal grammar of English. *Applied Linguistics*, 7, 1: 1–25.

Stuer, A. P. L. (1982). *The French in Australia*. Canberra: The National University Press.

Van Maanen, G. (2004). The invisible man. *Multicultural Communities Online*, 6, 3. www.multiculturalwa.net.au/wppuser/owamc/onlinenews_3_04. (online, accessed 2 February 2009)

The memory of objects: Eurasian women (re)creating identity and belonging in the post-migratory home

Michelle Barrett

CURTIN UNIVERSITY

Introduction

This chapter draws upon a larger study that examines the experiences of people in Australia who identify themselves as 'Eurasian' and how they negotiate this often ambiguous 'mixed' identity in everyday life. My focus is on people of mixed European and Asian heritage – specifically those who represent the legacy of the European colonial expansion throughout South and South East Asia – and so includes the Burghers of Sri Lanka (colonial Ceylon) and Eurasians who have migrated to Australia from countries like Malaysia (colonial Malaya) and Singapore. These two broad, post-colonial groups share a similar ancestry resulting from the intermixing between Portuguese, Dutch and other European colonists with local populations throughout South and South East Asia. Therefore the cultural boundaries between these two 'Eurasian' groups are often porous, leading to a certain fluidity when it comes to personal self-identification. Specifically, this chapter focuses on the role that objects and ornaments play in (re)creating identity and a sense of 'home' for a group of migrant Eurasian women residing in Perth, Western Australia. The chapter draws on the work of cultural geographer, Divya Tolia-Kelly, who posits that the visual and material cultures in the migrant home can be read as artefacts that are imbued with memory and are therefore involved in the creation of home and identity within the diaspora (2004a).

The findings from my semi-structured interviews with three women of varying background, all of whom broadly identify as Eurasian, reveal the subtle relationship between their objects of home decoration and the deployment of memory. The objects served a function during the women's migration journeys and they continue to do important 'identity work' in their lives. Using a simple definition by Michael L. Schwalbe and Douglas Mason-Schrock, 'identity work' constitutes 'anything people do, individually or collectively, to give meaning to themselves or others' and involves the use of signs, labels and definitions to evoke those meanings (1996: 115). The identity work of my informants includes the process of home decoration to create and recreate meaning through their objects as they negotiate their Eurasian identities during the transition from previous homelands to Australia.

In relation to their identity, these women's choice of which ornaments to buy, to keep, or to discard, goes far beyond issues of consumerism and a commodification of Europe and Asia, to involve a personal and often emotional process of defining what it is to be Eurasian. Raj Mehta and Russell W. Belk argue that possessions play an important role in the reconstruction of immigrant identity because they are attached to our sense of self and therefore can aid in our sense of belonging (1991: 398). When talking about their objects and the memories they evoke, the three informants invariably reveal how they view themselves and what aspects of identity they choose to represent. This chapter is concerned with the objects and ornaments that are associated with their conceptions of their ethnic identity and how they use home decoration to come to terms with their Eurasian-ness.

Eurasian-ness

'Eurasian' as a term is difficult to define and its ambiguity leads to a variety of meanings for different people in different contexts. Eurasians have varied backgrounds, experiences and histories. There is no singular Eurasian identity, as Christine Choo *et al.* point out (2004: 71). The latter also contend that the term 'Eurasian' inherits its ambiguity from the fluidity associated with the words 'Asian' and 'European', both of which refer to people from broad geographical areas, each with a wide range of often overlapping cultures and societies (Choo *et al.* 2004: 71). In simple terms, anyone with a configuration of 'mixed' Asian and European heritage can claim a Eurasian identity. However, in reality, the boundaries of Eurasian-ness are often contested by Eurasians themselves, with porous borders defined and reinforced through the use of notions of purity and cultural authenticity, and with Eurasian-ness contingent on the situational and political context within which an individual lives. Within the scope of my research, I focus on those people who can claim an ancestry based on the colonial encounter in South and South East Asia.

The Burghers of Sri Lanka and the Eurasians of Malaysia and Singapore both share a claim to Dutch and/or Portuguese ancestry (amongst other European ancestries), as well as Asian ancestry, resulting in an overlap of cultural practices that include the areas of food, language and religion. Specifically, the people known as the Burghers are the descendants of the Portuguese, Dutch and British colonial rulers who initially intermarried with the local Sinhalese and Tamil populations of Sri Lanka. Similarly, the Eurasians of Malaysia and Singapore are a legacy of Empire, with their ancestry derived from the descendants of the Portuguese, Dutch and British colonial rulers who intermarried with the various existing ethnic groups of the Malay Archipelago (De Witt 2006).[1]

Many Burghers migrated from Sri Lanka to Malaysia during the post-war period of decolonisation, where they were often subsumed into Malaysia's Eurasian ethnic group due to their similar ancestries and shared histories. One common factor identified by Lionel Caplan is that a Eurasian identity marks a historical meeting of separate and unequal streams along the line of a perceived East/West divide (1995: 745). I am interested in the different and shifting understandings of being Eurasian and how this notion of an East/West divide is negotiated in the Eurasian home.

Methodology

The three informants discussed in this chapter are drawn from a larger study involving twenty people, men and women, who broadly self-identify as 'Eurasian' – that is, as having a mixed European and Asian ancestry, whether that mixing occurred with their parents or as far back as the era of European colonial expansion throughout South and South East Asia. Due to the similar ancestries and considerable cultural cross-over between the two groups, I include both the Burghers of Sri Lanka and the Eurasians of Malaysia and Singapore under the broad category of 'Eurasian'. However, my fieldwork reveals that the register of who identifies as Eurasian and who as Burgher is fluid and subject to the complexities of identity formation. The ambiguities associated with a 'Eurasian' identity lead to a process of negotiation, as individuals construct and reconstruct their identities within the larger context of the Burgher and Eurasian communities.

For this reason, my study cannot present a history of Eurasians as a whole; rather it can only seek to gain an understanding of how a limited sample of Eurasians themselves understand being 'Eurasian'. Therefore I adopt a phenomenological approach that privileges my participants' understandings, expressions and explanations of their identities. This involves a close textual analysis of the narrative responses of each participant to a series of open-ended interview questions that focus on identity, the concept of 'mixed race', and their everyday life experiences inside and outside the home. After conducting these interviews in my participants' homes, it became evident that a Eurasian identity is represented in their homes in different ways, corresponding to the way in which they understand being Eurasian. For the purposes of this chapter, I am focusing on three women who identify as Eurasian in different ways and who take three different approaches in representing their identity through their home decoration. Although a Eurasian identity was conceived of in a number of ways by my larger group of participants, the different approaches taken by these three women are broadly representative of the ways in which identity was expressed within the home by the larger participant study group. I therefore use these women's narratives and home decoration approaches as case studies that can provide greater insight into some of the ways that identity has been conceived of and represented by my larger study group.[2]

The first woman is of Burgher origin, but has always identified primarily as Eurasian due to her upbringing in Malaysia and Brunei rather than in Sri Lanka. The second informant is a descendant of the Burghers on her mother's side, with a European father; and the third is of Eurasian origin from Malacca in Malaysia where there is a separate and distinct Portuguese-oriented Eurasian group with a distinctive culture. The first informant is in her fifties and the other two respondents are in their mid to late thirties. All three describe themselves as 'mixed race' with Portuguese and/or Dutch heritage combined with Asian heritage. It should be noted that the concept of race is used in this chapter from the point of view that it exists as a social construct and not as biological fact. I refer to race because all participants in the broader research project have described themselves as being 'mixed race' and used terms such as 'in-between', 'in the middle' and 'hybrid' when talking about themselves. The three informants have all lived in a variety of countries, and all three migrated to Perth, Western Australia during the 1980s. Significantly, they described this event as confusing with respect to their identity and sense of being Eurasian.

The migration process exposes the ambivalence of the Eurasian experience and calls into question the notion of identity for many of those who identify as Eurasian. All my participants said that they often had trouble explaining what they were to people in Australia. Migrating to a new country often involves an intercultural negotiation between the migrant's home culture and their new host culture (Mehta and Belk 1991: 399–400). The Eurasian experience adds another dimension to this, as migrants' lives in their 'home' country often already involved intercultural negotiation when it came to identity. To illustrate this point, many of my other study participants, beyond these three, grew up in very British-oriented households in Malaysia, despite not having any British heritage. As was common in many colonial countries, household effects and objects were specially ordered from Britain, constructing and reinforcing the perception of quality and status associated with British goods. In effect, their Eurasian homes represented a reversal of Edward Said's notion of orientalism (1979), whereby in this situation 'Europe' was imagined and constructed in 'the East'.

'Eurasian' identity in the new home

This chapter is not a definitive account of Eurasian migrants in Australia. Rather, it presents the narratives of three Eurasian women's migration experiences, particularly in relation to the ways in which they have created 'home' and a sense of belonging in Australia. This is significant, considering that they all revealed that they had already experienced a precarious sense of belonging in the other countries in which they lived. For the informants, belonging is linked to their understanding of their Eurasian-ness. A key theme amongst many of my participants in the larger study sample, and certainly these three, was the process of home decoration and the use of material objects and their link with memory, to construct and represent their Eurasian identities whilst 'making home'. Jules David Prown, a scholar who was at the forefront of the emergence of the field of material culture in the early 1980s, posits that just as we create material culture, so too are we shaped by the material culture around us. He goes further by saying that just as we can use oral histories as a source for interpreting material culture, we can use artefacts to enhance or shape the telling and remembering of oral histories (1982: 2). When talking about their objects and the memories they evoke, these respondents invariably reveal how they view themselves and what aspects of themselves they choose to represent.

Within the study of material culture, much has been written about everyday objects and their link to people. As early as the 1970s, Mary Douglas proclaimed 'goods are neutral, their uses are social' (1979: xv). Arjun Appadurai expanded on this notion with his assertion that 'commodities, like persons, have social lives' (1986: 3). The field of material culture has continued to explore the social meaning of objects, from Mihaly Csikszentmihalyi and Eugene Rochberg-Halton's (1981) socio-psychological study on the link between domestic items and their use as symbols of self, to Daniel Miller's (2001) examination of people's relationships with the material culture of the home. From the perspective of consumption studies, Marsha L. Richins (1994) examines the public and private meanings of possessions that invest them with personal value, and Mehta and Belk (1991) examine possession value from the perspective of immigrants. The latter argue that the possessions brought by immigrants to new countries of residence resonate deeply with conceptions of self and therefore aid in the adaptation process (Mehta and Belk 1991: 399). Adaptation and belonging are key themes in the writings of cultural geographer Divya Tolia-Kelly. She argues that visual cultures in the home are central to constructions of identity and 'ensure a positioning of diasporic groups through their metaphorical effect, their metonymical value and their accretion of meaning' (Tolia-Kelly 2001: 51). While I draw upon the work of these scholars, I also remain aware that the conclusions drawn below are my interpretations and these may not correspond with how my informants interpret the ways in which they represent their identities. Owing to the permeable and shifting boundaries associated with identity that make it hard to pin down as a concept, I can only use scholarship to offer some insights into how home decoration and identity can be linked.

The first informant is of Dutch Burgher origin from Sri Lanka, but was born in Singapore and grew up in Malaysia and Brunei. Her family were not active within the Eurasian community, but they identified as Eurasian so that they would fit in by using a term easily recognised in these countries. They would enter the community of Eurasians in Malaysia and Brunei from time to time by visiting their Eurasian relatives, some of whom were actually of Burgher origin and some of whom were Portuguese-origin Malaccans. She grew up in a very respectable British-oriented Eurasian household where roasts and curries were consumed off Wood's Ware crockery, using the finest silverware from England and surrounded by shelves of miniature porcelain figurines from England. She ended up in Brunei as a young adult where she met and married her European husband and started her family. During the 1980s her husband lost his job due to Malaysia's nationalist policies and their subsequent migration to Australia was primarily influenced by 'push' factors in order to protect their family's financial and social status and to secure what she termed a good education for her children. Her parents and siblings had previously migrated to Australia and the reunion of extended family there in the 1980s greatly aided in her sense of belonging in her new homeland.

Figure 1

The informant also remarked that it was a relief to finally settle in a country after the upheaval of the migration process that took her family to England to stay with her in-laws for almost a year while they waited for application processes to be accepted and finalised. As a result, she described her overall migration experience and life in Australia as positive. She also commented several times that she and her husband had made the right decision: 'I still say we did the right thing ... I love being in Australia, I think we're very lucky compared to so many parts of the world nowadays'. They had both taken their only trip back to Malaysia and Brunei in 1999, where she said she was greatly disappointed to see what she deemed to be a decline in the general quality of life. Old cherished places and buildings from her memory were now subject to neglect and decay, and old friends no longer lived there. She realised that she herself had changed since emigrating and that her life in Australia was a comfortable existence that she greatly appreciated. Despite this, she still strongly represents her Asian side through her home.

As previously stated, the first informant was a married woman with a young family when she migrated to Australia. Her objects, which she has always loved, were extremely important to her during this time. Mehta and Belk (1991) argue that possessions play an important role in the reconstruction of immigrant identity because they are attached to our sense of self – who we are, who we were and who we hope to become (398). This attachment becomes particularly relevant during periods of transition such as the migration process. *Figure 1* shows a cabinet in the first informant's dining room in her home in Malaysia in the early 1980s. The image shows some of her favourite material possessions – her carved wood dragon lamp, a blue and white glazed ceramic vase, a framed Chinese landscape painting, some brass Chinese characters, a wool rug from Nepal and some ornamental wooden chairs. It should be noted that most of the objects in her house were brought from Malaysia when she migrated to Australia in the mid-1980s, and therefore they are just a few examples. The informant's Dutch Indonesian lamp was bought almost 35 years ago and it has followed her to every house she has lived in since. She ritualistically hangs it above the dining table, often at great expense, owing to its difficult electrical installation. During the interview with the first respondent, it became evident that the lamp is of primary importance to her sense of 'home,' as it has acted as a highly visible constant in all of her places of residence.

Jean-Sebastien Marcoux states that while a person's objects may become mobile as they physically move in relation to a place, those objects can represent stability to that person. 'The role played by mobile possessions in securing memory in motion' appears throughout research on migration, exile and diaspora (Marcoux 2001: 71). Mehta and Belk argue that geographic movement places a burden on individual possessions for anchoring identity, and this is increased as the distance of the move increases. Prohibitive costs can restrict the movement of objects over long distances, meaning that only the most important objects are taken (1991: 400). The informant's Dutch Indonesian lamp and her other possessions were shipped to Australia at great cost, revealing their importance as anchors of identity. Marcoux argues that the constitution of memory through displacements, whether they involve life-threatening upheavals or the less dramatic circumstances within the same city, gives us important insights into what people deem to be important to who they are (2001: 69). Coming from a long line of Burghers in Sri Lanka and then Malaysia, the informant's Eurasian-ness is very much situated in being Asian, and this is what she chooses to represent through her objects.

At the start of the interview, my first informant claimed to have chosen her possessions purely on an aesthetic level as they had nothing to do with her identity, but she slowly revealed that in the months leading up to migration, she actively sought out and bought as many beautiful Asian ornaments as she could find because she wanted to 'bring Asia with her'. Towards the end of the interview, she admitted that the objects around her were extremely important to her ethnic or cultural identity, describing them *as* her. As such, her possessions must represent herself as an Asian. One example is that her blue and white china, which she finds aesthetically pleasing, can not be of European origin, but must be Asian because, as she states: 'I grew up in Asia. I feel more comfortable with the Asian side of things'. At another time she said, 'I just want that feeling of Asia'. While it would seem that Asia is in a sense being reduced and commodified by her, the informant's connection with her objects goes much deeper. It was only as an adult, inspired by her brother-in-law, that she started collecting Asian ornaments. However, they now act as memory aids and have symbolic value, as they loosely represent her idea of Asia and, by extension, herself. This represents a significant shift from the British-oriented household of her childhood which she admits to rejecting as an adult woman.

Writing on the visual cultures and textural landscapes of the British Asian home and the use of memory in diasporic positioning, Tolia-Kelly reveals the connection between objects and senses of place that become part of a collective, visual vocabulary for a migrant community (2004a: 319). The textures of the object contain 'a set of relationships between biographical and national and/or cultural identifications' (Tolia-Kelly 2004a: 319). The first informant's possessions act as metonymical symbols for her biographical and cultural identification with her loose idea of 'Asia'. Her insistence on Asian blue and white china signifies what Tolia-Kelly terms 'remembered landscapes', whereby the 'colour, texture or icons within visual forms can refract memories of the experience of a different continent, a journey or simply a moment' (2001: 51).

My second informant is in her mid-thirties and identifies as Eurasian because her mother is of Burgher origin and her father is British. She interprets 'Eurasian' as a more fluid umbrella term that can encompass her father's heritage. She has lived in both Malaysia and England, but called neither home. She migrated to Australia as a child with her parents in the mid-1980s. As with the first informant, she states that her parents could no longer afford her international school fees and sought a better education for their children in Australia, where they also had family. She admitted feeling like an outsider when some of her fellow classmates in primary school remarked on her mother's darker skin, and she actively avoided talking about her background to friends: 'When people didn't understand my background it made me feel unusual and excluded and a little bit ashamed'. She reversed this in high school when she became proud of her varied ancestry and felt as though Australia was becoming a more multicultural country. At the time of her interview, she stated that she moves back and forth between foregrounding or backgrounding her Asian ancestry depending on the company she is in. This process leaves her with a slightly precarious sense of belonging in Australia. Despite this, she stated that she valued her quality of life in Australia and, for the most part, has had positive experiences. She has never been back to Malaysia, nor England, but does plan to visit one day when she has children so that they can see the places where she has come from. This is something she deems important; it is also important for her to have reminders of her ancestry represented throughout her home.

As with my first informant, her objects act as visual reminders of the things she grew up seeing as a child both in her home in Malaysia and in her grandparent's home in England. She recalls objects like her British grandmother's oriental rugs, opium table and blue and white china as things with which she strongly identifies. Her grandmother's blue and white china was European but it would still remind her of her mother's Asian blue and whites. She migrated to Australia as a child and so actively sought out and bought these things in Australia, specifically for what is termed their symbolic value. According to Richins (1994), the important role of possessions in identity is that a possession's meaning is central to its value. Again, for this informant, it does not matter so much which Asian country these things come from, but for her they must symbolise 'Asia', as this has significant meaning for her. She has pale skin and so felt that she had to assert her Asian side, as it could easily go unnoticed by others and because she feared that she may forget as time goes on. She said: 'When I moved in with my very white Australian partner, I went around the house and put up all of my Asian ornaments, almost defiantly. I don't have that many really, but I have a few in each room and whenever I see them I think 'that's me. I live here and I am part Asian', and then I feel comfortable'.

In contrast to the first informant's approach, this woman placed small clusters of ornaments in most of her rooms and was very aware of her thought process when she was choosing them. She said that she was making a conscious effort to display her Asian side in her home, but preferred to do it in subtle ways. For Tolia-Kelly, this conscious positioning of aspects of visual culture within the home can be read as a means of fixing and negotiating residence in Australia – something that might be of great importance to the sense of belonging for a child migrant. Tolia-Kelly argues that there is a politics to the display of visual cultures as they 'express a visual grammar and allow a 'highly individualised presencing' through their existence' (2001: 51). By placing her Asian ornaments in small groupings around her home, the informant is symbolically moving into the entire space of her house, anchoring herself and displaying her individualised presence. Her objects are not only for her own reassertion of identity. They are also used to display her identity to visitors and she uses them as a way to introduce her Eurasian identity to those who comment on her objects and who do not already know her background. In this sense, her ornaments act as metonymical symbols of herself (Tolia-Kelly 2001: 51).

Figure 2

My second informant has a few objects that she bought recently to represent the other aspects of her identity. She did this because she realised that she had neglected to represent her Portuguese and Dutch heritage and wanted to pay tribute to her new homeland of Australia. On her kitchen windowsill there is a grouping of 'Asian' inspired tea caddies, pink sugar bowl and various other things, all of which are used everyday and have symbolic value (see *Figure 2*). Her windmill pepper shaker represents her Dutch blood and a brass kettle represents her Sri Lankan ancestry, because it was made in India and is therefore a close enough representation in her mind. Beside it she has placed a colourful plate that she describes as her tribute to Australia and being first and foremost Australian. She also talked of recently purchased items such as an Indonesian *batik* apron that reminded her of the fabric of her grandmother's dresses and a hand-painted plate from Portugal that she views as symbolic of her Portuguese blood.

These are the things that she pointed out as representing her ethnic or cultural identity and, even though admitting to a lack of affinity with the Dutch or the Portuguese, or with India or China where many of her ornaments come from, she felt it was important to have these visual reminders in her house. For Tolia-Kelly, these types of visual reminders constitute a 'post-colonial identification with landscape' (2004b: 676), whereby my second informant has created a collage of other environments through the display and collection of certain items that serve to ground her 'identification in tangible and textural engagements' (2004b: 676). In many ways she is still coming to terms with her definition of Eurasian, as the migration process confused her idea of self and ethnicity. She concedes that her pale skin tone has greatly aided her post-migration adjustment. However, at the same time, it has challenged her sense of Eurasian-ness. In this way, her identification with her Asian ornaments helps to ground her with something tangible.

My last informant, also in her thirties, is a Malaccan Eurasian who migrated to Australia as a child in the mid 1980s, arriving with few or no possessions of her own. After her father's death, her mother chose to bring her to Perth where she had family. This informant has lived in Australia ever since, with the exception of a year spent living in Canada in her twenties. She told me how she refused to take Australian citizenship for many years, believing Australia to be an inherently racist country which left her with a divided sense of belonging: '[It] took me 17 years because I didn't identify with being Australian. Mainly because it was very… you had to be Caucasian'. Her feelings turned and she became a citizen after she saw Indigenous Australian athlete Cathy Freeman lighting the cauldron at the 2000 Olympic Games in Sydney. However, deciding to give up her Malaysian citizenship was a hard decision for her, and she stated that she still has strong feelings for her homeland: 'I love Malaysia. I still love it and if I had lots of money I would probably have a holiday home there'. She had travelled back for the first time the year before the interview, and planned to go again in the future. She is also working on a self-definition of her identity – she has a Chinese grandfather and looks typically Chinese, so feels as though she has to assert that she is actually Eurasian. One of the ways that she does this is through her active membership of a Eurasian community group in Perth. She prefers subtlety, and when I went into her home it was not apparent at all that she used her objects to create a sense of being Eurasian. Aside from a wooden elephant and a black Chinese silk cushion, everything else was what is currently in vogue in home decorating shops. However, she revealed during the interview that many of her objects were chosen specifically because they acted as visual reminders of her Malaccan Eurasian heritage.

She moved around her flat and showed me little things such as some glass tea light holders with a black lacy pattern on them that reminded her strongly of the embroidery and lace that her grandmother and other Eurasian women used to make in Malacca. She said: 'A lot of the Eurasian houses have white lacy (curtains). I don't want to have that because it looks yucky, but I'll have other bits of it'. She pointed out all the other things that replicated this lacy pattern, including a black and white picture on the wall and a ceramic candle dish on her coffee table. She said: 'I really relate to these'. On the candle dish, she had placed three white artificially-scented blossoms that remind her of the flowers her grandmother and other Eurasian women wore in their hair. These objects act as metonymical symbols of both her grandmother and the larger Malaccan Eurasian culture in which she grew up. The symbol of her grandmother could again be found in her kitchen cupboard. Amongst the stark, white porcelain pieces of her angular, modern crockery set, she almost embarrassingly pointed out four floral tea cups in pastel colours. She told me of how she had to buy them when she saw them, as they reminded her of her grandmother's tea set. As a child she would have afternoon tea and small cakes with her grandmother in Malacca. Today, as a fairly regular ritual, she sits sipping her tea from her floral tea cup and eats a small cake and a curry puff while reading the paper. This story moves beyond the issue of consumption (the buying of her floral tea cups) to include a very personal account in which she incorporates the memories of her grandmother and growing up in Malacca into her post-migration home.

She does this further throughout her home. Her bedroom is full of heavy dark wooden furniture that reminds her of the colonial furniture in her Malaccan grandfather's house and she has a framed print of a Malaccan fort in her kitchen. Her most prized possessions are two framed sixteenth-century Portuguese coins from sunken Portuguese galleons. This last informant, more than the others, reflects Tolia-Kelly's notion of a 'culture of landscape' in relation to one specific place (2006: 343). For Tolia-Kelly, the metaphor of a cultural landscape re-presents the experience, memory or culture of a place/

homeland in the visual textures of the home. By solidifying 'cultural memories of place in representational form and in material textures', this informant has re-presented through a culture of landscape much of the experience, memory and culture of Malacca in her home objects (Tolia-Kelly 2006: 343).

The Eurasians of Malacca constitute a separate and distinct ethnic group that can trace its roots back to the Portuguese colonisation of Malacca in the 1500s. The Malaccan Eurasians now have *bumiputra* status in Malaysia – this literally translates as 'son of the soil' – and means that they are recognised as an indigenous ethnic group. My Malaccan Eurasian participant therefore experiences her Eurasian-ness in terms of a specific geographic location with a specific history and culture – one that was centred on the sea, on Catholicism, as well as on Portuguese cultural influences. She told me stories about the San Pedro festival and the blessing of the boats and playing in the sea as a child. It was in the muddy tides that she remembers finding similar coins and regretted never having kept one. When she went back to Malacca Town in recent years, she said she had to buy them as they were a piece of her past and she is extremely proud of them. Aside from photos of her deceased father, these coins were the only things she said she would hand down to her children or save in the event of a fire.

The very clearly defined boundaries of what constitutes a Malaccan Eurasian has led her to describe herself as a historical product of interracial marriages and multiculturalism, rather than describing herself as part-European and part-Asian as all my other participants have. As a result, she chooses to represent her identity through a Malaccan cultural landscape, using the subtle deployment of memory or visual triggers of memory throughout her house. Although not recognisably Asian, her ornaments were chosen for their symbolic value and possession meaning (Richins 1994). Furthermore, she wanted her possessions as a whole to represent the contrasts that she feels within herself. She illustrated this by describing the contrasts of the hard and soft of her fluffy rugs and wooden floors, the light and dark of her colour schemes (much of which was black and white), the old and new of her old wooden furniture with new white leather couch, and East meets West. These are the things that she believes represents herself, summing it up by happily stating: 'I have East and West!'.

Conclusion

There are many different configurations of Eurasian, and just as many ways to experience and assert Eurasian-ness. These configurations are contingent on many socio-historical factors that shape the biographical narratives of each individual. Certainly the narratives of my informants provided three examples of how being Eurasian is understood and expressed. The first informant lived in Asia for a longer period of her life, migrating to Australia as an adult. The migration process at this stage in her life seemed to affect her self-identity to a lesser degree than the two younger informants – her understanding of being Eurasian is grounded in being Asian. The second informant migrated to Australia as a child and it could be argued that her movements between Malaysia and England beforehand have shaped her understandings of being Eurasian in a more complex and hybrid way that seeks to incorporate all aspects of her ancestry. While also migrating to Australia as a child, the third informant's identity is more grounded in the location of Malacca which still figures largely in how she imagines herself. Her understanding of Malacca's cultural history has led her to understand being Eurasian in a more balanced way as a product of historical forces.

The different backgrounds of my three informants and how each views her Eurasian-ness is represented through her objects. Regardless of the age at which they migrated, memory plays an important role in their process of home decoration. As Attfield points out, the seemingly inconsequential objects including 'small personal effects collectively termed ornaments' belie the important role that they have in 'defining, performing, rehearsing and mediating aspects of subjectivity' (2000: 153). For these three women, their objects and the memories associated with them have helped to anchor them during the destabilising migration process. They have also aided the active (re) creation of a post-migration ethnic identity. Engaging with the objects daily ensures that the informants are involved in the ongoing process of self-definition.

The relationship between people and their objects is complex and multilayered – it is constantly renegotiated as personal, and cultural memory is deployed in the construction and constant reassertion of identities. Objects with symbolic value are chosen to evoke nostalgic recollections that are deemed useful in a person's identity work as they negotiate the complexities of identity and come to terms with how they understand 'Eurasian-ness'. Certainly for my participants, objects are bought, discarded, received from relatives and constantly rearranged so that some find themselves in places of importance within the house, while others are relegated to rooms of lesser importance. My first informant has always gone to great effort to install her Dutch Indonesian lamp in pride of place above the dining table, but less important objects, which have little meaning or symbolic value to her, go straight into the laundry.

The different approaches that these three informants have taken toward expressing their Eurasian identities throughout their homes is representative of the three broad ways in which the remaining 17 participants in my larger study approach their home decoration. The approaches involve either overt expressions that use ornaments and furniture to situate the Eurasian identity firmly within the cultural landscape of Asia, or a more subtle form that uses small clusters of ornaments or furniture that directly represent or visually symbolise aspects of a Eurasian identity that remains hybrid or draws specifically on a geographical location such as Colombo in Sri Lanka or Malacca in Malaysia. Regardless of which approach has been taken, the link between home objects and the memories and meanings that these evoke have significant value in the constant (re)creation of my participants' identity and helps to shape their senses of belonging and understanding of being Eurasian in Australia.

Notes

1 Arguably, the Portuguese can be credited with creating the foundation for most Eurasian ancestries, as their maritime trade routes marked the beginning of direct contact between East and West (Ryan 1976: 40–45 and Lewis 1995: 6–7). The global economy of the fifteenth century saw the rise in a desire for spices which essentially drove much of the European maritime expansion across the globe, particularly towards the East as more direct sea routes were sought in order to bypass the control of the Ottoman Empire (Keay 2005: xi and Ryan 1976: 40–42). The Portuguese were the first to reach South and South East Asia and they quickly sought to control the important seaport of Malacca on the south-east coast of the Malayan peninsula, located therefore at the nexus of the East-West trade routes. In the sixteenth century, the reach of the Portuguese Empire spanned from Macau to Goa, Ceylon to Malacca, and across parts of Africa and Brazil. Miscegenation was encouraged by the relatively small numbers of

Portuguese colonists in order to boost the number of Catholics in the region who were loyal to the Portuguese crown, and this saw the rapid growth of a racially mixed (*mestico*) population (Noonan 1968: 53 and Kraal 2005: 11). In the seventeenth century, the Dutch, under the auspices of the *Verenigde Oost-Indische Compagnie* (VOC) (United Dutch East Indies Company), established themselves throughout Asia by expelling and replacing the Portuguese in their colonies (Gelman Taylor 1983: xx and Ryan 1976: 67). Despite a reputation for being aloof rulers, the Dutch encouraged intermarriage between the employees of the VOC and local populations, which saw the creation of Eurasian communities of Dutch descent in colonies such as South Africa, Ceylon, where they were called the Burghers, and in particular Indonesia (Kraal 2005: 14). Dutch rule in the region lasted up until the British gradually replaced them in the nineteenth century (Lewis 1995: 123). Miscegenation also occurred during this last period of European rule in the region, and large movements of Eurasians occurred throughout the colonies as they sought employment and trading opportunities within the British Empire. Eurasians from Malacca and British India (Anglo-Indians) emigrated to Penang and Singapore and Burghers from Ceylon emigrated across to the Malayan peninsula where a large workforce was needed to aid in the expansion of Empire. The end of British rule coincided with the decolonisation period after World War II; however, all three waves of European colonial intrusions left their cultural mark on the present day countries within the region.

2 Although some approaches to representing identity throughout the home were overlapping, I was able to divide my group of 20 participants into three discernible groups. The first group (6) constitutes those who represent an overtly Asianised identity with an abundance of general 'Asian' ornaments spread throughout the home. This includes Chinese blue and white porcelain ornaments, wooden Elephants and textiles from India and Indonesia, Japanese tea sets often received as wedding gifts, and Chinese rosewood furniture. The second group (8) sought to represent their ethnic identity in a less overt way, choosing to display clusters of ornaments here and there throughout the home, some of which were generally 'Asian' and some of which represented other ethnic components of their identity or specific places, such as Dutch windmills, Portuguese cockerels, and paintings of Malacca or Colombo. The third group (6) used a more subtle approach to identity representation, which focused more on visual reminders to trigger memory of a certain place or time, or what they perceived to be symbolic of a certain ethnicity. This includes ornaments or objects that contained a certain pattern such as *batik*, or one that was reminiscent of patterns from Asian blue and white china.

References

Appadurai, A. (ed.) (1986). *The Social Life of Things: Commodities in Cultural Perspective*. Cambridge: Cambridge University Press.

Attfield, J. (2000). *Wild Things: The Material Culture of Everyday Life*. Oxford & New York: Berg.

Caplan, L. (1995). Creole World, Purist Rhetoric: Anglo-Indian Cultural Debates in Colonial and Contemporary Madras. *The Journal of the Royal Agricultural Institute* 1, 4: 743–762.

Choo, C., Carrier, A., Choo, C. & Choo, S. (2004). Being Eurasian: Transculturality or Transcultural Reality? *LifeWriting* 1, 1: 71–96.

Csikszentmihalyi, M. & Rochberg-Halton, E. (1981). *The Meaning of Things: Domestic Symbols and the Self.* Cambridge: Cambridge University Press.

De Witt, D. (2006). The Easternization of the West: Children of the VOC, *The Easternization of the West: The Role of Melaka, the Malay-Indonesian Archipelago and the Dutch (VOC) International Seminar*, Malacca, Malaysia, July 27. www.dutchmalaysia.net/press/Easternization.html [online, accessed 10 October 2008]

Douglas, M. (1996 [1979]). *The World of Goods*. London & New York: Routledge.

Gelman Taylor, J. (1983). *The Social World of Batavia: European and Eurasian in Dutch Asia*. Madison, Wisconsin: University of Wisconsin Press.

Keay, J. (2005). *The Spice Route: A History*. London: John Murray.

Kraal, D. (2005). *Gateway to Eurasian Culture*. Singapore: Asiapac Books.

Lewis, D. (1995). *Jan Compagnie in the Straits of Malacca, 1641–1795*. Athens, Ohio: Ohio University Center for International Studies.

Marcoux, J.-S. (2001). The Refurbishment of Memory. In D. Miller (ed.), *Home Possessions: Material Culture behind Closed Doors*. Oxford & New York: Berg, 69–86.

McGilvray, D. B. (1982). Dutch Burghers and Portuguese Mechanics: Eurasian Ethnicity in Sri Lanka. *Comparative Studies in Society and History* 24, 2: 235–263.

Mehta, R. & Belk, R. W. (1991). Artefacts, Identity, and Transition: Favourite Possessions of Indians and Indian Immigrants to the United States. *The Journal of Consumer Research* 17, 4: 398–411.

Miller, D. (ed.) (2001). *Home Possessions: Material Culture behind Closed Doors*. Oxford & New York: Berg.

Noonan, L. (1968). *The Portuguese in Malacca: A Study of the First Major European Impact on East Asia*. Lisbon: Centero de Estudios Historicos Ultramarinos.

Prown, J. D. (1982). Mind in Matter: An Introduction to Material Culture Theory and Method. *Winterthur Portfolio* 17, 1: 1–19.

Richins, M. L. (1994). Valuing Things: The Public and Private Meanings of Possessions. *The Journal of Consumer Research* 21, 3: 504–521.

Ryan, N. J. (1976). *A History of Malaysia and Singapore*. Kuala Lumpur: Oxford University Press.

Said, E. W. (1979). *Orientalism*. New York: Random House.

Schwalbe, M. L. & Mason-Schrock, D. (1996). Identity Work as Group Process. *Advances in Group Processes* 13, 1: 113–147.

Tolia-Kelly, D. P. (2001). Iconographies of Identity: Visual Cultures of the Everyday in the South Asian Diaspora. *Visual Culture in Britain* 1, 4: 49–67.

Tolia-Kelly, D. P. (2004a). Locating processes of identification: studying the precipitates of re-memory through artefacts in the British Asian home. *Transactions of the Institute of British Geographers* 29, 3: 314–329.

Tolia-Kelly, D. P. (2004b). Materializing post-colonial geographies: examining the textural landscapes of migration in the South Asian home. *Geoforum* 35: 675–688.

Tolia-Kelly, D. P. (2006). Mobility/stability: British Asian cultures of 'landscape and Englishness'. *Environment and Planning A* 38: 341–358.

PART 2

Migration, literature and media

Narratives of the long sea voyage: Journeying typologies and literary impulses

Diana Glenn
FLINDERS UNIVERSITY

Introduction

The chapter explores connections between metaphors of journeying in a selection of literary texts and representations of transnational journeying arising from a case study of the oral narratives of first-generation Italians who migrated by sea to South Australia from the region of Campania, Italy, in the post-WWII period. With the passage of time, the informants' evocations of the sea voyage provide a dynamic entering into the modalities of the migration experience during the 'ante-chamber' experience of travelling at sea prior to arrival and settlement. The recollection of the sea voyage remains a focal point in the informants' experiential narratives, and the discussion seeks to typify the migrants' journeying experience in the light of archetypal voyaging narratives.

Journeying metaphors

In our modern era, metaphors of journey have been explored according to archetypes such as those outlined by Georg Roppen and Richard Sommer, who examine two principal archetypes, the first stemming from 'an impulse toward renewal, restoration, rejuvenation' (Roppen and Sommer 1964: 17), thus constituting a journey of personal salvation, while the second may be regarded as 'an impulse after unity of knowledge, or understanding; in this respect it is, very simply, the product of man's desire to make sense out of his world' (18). My interest in journeying metaphors and the topology of the vessel crossing boundaries, thereby initiating a new discourse or renewal, stems from both a literary impulse and a metaphorical mapping of borderlines of identity. The topographical points of intersection are Campania in Southern

Italy, known by the ancient Romans as Campania Felix ('fortunate countryside'), and the state of South Australia.

In the years 1353 to 1355, there was a recruitment drive to attract residents from Provence in Southern France to Campania, specifically to the territory of the Fortore in the province of Benevento, considered a settlement zone with ideal climactic conditions (Fuschetto 1984: 25–26). Similarly, in the 1840s, a poster advertising the free colony of South Australia in the Royal Institute of Cornwall declared: 'The province of SA is a delightfully fertile and salubrious country, in every respect well adapted to the constitution of Englishmen, and is one of the most flourishing of all our colonies.' In that era, free emigration to Port Adelaide, South Australia, entailed leaving the 'old country' for the 'new world', travelling with one's family in married steerage accommodation. For over four months, 48 people in steerage lived, slept and ate together in a dark, confined space. However, the promise of a salubrious, 'fortunate' countryside and new beginnings encouraged them to endure the hardships of the voyage.

In exploring recollections of the sea voyage from Italy to Australia through oral testimonies, the research project draws upon a data set of 30 oral narratives collected in an interview format from a group of first generation Campanians who left Italy in the post-WWII period in order to settle in the city of Adelaide, in the state of South Australia. As the O'Connor database (36,357 names recorded on Alien Registration Cards) has demonstrated, there was a significant migration stream from Campania to South Australia after WWII: 'From the point of view of regional origins, the highest ranked, in terms of comparative percentage of birthplace of South Australia's Italians, is Campania (27.9%), followed by Calabria (23.5%), Veneto (10.5%) and Abruzzo (8.6%)' (O'Connor 2004: 59). In total, the number of arrivals from the five provinces of Campania is recorded in the database as 10,145 (5844 males and 4301 females), with the highest number (6,315) arriving from Benevento (O'Connor 2004: 60–62). In Campania, the project informants had resided in provincial centres and most had had access to at least two to five years of primary schooling. Prior to transnational migration, their lives were closely bound up in the exigencies and rhythms of daily family life and work, the provision of sustenance, devotion to the Church and the enactment of rituals connected to family and community life. However, once the decision to emigrate overseas had been taken, in the majority of cases through the mechanism of family-based chain migration, the informants' destinies were then linked inexorably to the faraway outpost wherein resided the migrants from family and community networks who had paved the way. For the Campanian informants, settlement in the city of Adelaide represented a profound dislocation, as they were forced to adapt quickly to life in an urban Anglo-British setting. At the same time, it offered an impetus for personal change.

Many of the project informants are now in their seventies and eighties (one is a centenarian), and their stories recall events from their childhood and youth in pre-war Italy, as well as their life after migrating to and settling in South Australia. Portelli observes: 'oral history expresses the awareness of the historicity of personal experience and of the individual's role in the history of society' (Portelli 1997: 6). Oral-based interactions are personalised, reflective of past and present vicissitudes, and evoke the effects of cross-cultural communication across a broad arc of time. The majority of the project participants were interviewed in Adelaide, where they have been residing since their arrival from Italy, while others were interviewed in Campania, where they repatriated after a period of time spent working in South Australia. The informants were asked to respond to a questionnaire in Italian surveying information across three or four categories: life in Italy prior to migration, the sea crossing to Australia and settlement in Adelaide, with an extra set of questions for return migrants.

In these narratives of memory embracing a 50-year or 60-year period, remembrance of the sea crossing looms with clarity and profound emotive and psychological resonance as a key point of reference from which the informants seek to understand a transformative experience from their youth. The narratives evoke the impulses that motivated their migration journey, the profound loss of traditional community life, the intricacies and permutations of the kinship ties that fed the phenomenon of chain migration, and the fracturing and reformulation of identity in an unfamiliar land. In narrating the sea crossing, the informants trace the key moments of physical dislocation from the old world. The sea voyage from northern climes across the vast southern ocean looms large in the Campanian experiential narratives wherein the remembrance of the journey by ship represents a signal moment of moral agency from which all else flows. As one informant recalls, the ocean crossing represents the realisation of the loss of 'home' and the commencement of a reconstruction of self in the unknown continent: 'When I arrived at Fremantle, I saw all that water that I had crossed and I looked back and I thought: 'I have come to a prison, I don't believe that I will ever return'.' From this voyaging experience, activated through the physical and material separation from the old world, site of a profound emotional and psychological attachment and belonging, the project narrators seek to understand and map their journey of displacement by means of journeying typologies such as a departure through necessity, the irrevocable loss of a collective and familial sense of belonging, inner transformation, risk-taking, the traversing of boundaries and, in the case of returned migrants, a return to the homeland following a remapping of temporal and spatial coordinates.

Literary typologies of the horizontal voyage

Narratives of sea voyages to unknown lands have captured the imaginative spirit for millennia. It is argued in this chapter that the real-life experiences of the Campanian migrants reflect journeying typologies from the literary world of seafaring tales. In the European cultural tradition, two types of voyage from classical literature and biblical exegesis have held sway: the horizontal and the vertical voyage. The archetypal horizontal voyage takes the form of either a physical pilgrimage on land, or a voyage undertaken in a seafaring vessel from landmass to open sea, which is followed by a return to land. In the Judeo-Christian tradition, the vertical voyage constitutes a metaphysical journey into a spiritual realm, such as the one experienced by Saint Paul (God's chosen vessel, Acts 9:15), who underwent a *raptus* whereby he was 'caught up into paradise' (taken up to heaven in his bodily state, 2 Corinthians 12:2–4) and saw heaven by means of a direct vision and not *per speculum*. The archetypal sea voyage, that is, the horizontal voyage found in classical literature, is well known from celebrated poetic texts. Three such literary examples representing different facets of human experience linked to a horizontal sea voyage are *The Odyssey* by Homer, *The Aeneid* by Virgil and *Inferno* XXVI, the ill-fated voyage of Ulysses in Dante's *Comedy*. As exempla of voyages, these texts involve diverse themes and typologies: a prolonged return to the homeland, departure through necessity, an escape from the destruction of one's home, never to return, and a voyage of discovery, undertaken as a search for the unknown that ends in tragedy.

In *The Odyssey,* the Greek hero, Odysseus, has been away from his island kingdom of Ithaca for twenty years: ten years fighting the Trojans, followed by ten years of wandering before returning home. His is a sea voyage of return in order to recover his true identity and take his rightful place among his people as their sovereign. For the Trojan prince Aeneas, the hero of Virgil's epic, *The Aeneid,* a long sea voyage takes him away from the burning remains of his city, Troy, which has been overrun by the Greek army after the stratagem of the Trojan Horse. Aeneas's journey sees him, a stranger and refugee who is displaced and has lost his home, arrive on the shores of Latium whence he will eventually found the Roman Empire. Aeneas can never return home because 'home' has ceased to exist. He must construct a new life and a new identity in an unfamiliar territory. His story is underpinned by the exemplum of *pietas* and the need to undertake enormous personal sacrifice. In the third example, Dante imagines Ulysses as an old king who craves one last voyage of discovery and adventure with his faithful crew. Dante's Ulysses embarks on a foolhardy sea voyage beyond the markers of the known world, the Pillars of Hercules, heading west in his ship across an uncharted sea. He urges his crew to follow him, telling them that they were not 'made to live as brutes but to pursue virtue and knowledge' [*fatti non foste a viver come bruti, / ma per seguir virtute e canoscenza*] (*Inf.* XXVI, 119–120).[1] However, in Dante's fictional rendering, Ulysses transgresses divine boundaries and his ship sinks beneath a mighty wave, with all souls on board perishing.[2] In the metaphysical journey of the Pilgrim Dante in the *Comedy*, self-knowledge, self-determination and inner transformation are key elements in a poetic narration of memory and the quest for identity.

In the narratives of migration of the Campanians who settled in Adelaide in the 1950s and 1960s, the sea voyage represents not only the spatial relocation of the corporeal self beyond the Pillars of Hercules, but also the redefinition of the known and unknown, the obedient self and the unshackled other who must explore new relationships of moral responsibility and redefinitions of selfhood and belonging. As with the travails of their literary precursors, one can identify in the Campanian stories a number of journeying archetypes such as the displacement of self, a departure through necessity to an unknown land, the need for personal sacrifice, and the cognisance of an inner transformation that unfolds in the search for a new way of being.

Experiental journeying narratives

In the oral narratives of the Campanian informants, the sea voyage represents not only a physical relocation but a reconfiguration of the self within a transient experience that remains a central focus for narratives of self-realisation and belonging linked to fragmentation and loss, where previously there was continuity, interactivity, shared knowledge and cohesiveness of family mores, gender-based and community roles. For the project interviewees, the end of WWII marked the demise of a former way of life that had been based on time-honoured traditions connected to the land, family, community and religious values that had been preserved over generations. The society was in upheaval, and migration to an unknown land offered a future of promise and enterprise for many family groups. Sponsorship by close family members, spouses or *paesani* was a strong feature of transnational immigration by Campanians to South Australia during the post-WWII period. Thus the journeying and resettlement experiences of the project informants were predominantly influenced by family kinship networks operating within an open and flexible system of chain migration. The majority of interviewees had never crossed regional borders prior to their transnational migration.

During the interviews it became clear that, despite the passage of time, the departure from Italy, the sea voyage and the moment of disembarkation constituted three focal points in the narratives; these represented, respectively, an experience of loss and enormous change (a turning away from the elemental site of identity and belonging), a period of waiting in a neutral spatial and temporal zone and, finally, the shifting, interactive contesting of spaces, parameters and tensions in which to construct a reconfigured, more fluid identity by means of which the individual would be able to articulate and express future aspirations and autonomous agency. As Andreina De Clementi has noted: 'i comportamenti degli emigranti si segnalano … per disponibilità a cambiare registro, progetto, strategie di vita e di sopravvivenza' [migrant behaviour has been characterised by a willingness to modify language codes, life-plans and survival strategies]

(De Clementi 2007: 30, *translation mine*). In the case of Italian migration to Australia, John Gatt-Rutter observes: 'The overwhelming majority of Italians coming to Australia have had to face that challenge or trauma of crossing the linguistic and cultural divide' (Gatt-Rutter 2006: 115). For the project informants, adherence and obedience to cultural norms in Italy ensured one's place in the family and local community. The individual's centre of existence was located within the family unit and the lives of family members were bound up together in daily ritual and activity. The codification of collective values and practices took place in a provincial, pre-industrial setting. In the 1940s, the agrarian landscape of Campania was dominated by a share-cropping system (*mezzadria*), in which landholdings were traditionally patriarchal and the majority of the informants maintained a close connection with the land. The centre of community life comprised the *piazza* and the parish church, where meaningful exchange and significant rituals were carried out, in accordance with the cyclical nature of the liturgical calendar. Therefore, selfhood was linked to notions of collectivity, e.g. the *paese d'origine,* blood-kin networks, public and private worship of the local saints and madonnas, adherence to the parish community, pilgrimages, and strict observance of the typologies of courtship, marriage and child-bearing.

The migration of the informants to Australia occurred prior to Italy's economic miracle and the atomisation of Italian culture. During the economic boom in the 1960s, Italy underwent a period of unprecedented social change, together with rapid industrial and technological advancements. However, these profound social changes did not have the same impact on the lives of the Campanian migrants who had settled definitively in South Australia. Through the experience of migration, the engendered social norms and codes of the project participants were destabilised and their sense of belonging was reconfigured within the context of cultural dislocation in the great southern land.

Recollections of the sea voyage

The sea-route for the project participants commenced in Naples. From there they travelled to Messina, Port Said, Colombo, Aiden, Fremantle and Melbourne, with an inland crossing to Adelaide. On board the vessel, down in steerage, people were sharing living quarters. Some spoke about the discomfort of sharing space with people who had never seen a modern toilet or shower. Thus, with fellow-passengers suffering sea sickness, others improvising their personal hygiene routines, or lack thereof, in dormitories sleeping 30–40 people at a time with bunk bedding, men's and women's quarters separated, one informant described bed-time as having to face a nightly guillotine. Another recalled fruit, in particular a pineapple, being purchased at one of the ports and then not being consumed and the smell of the rotting fruit at night wafting through the sleeping quarters. One female informant expressed strong feelings of trepidation while at sea:

> I was sick with fear on board that ship. I was worried about my husband and small child who had been separated from me. And it stank down there ... I never thought that I was going to survive. But what choice did we have? We were leaving to find work, to change our lives. In Italy there was always the fear that you would not survive.

The trip from Fremantle to Melbourne was unpleasantly memorable for the roughness of the sea, when even the tables in the eating areas had to be fastened down and secured to stop them sliding about. Others spoke of the friendliness and helpfulness of the crew, the pleasant holiday atmosphere, the generous facilities, recreational activities, festivities when they crossed the equator, dancing, laughing together and the abundance of food. One informant reported the dramatic impact of having enormous quantities of food available for consumption:

> We had never seen so much food in all our lives! We were eating huge blocks of ice-cream. There was American-style breakfast with boiled eggs, fried eggs, scrambled eggs. When the sea was rough, the eggs went flying in all directions!

However amusing the anecdotes about food and festivities were during the interview process, they served as ice-breakers in order to drill down into the complex labile state that the sea crossing engendered psychologically for the informants. Through journeying, each individual maps out a new mental cartography that enables not only the reconceptualisation of geographical determinants, but also a revalorisation of paradigms of millennial culture and encoded behaviour in order to construct a meaningful relationship and form of communication in the new landscape. Fundamental to the experience is a moving out of the self, the known, the recognisable, to a realigned notion of selfhood within the new social context. For the project informants, the sea voyage from Italy to Australia represented an experience of liminality, that is, the sensation of being in a threshold state, caught between two realities: the former life and the new state of existence. For many this represented an emotionally harrowing separation from the community of origin, either temporarily or definitively, and the entering into a type of ante-chamber before the resettlement into a foreign territory of unknown physical and cultural dimensions.

The vessel that enclosed them and sheltered them from the vast unknown southern ocean afforded a time of reflection and of the nurturing of dreams and aspirations in a neutral cultural space that was disconnected from their former reality and foreshadowed disembarkation at a new cultural frontier: 'the journey by sea means uncertainty' [*il viaggio per mare dice incertezza*] (Gasparini 2000: 127). Transnational migration involves a movement outwards from the nucleus of time-worn ritual and engendered social norms. Thus, the sea voyage is both a physical journey of dislocation from the place of origin to the new settlement and also represents a time of re-evaluation of self and belonging, allowing those on the journey to project themselves spatially in order to move forwards into a modern lifestyle occurring in a cultural outpost wherein lay a future of possibilities and progress: a blind faith in order to forge a new identity within the host culture.

As the informants reported: 'People used to say: Saint Australia. People were leaving to find work, to change their lives.' The interviews captured perceptions shaped by both transnational epistolary narratives, themselves embedded in metaphor drawing on realia and myth-making within the alien landscape, and by narratives of plenty, of bounty, of streetscapes covered in lollies. Some of the interviewees had been told to expect in Australia a land where there were so many lollies on the street that no one even bothered to pick them up. Alternatively, others were told that Australia was a land forsaken by God where there was nothing and people survived on green leaf vegetables. An anecdote by a second-generation Italian-Australian woman recalls that her father, while waiting on the docks for she, her mother and brother to disembark from the ship, began throwing sweets up into the air for her to catch. The distance being so great, all the sweets fell into the deep waters in front of the vessel. This proved to be a distressing experience for the child: a microcosmic moment capturing the loss of a desired object that on the broader canvas signified the enormity of the loss of home, family, friends and all that was familiar.

In Italy, I interviewed a man who worked as a migration agent in Campania during the 1950s and who often drove prospective migrants to the port in Naples where they embarked on their ship. He recalled harrowing scenes of family members who were desperate to let go in order to carve out a better future, while at the same time they were equally desperate to remain in Italy in their unified family groups. One informant who emigrated to Adelaide in 1962, in order to find work, conveyed a sense of bewilderment and of losing his internal compass. In his interview he repeatedly said, 'Where were we going?'. I asked him: 'How had you imagined Australia to be?'. 'A dream', he replied, 'I really knew nothing about where I was going. I was on board the *Sydney* for 32 days, food and water, but where was I going? There was a pool, there were games, there was a cinema, there was everything, but I just didn't know where I was going. It took me two years to pay off my debts'. This informant communicated his strong sense of unease about Australia and he continued to repeat the phrase, 'There was nothing there', even though this is precisely what he had said about the employment situation in his village in Italy before emigrating to Australia: 'There was no money. Nobody paid you and so we emigrated'. He returned definitively to Italy in 1973.

For a number of informants, upon arrival, the songlines in the landscape of home that had been traversed and meditated upon by generations were replaced by a sense of emptiness and cultural void. This sense of emptiness, nothingness, unfamiliarity and shock, is lucidly expressed by Raimond Gaita in *Romulus, My Father*, when he describes his father's reaction to the landscape in north-eastern Victoria after the family's arrival in 1950:

> Though the landscape is one of rare beauty, to a European or English eye it seems desolate, and even after more than forty years my father could not become reconciled to it. He longed for the generous and soft European foliage, but the eucalypts of Baringhup, scraggy except for the noble red gums on the river bank, seemed symbols of deprivation and barrenness. In this he was typical of many of the immigrants whose eyes looked directly at the foliage and always turned away offended. (Gaita 1998: 14)

As one of the informants candidly stated: 'People had told me that Australia was 'bella' but when we arrived, oh my God, I didn't like it but I couldn't go back'. The feeling of entrapment expressed by some informants translated into a determined effort to overcome the negative sense of disorientation and move forwards: 'When I disembarked from the ship I said: 'Croce nera, no more viaggio per me (*Black cross, no more voyages for me*)''. This informant became a dynamic negotiator for the family in the new land. On a more humorous note, an interviewee who was employed as a radio officer on the *Oceania* and the *Neptunia*, passenger liners taking Europeans to Australia recalled a particular trip on the *Oceania* with, as he put it, 'a ship full of proxy women coming to Australia to meet their husbands'. He relates the following anecdote:

> As we were approaching Melbourne and Sydney, we were getting telephone calls from the husbands wanting to talk to their proxy brides. And this poor girl, she came when we sent a notice down that her husband was calling her from Sydney. She came to the radio station and she went to the telephone in the cabin but she had never seen a telephone before and so she wouldn't speak. She was absolutely terrified. And then, of course, the husband was saying, 'Giuseppina! Parlami! Parlami! Dimmi qualcosa!' (*Giuseppina! Speak to me! Speak to me! Say something!*). And I sort of went into the cabin and I said to her, 'Just calm down, just try to talk to your husband'. And suddenly the man at the other end starting shouting out: 'Who's there? What are you doing with my wife?' I said, 'Look, I am just the radio officer. I am just trying to explain. She is terrified. Calm down'. But the man became angrier and angrier. And that was just one of the many stories we had on the ship.

Women's roles and the crossing of borderlines

The set of oral testimonies provides a special focus on the narratives of female informants, who formerly held marginal status within a cultural landscape characterised by long-standing models of patrilineal dominance. Most of the women who were interviewed grew up during the period of fascism, that is, of ideology shaped by hegemonic discourse, the lack of a free press and the relegation of women to domestic roles as exemplary housekeepers and breeders of military fodder for the Empire, the latter encouraged formally by the regime by means of fiscal incentives. For a number of the women informants, the three-pronged experience of departure, sea voyage and physical relocation provided a fertile (in the case of some who assumed quasi-masculine roles as chief providers for their families, a vigorous) cultural context for the delineating of new borderlines of female identity and work practices, earlier threads of which have been traced at the turn of last century in village-based practices in Italy where the men had emigrated (Bianchi 2009 [2001]: 257–274).

In recollections of the sea voyage, representing a physical detachment and fracturing from the encoded behaviours and strictures of the past, metaphors of self-transformation suggest that the journey served as a catalyst for the exploration of less conventional gender roles and the assumption of greater responsibility and moral agency on arrival. The spatial re-contextualising allowed for a realignment of cultural codes that might have appeared to be predetermined and fixed. However, the ramifications of transnational migration were played out fast and furiously and in unexpected ways in the place of settlement. Where the women may initially have felt constrained to migrate for family reasons and pressures, after settlement they quickly adopted unexpected social roles, sometimes participating in joint enterprises or enacting a dynamic of economic engagement beyond domestic walls, just as the menfolk were doing. They found themselves bartering and selling goods and services, or negotiating mortgages and contracts. They experienced a new mobility by driving motor vehicles and catching taxis to work-places in an Anglo-British urban environment in which they were forging relationships within the mainstream culture through daily discourses of survival. They seized opportunities to adapt their skills and ingenuity to new social domains and a radically different labour market.

This determination by the women informants to succeed and overcome obstacles worked in tandem with a recognition of the unsustainability of the traditional gender-based practice of silence and obedience, and the rigid maintenance of engrained cultural values and narrow endogamous practices in the face of a foreign, multicultural, social mix such as the one they encountered in Adelaide. On the whole, the Campanian female informants expected to recreate the social practices and fulfil the patrilineal expectations of their town or village identity in the place of settlement. Unexpectedly, for a number of them, upon arrival, the dichotomies determining social roles and filial relations were sometimes in flux. Like the male informants, in Adelaide they found themselves in situations that facilitated connection with the Anglo-British world, the outside world of foreign interactions. Therefore, women had to contest spaces, express autonomous agency, revitalise power relations formerly tied to gender, articulate a widening of their range of social roles and responsibilities and renegotiate the terms of conduct removed from the strictures of the cultural territory of origin. In their community of origin, travel was traditionally a male preserve. Moreover, women's status was determined by male members of the family and they were required to express their loyalty to the collectivity. In Adelaide, the female informants acquired a moral agency that they would have been denied back home. In Australia, the patrilineal codes had been irrevocably altered. Thus they tell and retell their stories in order to extract meaning from their life journey, constantly renegotiating their place in the social order of the dislocated community, where the old strictures of a millennial culture lack the same degree of authority.

Foodways, family ritual, the conservation of linguistic structures and adherence to moral codes, all constituted the underpinnings of identity. Bringing with them social capital, a willingness to work, hope for the future and a capacity to adapt to unfamiliar situations, the female informants altered their cultural purview. The traditional ways were shaped by the impact of the new cultural landscape, itself endowed with constructs and typologies. From *contadine* or provincial dressmakers and housewives they moved to new constructions of identity as bread-winners. In their roles as micro-managers, they became mediators who were resistant to factors that undermined or challenged the successful integration of the next generation, their own Australian-born offspring.

Conclusion

Oral narrative has preserved a varied social discourse and created a history that gives legitimacy to 'the significance of the *subject* in historical enquiry' (Young 2006: 5). Through the migration experience, as journeyers and mediators between two diverse worlds, many of the Campanian informants sought out opportunities to redefine the parameters of their social reality and embrace change. In

Boncompagni's terms, the migration process can function as 'a powerful engine for cultural change' [*un potente motore di cambiamento culturale*] (Boncompagni 2009 [2002]: 118). The Campanian narratives of the long sea voyage constitute the connecting narrative between two social constructs. They represent both a bridge of interconnection and a leap of faith into the unknown future. In this context, transnational migration can be seen as a transforming element that re-aligns relationships of power, destabilising the status quo and providing flexibility of opportunity for self-determination. Each retelling of the story gives rise to a reassessment and revalorisation of the experience of migration in the present temporality.

What emerges strongly from the set of oral narratives is the typology of inner transformation; of becoming; an openness of stance and the adoption of modalities of change and self-determination. One notes a new consciousness through which the protagonists initiate a more open dialogue that incorporates an outward gaze and a non-passivity, thus allow a dynamic entering into the new and unfamiliar multicultural and multilingual landscape. In tracing features of the sea voyage, one recognises in the informants' narratives elements of the archetypal horizontal voyage: a departure through necessity, for some a journey with overtones of despair and loss. For most, however, the journey to Australia ultimately proved to be a voyage of self-discovery and self-realisation within a spatial recontextualisation, the essence of which is renewed in every retelling of the story across generations.

Notes

1 Quotations taken from Dante Alighieri. *La Commedia secondo l'antica vulgata*, ed. G. Petrocchi, 4 vols, Milan: Mondadori, 1966–67 and Dante Alighieri. *The Divine Comedy*, translated by Charles Singleton, Bollingen Series LXXX, U.S.A.: Princeton University Press, 1980.

2 The tale of Ulysses has served as an inspiration for countless readers, not least of which was Primo Levi in Auschwitz in 1945 who, as he recalls in *If This is a Man,* recited parts of Dante's *Ulysses* canto by heart to an inmate, compelled as he was to salvage the remnants of his humanity from the brutality of the concentration camp, or as Margaret Baker has observed, 'to resist succumbing to dehumanising oppression' (Baker 2000: 44)

References

Alighieri, D. (1966–67). *La Commedia secondo l'antica vulgata*, G. Petrocchi (ed.), 4 vols. Milan: Mondadori.

Alighieri, D. (1980). *The Divine Comedy*, C. Singleton (trans.), Bollingen Series LXXX. U.S.A.: Princeton University Press.

Baker, M. (2000). Reflections Cast on *Inferno* XXXI-XXXIV by Primo Levi's Account of Auschwitz. In M. Baker & D. Glenn (eds), *Dante Colloquia in Australia 1982–1999*. Adelaide, SA: Australian Humanities Press, 43–52.

Bianchi, B. (2009 [2001]). IV. Lavoro ed emigrazione femminile (1880–1915). In P. Bevilacqua, A. De Clementi & E. Franzina (eds), *Storia dell'emigrazione italiana, Vol. I. Partenze*. Rome: Donzelli Editore, 257–274.

Boncompagni, A. (2009 [2002]). IV. In Australia. In P. Bevilacqua, A. De Clementi & E. Franzina (eds), *Storia dell'emigrazione italiana, Vol. II. Arrivi*. Rome: Donzelli Editore, 111–119.

De Clementi, A. (2007). Caratteri storico-antropologici dell'emigrazione italiana. In O. De Rosa & D. Verrastro (eds), *Appunti di viaggio. L'emigrazione italiana tra attualità e memoria*. Bologna: Società Editrice Il Mulino, 27–34.

Fuschetto, A. (1984). *S. Marco dei Cavoti dall'antica S. Severo Beneventana alla scomparsa del feudo*. Benevento: Edizioni Centro Culturale Sannita.

Gaita, R. (1998). *Romulus, My Father*. Melbourne: Text Publishing.

Gasparini, G. (ed.) (2000). *Il viaggio*. Roma: Edizioni Lavoro.

Gatt-Rutter, J. (2006). Bello the Bilingual Cockatoo: Writing Italian Lives in Australia. *Annali d'Italianistica. Negotiating Italian Identities* 24: 107–131.

Holy Bible. Revised Standard Version (Catholic Biblical Association of Great Britain, 1966). London: Nelson.

O'Connor, D. (2004). The post-war settlement of Italians in South Australia. In D. O'Connor (ed.), *Memories & Identities. Proceedings of the Second Conference on the Impact of Italians in South Australia*. Adelaide: Australian Humanities Press, 57–78.

Portelli, A. (1997). *The Battle of Valle Giulia: Oral History and the Art of Dialogue*. London & Wisconsin: The University of Wisconsin Press.

Roppen, G. & Sommer, R. (1964). *Strangers and Pilgrims: An Essay on the Metaphor of* Journey. Oslo: Norwegian Universities Press.

Young, A. (2006). Oral history as emergent paradigm. Oral History and its Challenge(r)s, *Oral History Association of Australia Journal* 28: 1–6.

Journeying South: the contribution of contemporary Australian literature for migration research

Keith Jacobs

UNIVERSITY OF TASMANIA

Introduction

This chapter explores the experiences of migration through the prism of contemporary Australian literature. Though literary texts have been viewed as unreliable sources of evidence,[1] I argue that a more active investigation of the literary form is important because of the ways it can encapsulate the complex feelings that arise in the course of migration. Migrant experience has long appealed to artists and writers seeking to get to the heart of the human condition. Authors such as Franz Kafka, John Steinbeck and Henry Handel Richardson have crafted powerful and influential fictional narratives from the raw material of migration. In their respective texts, these authors demonstrate a nuanced understanding of the ways migration can change lives, shape personalities and transform the structure of families, communities and even whole societies.

Migration is so often a momentous process. For the most part, it has a dramatic impact on those who choose it or have it thrust upon them. Ward and Styles provide the following formulation in their study of contemporary experiences of migration:

> The impact of leaving the homeland and the subsequent process of migration [can] prove to be daunting … a person may experience … [the] loss of family, friendships (social and work), language, cultural heritage, and familiar environment, and these losses could impact negatively on the identity of the person. (2003: 350)

Ward and Styles argue that the place and idea of home are constructs around which humans build their lives. They suggest that most human beings are attached in some way to their place of address. Because we still gravitate toward hard matter and enduring, decipherable cultural frameworks, moving away from home can be traumatic.

Place and space, home and hearth, however, do not provide succour to all people in all places at all times. As Williams and McIntyre point out, 'studies of such topics as community, home, migration and tourism remain infused with outdated assumptions of a geographically rooted subject' (2001: 392). Williams and McIntyre contend that we are not as firmly entrenched in our homes as we might like to think.

As an alternative, scholars have posed a countervailing question: should we not accept that we are actually becoming nomadic, de-territorialised, cosmopolitan subjects at home nowhere and everywhere? Blunt, for instance, has argued that this emerging empirical truth has informed variegated and dispersed attempts to prioritise flux over stasis in the construction of epistemologies. These attempts, when gathered together, might be said to constitute a 'mobilities turn' in the social sciences (Blunt 2007: 684). Mac Éinrí works within this tradition:

> The old assumption was that place, culture and identity were fixed and interrelated in a definable, consistent way ... In the world in which we find ourselves today, there is an increasing stress on interconnectivity, accompanied by an emphasis on the permeability of borders, whether of the self or of the community in which one lives. (1994: 91)

Though the 'mobilities turn' offers a new lens through which to understand nascent and possibly definitive complexities integral to the contemporary era, I still want to maintain that location, home, place, belonging and ontological security nest within one another. This, however, is not the case for everyone at every time; many people are not able to live where they feel they belong, or, vice versa, to belong where they feel they must live.

Migration forges new subjectivities, augments existing identities, changes world-views, builds tension and precipitates release. It can be a transformative, euphoric, ecstatic, cathartic, or traumatic process. It can reorder regimes of apprehension. As Chamberlain and Leydesdorff write: 'For the migrant, perspective and distance, tension and adjustment, jostle in the imaginary, abstract actors in the drama of belonging, identity and nationhood' (2004: 227). It is little wonder then, that artists of all types have drawn so heavily on internal, transnational and diasporic mobility as the impetus for their work.

My intention in this chapter is to argue that a close reading of literary fiction can enhance our understanding of the varieties and often unidentified aspects of migratory experiences. To develop my claim, I begin with a short discussion of some of the conceptual challenges that confront those commencing a critical reading of literary texts, and then proceed to discuss specific examples from the genre of migrant Australian literature as a basis to support my argument. The chapter concludes with a discussion of how we can engage in more productive encounters with literary sources.

At first glance, a claim that literary texts provide a useful empirical source might appear foolhardy, since literary fiction and autobiography have often been seen as unreliable.[2] Literary works are generally authored by a single person, which implies a single interpretation, whereas social scientists are committed to collecting a large body of evidence and using multiple sources before making generalisations. We are usually reluctant to extrapolate too much meaning from singular interpretations, in any genre, for fear that any subsequent analysis will be too narrow or myopic. Of course, this apprehension is understandable, as it would be poor scholarship to base far-reaching claims on dubious or limited evidence. It is important to note, too, that a substantial proportion of social policy migration research seeks to explore migration issues within the frame of administrative jurisdictions. Researchers engaging with social policy are, in the main, interested in interpreting the economic and social implications of large-scale migration rather than the stories of individual migrants.

The perceived unreliability of fiction helps to explain why scholars are so reluctant to engage with literary sources except tangentially, that is, as adjuncts to more systematic modes of investigation. However, for those willing to probe, literary texts can provide rich sources of material that are representative of very complex human behaviours and histories. A useful starting point, therefore, is the work of White (1995) who claims that migration literature foregrounds the complex worlds that we all inhabit. White contends that accounts that are deliberately fictitious can provide important insights about the way in which self-identity is enacted and the context which shapes identity formation:

> Creative or imaginative literature has a power to reflect complex and ambiguous realities that make it a far more plausible representation of human feelings and understandings than many of the artefacts used by academic researchers. (1995: 15)

White's conception of self-identity is multiple rather than singular – he views the self as contingent and shaped by new experiences rather than as fixed or essentialised. Migrant literature is of special interest because it makes explicit the way in which our sense of self can be destabilised by dramatic change such as moving from one country to another. Literature in this genre provides an excellent vantage point to reveal the fragmentation of the self and the effusion of feeling that can be stirred up by migration. Some of these feelings, argues White, include ambivalence, alienation, excitement and joy. In other words, the experience of migration acts as a catalyst and conduit for nascent feelings, a re-conception of our sense of self and our relationships with others.

Although the label 'migrant literature' might be deemed problematic in so far as many of the texts extend beyond issues related to migration, White's work does provide a way to categorise the different contexts in which migrant literature is produced. He points out that a large amount of migrant literature is autobiographical and often written for the purposes of catharsis (White 1995: 9). Artistic considerations also play a part; for instance, migrant writing can be a way to capture the experience of dramatic change. White also notes that some authors write for a political objective, that is to acquire cultural legitimacy and to use their work as a platform to highlight issues such as poverty and discrimination. Some of the thematic categories that White identifies in contemporary migration literature are: 'acts of flight', that explore the outward-bound journey; 'ambivalence and adjustment', involving the period after moving, during which the new migrant encounters different experiences; and 'notions of return', where the literature engages with feelings aroused by a visit to the former home (White 1995: 2–15).

The third reason that White's chapter has value is provided in the discussion on the ways that literary and sociological interpretations differ. Those studying literature seek understanding mainly through the text, while the social scientist seeks to explore wider social contexts and power relationships. Hence social scientists, if they cite literature, seek to anchor those texts within a broader cultural milieu. White is correct in arguing that there is a difference in emphasis placed on texts by social scientists and literary critics, rather than major differences *per se.*

White's suggestion that we can treat literature as a source of evidence is compelling, but there is a need to elaborate more specifically on the connection between literature and its place in the social realm, as this connection is more complex than first appears. Literature does not just reflect; it is also a constitutive force that influences society. In this sense, literature actively produces new ways of seeing and shapes the way we forge our social relationships. As Marcel Proust writes in *A la recherche du temps perdu*:

> Actually when he reads, every reader is only a reader of himself. The work of the author is simply a kind of optical instrument, that the author offers the reader so that he might appreciate what he would perhaps not have been able to see himself. (1913–1922 [1996]: 329)

Fiction and autobiography: a blurring of the boundaries

If we accept White's arguments about the significance of the migrant experience, then a key conceptual task is to consider the different approaches that can be taken to migrant literature. In his discussion, Carter makes a distinction between pre-structuralist and post-structuralist readings of migrant literature. Pre-structuralist interpretations consider migrant autobiography as analogous to oral testimony; it is generally regarded as an 'unproblematic addition to or assimilation of the migrant into the majority culture' (1997: 3). In contrast, a post-structuralist reading contends that 'migrant literature is (potentially) a site of the transgressive, or resistance to or subversion of a dominant culture' (Carter 1997: 3).

Carter's observation is useful, but it fails to problematise the conventional distinction between fiction and autobiography. A rigid distinction of this kind is difficult to maintain in the light of recent scholarship. As Döring has commented, the relation between the two 'has never been an easy one' (2006: 71). There is a wide range of views, from those who see autobiographical writing as unproblematic in that it provides a representation of the author's life, to post-structuralist theorists who construe autobiography less in terms of reference or description of the past and more in relation to active self-formation. As

Döring writes: 'through telling his or her own life, the autobiographer therefore turns into the author of his or her own self' (2006: 71). The unstable aspects of autobiographical writing were the focus of de Man's essay 'Autobiography as De-Facement'. De Man resisted the idea that fiction and autobiography can be analytically distinguished in the way that many critics presume. For de Man, autobiography cannot be seen as descriptive, since it actively produces new ways of presenting the self. In this sense, autobiography problematises the distinction between factual events and fiction:

> We assume that life *produces* the autobiography as an act produces its consequences, but can we not suggest, with equal justice, that the autobiographical project may itself produce and determine the life and that whatever the writer *does* is in fact governed by the technical demands of self-portraiture and thus determined in all its aspects, by the resources of his medium? (de Man 1979: 920)

The observations of Döring and de Man are important as they question the usual distinctions that are made to demarcate migrant autobiography from migrant literary fiction. In fiction, there is no necessary commitment to provide a literal interpretation, and instead, writers use their imagination to portray events that may or may not have a basis in reality. While fiction does not require any self-imposed restraint by the author for accuracy, its artistic merit is, in part, contingent on the degree to which the work is able to provide insights into the human condition and the ways in which we understand the world. In this sense, fiction, including science fiction and fantasy, is always drawing from reality even if, by definition, it remains fictitious.

In autobiographical works, there is at least some commitment to representation, as authors reflect on their own experiences. There is an attempt to *represent* important issues of the past, so there is a connection between the act of writing and the events that have taken place. Yet the degree to which autobiographical writing can be viewed as accurate is unclear, for while it entails recollection of the past, it is reliant on memory and necessarily selective, in that the author has to decide what to leave in and what to leave out.

In general terms, a post-structuralist interpretation of migrant writing challenges common sense convictions about the stability of the self and the enduring aspects of our personality. From this vantage point, migration can accentuate the sense of instability surrounding self-identity:

> Stories and images of the self, on what ground do they rest when the 'I' has been dislocated from home? Who is represented under the sign of 'I' when the boundaries of the self seem unstable and the history of identity seem so uncertain? (Papastergiadis 1998: 71)

Up to this point, the chapter has probed the range of different forms of migrant writing and explored the ways it can be conceptualised. In what follows, the focus of the discussion moves to an exploration of the diversity of approaches that contemporary authors have taken to the task of writing migrant experience in Australia. The selected examples embrace different perspectives on post-war Australian migration including British, continental European and Asian vantage points.[3] The texts are used as sources to explore the disruption that can follow migration, and the attempt by individual characters to negotiate the changes they encounter. Specific themes relating to migration sensibility are used to draw out their wider significance both as a response to the particularities of the Australian physical and cultural landscape and also in terms of individual migrant experiences. These themes include: 'the moment of arrival'; 'belonging and exile'; 'the quandary of return'; 'cultural ambivalence'; and 'the meaning of home'.

The moment of arrival

An interesting component of Australian migration literature is those texts that recount the experiences of children. For most children, migration is not a choice of their own making and this has meant they can often have a quite different take on its significance. The emotional issues that arise in the course of migration are the focus of Mary Rose Liverani's *The Winter Sparrows*. Liverani's novel is based on her life as a child growing up in a working-class area of Glasgow and her move to Wollongong when she was thirteen. In *The Winter Sparrows*, the author describes how her close family relationships were altered dramatically following her move. After living in a migrant hostel, Liverani moved to a suburban housing estate where she dealt with her sense of social isolation by expending her energy on the study of literature and schoolwork. Liverani describes the excitement that she and her siblings felt when they discovered that they were moving to Australia:

> We somersaulted all over the beds and threw the pillows up in the air. We're off to see the beaches of Aus. Then we ran out of the house half dressed and knocked on all the doors and windows like Wee Willie Winkie. (1984: 189)

The intense emotional responses are explored further when, after arriving by boat, Liverani describes her reaction. She notes a sense in which her anticipation of what Australia would mean exceeded her initial experience of the new world: 'I am waiting for Australia to enchant me. To distract me from the past. To become the hypnotic present' (1984: 195). In the passage below, Liverani recalls her attitude to her Australian school, and her sense of isolation:

> Loneliness made me hate school … There was no one left for me to talk with easily; nothing to stop me from spending recesses in the school library, reading or doing my homework. But I shivered in my isolation, sick to belong to any group, no matter what, to be included in the laughter. (1984: 315)

There is little room for sentimentality in Liverani's account and she does not dwell on describing her feelings in any elaborate way. Instead, she reports on daily encounters, and uses the Glaswegian dialect to portray her upbringing in Scotland and Australia. Many of the early sections of the book describe her friendships and encounters with teachers at school in Scotland. The Australian scenes depict life in the hostel and her family's new home in Wollongong.

The drama of childhood migration is also taken up in an autobiography by Paul Kraus, *A New Australia, A New Australian*, in which the author describes his move from Hungary to Australia in 1949 as a five-year-old. Kraus contrasts his own experiences with those of his parents whom he felt were traumatised by the experience of leaving Europe. Kraus writes:

> The reality of having reached Australia had not dawned. They were bewildered at being half a world away from their birthplace, from being away from the Europe they had never previously left. They were in a trance. Australia represented deliverance from the hates and torments of the past – yet there were no images upon which to place their dreams. (1994: 17)

This focus on the emptiness of arrival recasts Liverani's observations. It is as if the anticipation of arrival has been so enormous that when it does finally happen, the emotions aroused are just too overwhelming to fathom. Kraus attributes his ambivalence about Australia to his family being Holocaust survivors and their embracing of Christianity. His loneliness prompted him to leave Australia in his early twenties to live in England for a short while to pursue his career as a teacher. Kraus's story is representative in that it follows a similar trajectory to many migrant life stories. He describes the ambivalence of living in a country that is not home, yet at the same time he feels a desire to assimilate. Kraus runs a political commentary alongside the autobiographical aspects of *A New Australia, A New Australian*. This impersonal social narrative focuses on the politics of Australian migration, in charting the major events such as street protests against Australia's involvement in the Vietnam War and the change in migration policy in the 1970s that precipitated larger numbers of non-Europeans to settle in Australia.

Liverani's and Kraus's responses to their arrival in Australia provide a basis for comparison with a more contemporary novel by Chandani Lokugé, *If the Moon Smiled*. Lokugé grew up in Sri Lanka and moved to Australia in the early 1990s. In the passage below, the author describes the feelings of the main character, Manthri, who moves to Australia with her husband and two children:

> One grey dawn in February, I gaze down from the clouds at the brown and green jigsaw puzzle of Australia. It seems complete without us. How will it fit us in? Would we be sawed into new shapes? I think of falling away to the surrounding emptiness: a being without centre or circumference, to disintegrate like ash in the air. (2000: 48)

In this passage, there is little sense of excitement at the prospect of moving. Lokugé's novel conveys the initial sense of separation that many migrants experience. In the following passage, Manthri is isolated and uncertain about how to interpret her new encounters:

> I have talked to no one today. I reflect on people I know. I go over conversations that I have absorbed on visits, an unguarded look on the face of an acquaintance. What was she really thinking? What was behind her smile? Perhaps it was just put on. I study other wives and mothers.

> Some of them are at least mistresses of their own homes, if nowhere else. (2000: 75)

The novels by Liverani and Lokugé, as well as Kraus's autobiography, capture some of the ways that migrants develop a very conscious sense of their own difference in relation to other people, as well as how a sense of self unfolds through contact with others, following the act of moving. Their narratives also bring to the fore how migration that is not clearly chosen, for example, where individuals such as children or spouses accompany their families, creates an additional sense of powerlessness.

Belonging and exile

Both *Café Scheherazade* by Arnold Zable and *The Sound of One Hand Clapping* by Richard Flanagan explore the possibility of connection and disappointment aroused by a sense of disconnection that can accompany forced migration or exile following a period of war. The central character in *Café Scheherazade* is a journalist who recounts the wartime experiences of three Jewish refugees from the Second World War. The characters congregate around the eponymously titled Melbourne café. Zable's book interweaves the narrator's own perspective with the stories of the three principal characters. For Zable, the geographical space that separates Melbourne from central Europe is used as a literary device to explore his characters' feelings. The narrator explains:

> This is a tale of many cities: each one consumed by the momentum of history. Each one recalled at a table in a cafe called Scheherazade, in a seaside suburb that sprawls upon the very ends of the earth, within a city that contains the traces of many cities. (2001: 7)

In this account, Melbourne is a far-off place but one that provides the possibility for making connections with the past. Zable's portrayal of migration is not one of disjuncture or rupture but of psychic continuity with previous selves, lived out in another country. Towards the end of the novel, the narrator describes Port Phillip as an emblematic place of arrival. In the passage below, the bay is re-imagined ontologically, as a site of sublime security:

> A place of refuge. An ample embrace. A seabird's graceful glide. These are the images that come to mind. This is how I like to imagine the moment of arrival. (2001: 215)

In the following excerpts, the impressions of the migrants are enunciated. Zable explores the contrasting emotions that are encountered as a way of illustrating the sensibilities of each of his four principal characters:

> It was just another city coming into view. I did not see myself as coming here to build a new life. I had no ambition. I just came. I wanted to drink, make merry and pass the time. I wanted only to live for the day. (2001: 216)

> The city was yet another arena of opportunity to revel in, to impress upon with his cunning and charm. A place for future fortunes made, fortunes lost, wealth squandered, wealth regained. (2001: 217)

> But for the most part he was captive to a mind filled with jousting images of the past; a mind leached by Siberian snows, bleached by Arctic winds. And a heart swamped by the feelings which had overwhelmed him when he returned to the streets of the city of his birth to find his house erased from the face of the earth. (2001: 216)

> A sense of isolation was her dominant feeling. The surrounding land seemed to reflect it: the empty beaches, the windswept dunes, the expanse of low-slung houses squatting by the coast. She felt adrift, disconnected from the vibrant cities of her past. She saw the new city as a wasteland. She had a baby to nurse. And she harboured regrets, resentment over ambitions thwarted. (2001: 217)

The feelings that surface towards the end of a migratory journey are used by Zable to reveal different aspects of the inner lives of his characters. Zable uses the city as a setting to enable his characters to reflect on their experiences.

Similar themes are captured in Richard Flanagan's *The Sound of One Hand Clapping*, but from the perspective of affective disconnection. Flanagan's novel depicts the harsh realities for Eastern European migrants working in hydro-electrical schemes in Tasmania in the 1950s. His story describes a daughter's (Sonja) encounter with her father following the suicide of her mother (Maria). The novel's chronology moves back and forth from the 1950s to the 1990s and depicts the anguished lives of the migrants, their isolation in living in such a remote part of Tasmania, and the harsh conditions they found there. There is nothing in Flanagan's novel that romanticises migrants' lives; his story is one of solitude, loneliness, and bitter family violence. It is as if the dark legacy of migration is destined to reverberate through and across generations. His characters are alienated from their environment because of the painful associations with the past and their sense of being marginal to the main culture:

> Well it's a funny thing, thought Jiri as he lay down in his bed, this life of mine. In Czechoslovakia he had drunk with the Gypsies. In Tasmania he drank with the Aborigines. He was never accepted by either, but then he, being half Sudeten German, half Czech, had never felt accepted anywhere. (1997: 114)

In another passage, Flanagan goes on to describe the views of those arriving in Australia as refugees in the 1950s. Again, there is a sense in which the expectations of their new country were limited to living in a society free from conflict:

> Australia was ordinary, and even if it wasn't, they didn't want to know about that. They simply wanted a world that might be ordered with the hope that the order might last long enough to build a home and raise a family and have them in turn bring their children back, and then die knowing one had as much as one could rightfully expect out of life without having to suffer cataclysmic wars, occupations, revolutions, destruction of homes, cities, nations, countries, languages, peoples. (1997: 116)

For this discussion, the significance of Zable's and Flanagan's novels is in their exploration of the linkages between the experiences of migration and turbulent events of the past. For Zable, there is a sense of optimism about the legacy of migration, while for Flanagan there is a sense in which his characters are so overwhelmed by the legacy of the Second World War that they are resigned to never being able to break out of the despondency they experienced as refugees. The novels by Zable and Flanagan are also of interest because of the ways they foreground how economic and social dislocation can reverberate within the lives of individual migrants. The political context becomes subsumed and subsequently reinterpreted by their characters.

The quandary of return

Contemporary migration in an increasingly interconnected world has meant that the choice of returning or staying is more tangible than in previous periods. The dilemmas of migration are made explicit in Graham Kershaw's novel *The Home Crowd*. In a different way from the other texts discussed, Kershaw is able to explore the emotional responses generated by the act of returning. His novel is narrated by a character called George, who describes his journey back to the outskirts of Manchester, following the death of his father. It transpires that George's move to Australia was hasty and he had left a pregnant girlfriend (Kate). The novel centres on George's desire to return to England to reconnect with his former life and makes explicit the quandary experienced by George. He has a life in Australia but still feels a desire to relive his earlier experiences prior to migrating:

> In Fremantle it would be different, I knew: the humid aftermath of summer would be blowing away. Fresh afternoon breezes and maybe showers at last, giving the lawns some respite. 'Three days,' I kept saying to myself, 'I'll be there in three days.' But no matter how sweet the thought of sunrise there, and no matter how cold my aching feet, the thought brought no joy, only the creeping sense of time overtaking me, panicking me, pushing me to … what? What was I rushing back to? (2002: 112)

Kershaw's novel can be read as a meditation on the ties and bonds arising from intense relationships that can be so difficult to break. In the novel, it is the emotional entanglement with his former partner in England and his son Tom that proves, in the end, more compelling than his life in Australia with his fiancée.

Conclusion: home – the centre of the world

Finally, I want to suggest that it is possible to view migrant writing as a whole, whether fictional or autobiographical, as a response to and contemplation of the meaning of 'home'. For in the context of migration, the home is the place one moves away from, but its symbolic significance remains in that it provides a backdrop against which new experiences can be compared. As Papastergiadis has written:

> Our outward adventures are measured in relation to home. Dreams of journeys begin from home and the rest of the world extends outwardly from this radix. Mapping elsewhere is also a homing device. Our inward returns are read as confirmations of an incontrovertible dynamism. The meaning of the home has both a centrifugal and centripetal force, it combines both our inner and outer trajectories. Home is the centre of the world. (1998: 2)

Home provides a symbolic space for all the writers engaging in literature to articulate the emotional responses of their subjects, or in the case of autobiography, to express how different aspects of identity are transformed by migration. To progress this line of argument, it is helpful to consider Paul Carter's book *On Living in a New Country*. Carter explores his own experience as a migrant to Australia in middle age. In his introduction, he cites the work of the British painter, Adrian Stokes, whose departure from London to Italy enabled him to begin a new life:

> The novelty of Italy was proportional to the freedom it offered him from his old self. Impressed by the outwardness of Italian life, a quality as much aesthetic as temperamental, Stokes found the strength to turn his own psychic life inside out. The new country did not erase the old one – 'Rapallo could not oust Hyde Park' – but it did supply a position from which to speak, to begin again the laying down of habits. (1992: 1)

Carter's argument is that new countries are in a sense 'autobiographical fictions'; from a psychic perspective, the migrant does not arrive, just once, but 'continues to arrive, each new situation demanding a new set of responses, almost a new identity' (1992: 3). Migration is therefore something akin to universal experience in that all of us construct notions of a journey in some form or other:

> We are almost all migrants; and even if we have tried to stay at home, the conditions of life have changed so utterly in this century that we find ourselves strangers in our own house. (Carter, 1992: 7)

Thus, the sense of dislocation that all migrants feel at some point is something we all have to negotiate in differing degrees as we adapt to the changes that confront us in our everyday lives. Carter's argument provides a basis to categorise migration literature by making this connection between individual experience and the shared aspects of our existence.

All of the novels discussed in this chapter encapsulate the migrant's sense of dislocation and strangeness. The works by Liverani, Kraus and Lokugé foreground the way in which significant life-changing events impact on a sense of self. Themes of exile and belonging are evident in the work of Zable and Flanagan, both of whom highlight the psychic turmoil that remains long after the actual act of migration. The quandaries surrounding the return visit are fruitfully tackled in Kershaw's novel. He engages with the predicament that many migrants experience in relation to the feelings towards their former home and, for this reason, his work provides an insight into the lived experience of transnationalism and different modes of 'belonging'.

The opportunities afforded by fiction are considerable in that they provide a wider contextual and discursive space in which to consider the complexity of experience, the unstable boundaries of the self and shifting histories of identity. I have used recent Australian novels to contend that literary fiction provides a basis to interpret and explore certain aspects of the migrant condition. In making this claim, I am not suggesting that the study of literature provides an alternative to detailed empirical analysis; rather it offers the possibility to establish both a new vantage point and a different mode of evidence for considering the nature of identity and its generative effects.[4]

In terms of an academic enquiry, there is a shared commitment within the fields of sociology and literature to explore the ways in which individual identity is enunciated within cultural practice. While the distinction between migrant fiction and non-fiction autobiographical writing is an important one, the boundaries that delineate these forms of writing are often blurred when it comes to representing notions of self-identity. For this reason, literature provides a valuable resource for academic scholarship because of the prism it provides for highlighting the contingent aspects of self-identity and the sensibilities aroused through migration.

Acknowledgements

I would like to thank Jesse Shipway for his helpful advice on an earlier draft of this chapter. I also want to acknowledge the Imagining Home Editorial Committee for their permission to allow this chapter to be reproduced in a monograph titled 'Representation and Experience: Contemporary Perspectives on Australian Migration' (Ashgate Press 2011).

Notes

1 In 'Placing the Migrant', Silvey and Lawson (1999: 121) argue that there has been a tendency to sort geographical work on migration into two groups, an early group that was predominantly quantitative and a current group that is qualitative and ethnographic.

2 Though I will be discussing in more precise terms what literary texts on migration entail, at this point in the chapter some elaboration on the difference between literary and academic texts is required. For the purposes of this discussion, literary texts are viewed as works that are artistic in intention; by contrast, academic texts are generally aimed at enhancing our knowledge of the world either through empirical investigation or by enhancing the concepts and precepts that are used for investigation. A large part of academic writing on migration also engages in social policy prescription.

3 The selection of literary texts is limited to fiction published over the last 25 years. Examples of migrant poetry and drama are not included because of limited space.

4 An example of how fiction can provide an access point for social and cultural investigation may be found in the writings of Edward Said (1993). His study of Jane Austen's novels provided a basis to mount a subtle reading of eighteenth-century British imperialism.

References

Blunt, A. (2007). Cultural geographies of migration: mobility, transnationality and diaspora. *Progress in Human Geography* 31,5: 684–694.

Carter, D. (1997). *A Career in Writing: Judah Waten and the Cultural Politics of a Literary Career.* Toowoomba: Association for the Study of Australian Literature.

Carter, P. (1992). *On Living in a New Country.* London: Faber.

Castles, S. & Davidson, A. (2000). *Citizenship and Migration: Globalization and the Politics of Belonging.* Basingstoke: Palgrave.

Chamberlain, M. & Leydesdorff, S. (2004). Transnational families: Memories and narratives. *Global Networks* 4,3: 227–241.

de Man, P. (1979). Autobiography as De-Facement. *Modern Language Notes* 94,5: 919–930.

Döring, T. (2006). Edward Said and the fiction of autobiography. *Wasafiri* 21,2: 71–78.

Flanagan, R. (1997). *The Sound of One Hand Clapping.* Sydney: Macmillan.

Hall, S. (1994). Cultural identity and diaspora. In P. Williams & L. Chrisman (eds), *Colonial discourse and postcolonial theory: A reader*. New York: Columbia University Press, 392–402.

Kershaw, G. (2002). *The Home Crowd*. Fremantle: Fremantle Arts Centre Press.

Kraus, P. (1994). *A New Australia, A New Australian*. Leichhardt: The Federation Press.

Lawson, V. (2000). Arguments within geographies of movement: the theoretical potential of migrants' stories. *Progress in Human Geography* 24,3: 173–189.

Liverani, M. (1984). *The Winter Sparrows*. Melbourne: Thomas Nelson Press.

Lokugé, C. (2000). *If The Moon Smiled*. Ringwood Vic.: Penguin.

Mac Éinrí, P. (1994). How does it feel? Migrants and the postmodern condition. *Chimera* 87–94. http://migration.ucc.ie/Howdoesitfeel.htm [online, accessed 25 November 2009]

Papastergiadis. N. (1998). *Dialogues in the Diaspora*. London: Rivers Oram Press.

Papastergiadis, N. (2000). *The Turbulence of Migration*. Cambridge: Polity Press.

Proust, M. (1913–1922 [1996]). *A la recherche du temps perdu*. (translated by C. K. Scott Moncrieff, revised by D. J. Enright) London: Vintage.

Said, E. (1993). *Culture and Imperialism*. New York: Knopf.

Silvey, R. and Lawson, V. (1999). Placing the migrant. *Annals of the Association of American Geographers* 89,1: 121–132.

Ward, C. and Styles, I. (2003). Lost and found: reinvention of the self following migration, *Journal of Applied Psychoanalytical Studies* 5,3: 349–367.

Williams, D. & McIntyre, N. (2001). Where heart and home reside: changing constructions of place and identity. In K. Luft & S. MacDonald (eds), *Trends 2000: shaping the future: The 5th outdoor recreation & tourism trends symposium*. Department of Parks, Recreation and Tourism Resources: Michigan State University, 392–403. http://www.treesearch.fs.fed.us/pubs/23755 [online, accessed 1 August 2008]

White, P. (1995). Geography, literature and migration. In R. King, J. Connell & P. White (eds), *Writing Across Worlds*. London: Routledge, 1–19.

Whitlock, G. (2000). From biography to autobiography. In E. Webby (ed.), *The Cambridge Guide to Australian Literature*. Cambridge: Cambridge University Press, 232–257.

Zable, A. (2001). *Café Scheherazade*. Melbourne: Text Publishing.

Quack or talk: Varieties of storytelling and identity formation in Maxine Hong Kingston's *The Woman Warrior*

Venus Tsang
UNIVERSITY OF OXFORD

Introduction

This chapter explores how identities are created through different kinds of storytelling in the context of Maxine Hong Kingston's *The Woman Warrior* (1981). In the storytelling process, storytellers are at the same time communicating their world views and self-conception to their listeners. This concept of 'self-creation' is compatible with Stuart Hall's definition of identity as in a state of becoming, an identity which is constantly undergoing transformation due to the intervention of different histories and cultures (1996: 112). To illustrate the implications of storytelling on identity negotiation and formation, this chapter analyses storytelling as a conversational activity predicated on the interactions between storytellers and listeners. Four types of conversational storytelling will be discussed: solicited, response, collaborative and performative storytelling. The first of these, solicited storytelling, is the deliberate production of a story for particular listeners to effect specific purposes. Response storytelling is a reply or a reaction to previously told stories, while collaborative storytelling involves two or more storytellers co-narrating a story deliberately or spontaneously. Lastly, performative storytelling involves storytellers trying to engage their audience. Through an examination of the four varieties of storytelling, and informed by Hall's concept of cultural identity, I argue that storytelling functions as a significant means for the characters in *The Woman Warrior* to articulate and rearticulate their identities.

Storytelling and the reconstruction of identity

Storytelling is a means for us to negotiate and utter our shifting identities, to identify others and to respond to others' identification of us.

By telling a story about ourselves or others, we try to understand 'who we are, who others are, and how we are to be related' (Brockmeier and Carbaugh 2001: 10). The weaving of our world views and self-conception into stories is thus a way for us to reconstruct identities of ourselves and others. This idea about self-construction corresponds to Hall's theorisation of cultural identity. He argues that identity is never accomplished, but is 'a matter of "becoming"' (1996: 112). It is constantly being transformed according to how we position and reposition ourselves in relation to the discourses of history and memory, past and present and different cultures.

By adopting an interactional approach to the analysis of storytelling, I will consider storytelling as a conversational activity between storytellers and listeners. A conversational story is a story that 'arose in the course of natural everyday talk' (Norrick 2000: 27) and may involve two or more conversationalists in different contexts. The content of a conversational story ranges from personal anecdotes, others' life experience, legends, and myths, to imagination and fantasy, or a mixture of the above. Regarding storytelling as conversational allows a more inclusive review of the different types of story and storyteller.

Commenting on autobiographical writing, Bruner states that since not everything is worth telling, the teller of a narrative must justify its value by demonstrating 'a commitment to a certain set of presuppositions about oneself, one's relation to others, one's view of the world and one's place in it' (2001: 35). This is what Fludernik calls the '*tellability*' (1996: 63 [emphasis in the original]) requirement for a narrative, which is also applicable to conversational storytelling. By evaluating the content of the stories, the intent of the storytellers and the response of the listeners, I examine the interpersonal and communal functions of storytelling and their implications on identity formation, thus offering a micro-analysis of the varieties of storytelling recorded in *The Woman Warrior*.

The four types of storytelling outlined previously – solicited, response, collaborative and performative – though by no means clear-cut in their categorisation, will provide a framework for the study of storytelling that takes place in different contexts. The first type of storytelling is solicited storytelling. Solicited stories, which Norrick distinguishes from 'spontaneously told stories' (2000: 2), are usually more carefully structured with the selection of content and adoption of tone considered in advance. Addressed to particular listeners, these stories are usually deliberately produced to effect specific purposes, such as conveying a message or sanctioning an action.

The second type of storytelling is response storytelling, which serves to engage previously told stories in dialogue. They can be a reply or a reaction to the content or the morals of previously told stories and they can appear in the form of a brand new story or a revisionist version of previously told stories.

The third type of storytelling is collaborative storytelling. This refers to the co-narration of a story by two or more storytellers who both contribute content to the story. In some cases, the storytellers take turns to speak making it 'impossible to say just who is the teller or even the primary teller' (Norrick 2000: 168). In the process of collaborative storytelling, the co-tellers are engaged in a dialogical interplay, through which they may articulate shared or diverging values and world views. There can also be cases where the co-tellers do not deliberately cooperate to tell a story *per se*, but through their conversation, a story emerges.

The fourth type of storytelling is performative storytelling. This usually involves one or a few primary storytellers and a relatively large audience. The audience mainly participates in the storytelling performance by listening or giving verbal responses (e.g. asking and answering questions) or nonverbal responses (e.g. laughing and applauding). In order to justify their right to maintain a long turn and to gain their audience's attention, performative storytellers must carefully select and sequence the content of the stories. These four types of storytelling will be elaborated below with reference to *The Woman Warrior*. To distinguish Maxine the protagonist from Maxine the narrator, I will refer to the former as 'Maxine' and the latter as 'the narrator'.

Solicited storytelling

The story of the no-name aunt in 'No Name Woman' is an example of a solicited story told by Brave Orchid to Maxine. This is a story about Maxine's pregnant aunt who has an illegitimate child. On the night when she is about to give birth to her baby, the villagers raid her home. She ends up drowning herself and her baby in the family well. This story, told after Maxine has reached puberty, is carefully structured and is bracketed with imperatives. It begins with an order to silence about the family's past: 'You must not tell anyone … what I am about to tell you' (11). The ending also comes in the form of an admonishment about the consequences of adultery, dishonour and the loss of identity:

> Now that you have started to menstruate, what happened to her could happen to you. Don't humiliate us. You wouldn't like to be forgotten as if you had never been born. (*The Woman Warrior*: 13)

For the pragmatic Brave Orchid, this story is solicited to explain to her daughter, Maxine, such traditional Chinese values as loyalty to one's husband and family. By issuing a warning against sexual subversiveness, the mother erects a patriarchal wall to restrict the daughter's development of her female identity. This story is told as a secret between the mother and the daughter, as Brave Orchid says: 'Don't let your father know that I told you. He denies her.' (13). Upon the revelation of this family secret, Maxine gains access to the place her parents call home, a place dominated by misogynist values. She is obliged to share the communal values that suppress female sexuality, as she is told to join the family's effort to erase the existence of the aunt by remaining silent about her violent death.

Brave Orchid's solicited storytelling only reveals part of the no-name aunt's life story in which she is identified as a silent victim who sacrifices herself for her baby's father (whose identity she has never disclosed). Many details about the aunt's life are omitted. The story told by Brave Orchid creates an 'invisible world' (13) of China for the Chinese American Maxine who has to establish realities from stories about her parents' home in China and fit them into 'solid America' (13). Maxine's imaginary China is comparable to Rushdie's (1991) 'imaginary homelands' (10) and, to paraphrase his phrase 'Indias of the mind' (10), it is a case of 'Chinas of the mind'. Maxine has difficulty imagining her parents' home country in China, as the China depicted is only one of the hundreds of thousands of possible representations. It is, to use Rushdie's metaphor, an image reflected by 'broken mirrors' (1991: 11), an image composed of the fragments of memory, which may undergo different kinds of transformation and engender symbolic meanings. Thus the broken mirror does not reflect a nostalgic past, but calls for a construction of the present. In Maxine's case, China is composed of the remnants of her memory based on those of her mother's. The representation of China is therefore rendered even more partial but it is precisely this partial perception that gives space for the proliferation of fracturing perspectives and the engendering of response stories.

Response storytelling

In response to Brave Orchid's solicited story, the narrator retells the no-name aunt's ordeal by filling the gaps in her mother's story. The narrator's response story about the no-name aunt is characterised by open-endedness and filled with uncertainties (e.g. 'perhaps', 'could have been', 'may have been' and 'probably'). The narrator's use of a tentative tone in her response story is very different from Brave Orchid's use of imperatives (e.g. 'must not') in her solicited story. In the narrator's version, a number of possibilities about the baby's father is provided. He could be someone whom she has met in the fields or mountains, someone she has dealings with in the marketplace, someone who works in an adjoining field or someone in her own household.

The narrator imagines a number of possibilities about the aunt's role in her relationship with the man: a victim of rape, a romantic who is in love or a wild woman who is free with sex. The aunt is even given direct speech: 'I think I'm pregnant' (14), which is absent in her mother's version. By recreating the story of the no-name aunt, the narrator tries to reconstruct the aunt's life story and restore for her a voice. This displaces the moral function of Brave Orchid's monolithic story about an adulteress. The narrator's version no longer serves as a warning against female sexuality, but opens up possibilities for the recreation of the aunt's female self.

The retelling of the no-name aunt's story is a means for the narrator to engage in dialogue with her mother. Through response storytelling, the narrator voices her refusal to inherit the sexist Chinese values and her unwillingness to develop her self within the patriarchal boundary. As Cheung (1993) argues, through imagination, the narrator is able to 'test her own power to talk story and to play with different identities' (85). By touching on this taboo subject of the family, the narrator breaks silence, breaches the family teachings and deviates from the traditional understanding of filiality. She displaces the communal values her parents have transported from their home in China to America. In this way, the narrator asserts herself as a nonconformist.

The narrator's response story is mainly imaginary, but intermingled with it are stories featuring the experience of herself, her mother and other women in the community. For example, in fantasising how the aunt would comb 'individuality into her bob' (16) in front of the mirror, the narrator recalls Brave Orchid's story about her long braided hair, which has to be bound up in tight buns after marriage to efface her feminine charm. In describing how the aunt would attend to her looks by removing the little hairs on her forehead, the narrator threads into the storyline her childhood experience about her hair being painfully ripped along the hairline and the communal story about women's foot-binding. In guessing the identity of the man to whom the aunt is attracted, the narrator recalls her frustration about having 'no dates' (18) at school and her confusion about such notions as Chinese-feminine and American-pretty.

By inserting the different stories about feminine beauty into the no-name aunt's story, the narrator draws an affinity among women from the past to the present and from her parents' home in mainland China to her home in America. In her revisionist story, the juxtaposition of those episodes enables her to complain about the confining nature of the Chinese and American cultural values that dictate the definition of femininity. It is through this response storytelling that she utters her difficulty in asserting her female identity as a Chinese American.

Another response story is the tale of Fa Mu Lan in 'White Tigers'. Glorifying a woman warrior's heroic deeds, this story is first told by Brave Orchid to Maxine. Along with this one are other stories that deny female agency. In response to her mother's contradictory teachings of women's potential, the narrator retells the woman warrior's story in order to create a powerful female predecessor for herself. Similar to the retelling of the no-name aunt's story, the narrator's version is revisionist in nature. The difference, however, lies in the opening of the two stories. In 'No Name Woman', the narrator gives space for her mother to tell the story in the first person and to spell out the lesson to be learned. The mother's story about the no-name aunt is then followed by the narrator's interpretations and revisions, making the mother's story the beginning of a chain of stories to be continued by herself, the listener. 'White Tigers' does not begin with the mother's words, but with the narrator's summary of the lesson learned from stories told by the adults:

> When we Chinese girls listened to the adults' talking-story, we learned that we failed if we grew up to be but wives or slaves. We could be heroines, swordswomen. (*The Woman Warrior*: 25)

This lesson is not spelt out by Brave Orchid, but is a result of the narrator's reflection. The narrator's belief that she can be a heroine is contrary to Brave Orchid's conclusion that her daughter 'would grow up a wife and slave' (26). Choosing not to believe in her mother's ominous prediction, but rather, the stories of female empowerment, the narrator retells the story of Fa Mu Lan in the first person. The narrator has the conviction that she will 'grow up a warrior woman' (26). By using 'I' rather than 'she' to designate Fa Mu Lan, the narrator 'goes further, appropriating not only the chant but also the very body of that legendary woman warrior' (Smith 1999: 64). This allows the narrator to project her identity onto Fa Mu Lan – a heroine whose name is passed down from generation to generation, unlike the no-name aunt who dies with her name buried.

In the narrator's response story, Fa Mu Lan grows from being a martial arts apprentice to a powerful general who leads her soldiers towards victory in the battlefield. While the traditional chant mentions nothing about the woman warrior's love life, in the narrator's version, Fa Mu Lan encounters her husband in her tent and gives birth to a son when she is fighting her way northward. These significantly revised details in the narrator's story serve to demonstrate the narrator's belief that a wife does not necessarily become a slave. A woman can be a wife, a mother and a heroine at the same time.

This belief, however, is contradicted by the ending of Fa Mu Lan's story in which she returns home, giving up her 'public duties' (47) and becoming domesticated. There have been divergent interpretations of the story's ending among critics. While some dismiss it as a conservative story that restores power to the patriarch, some argue that the story celebrates women's liberation. For example, Huntley suggests that Fa Mu Lan is 'a heroine who balances family and career, fulfilling both her domestic roles and her duty to her people and country' (2001: 99). This is a reasonable comment given what Fa Mu Lan has contributed to her country and her family. However, the story is still far from liberating, especially when the ending of the story is taken into account. As Lan suggests, the new nation that is born after the woman warrior's victory only 'repeats an age-old pattern of dynastic replacement and retains an equally old system of imperial dictatorship' (2003: 239). Upon returning home after the triumphant battle, Fa Mu Lan promises her parents-in-law, 'I will stay with you, doing farmwork and housework, and giving you more sons' (47). This confirms the sexist belief that a woman must choose between public and private duties. In addition, her name is remembered not because of her prowess, but as the result of her fulfilment of her parents' wish, for Fa Mu Lan declares in the end: 'From the words on my back, and how they were fulfilled, the villagers would make a legend about my perfect filiality' (47).

That the story of Fa Mu Lan ends by celebrating filiality, rather than female power, reminds us of the no-name aunt's story used by Brave Orchid to preach family values and filial piety. In spite of this, the narrator has done something different from her mother. She has adapted the Chinese legends and myths, and added feminist perspectives to her story. This can be interpreted as her attempt to juggle the often contradictory traditional Chinese and Western values and to reconcile the psychic discord in her selfhood. Commenting on the self-production of the protagonists in Chinese American works, Cutter argues that they

> must learn to interact with, and finally recreate, the 'source text,' the parents' linguistic and cultural heritage, and they must also learn to recreate the 'target text,' their own cultural and linguistic horizons. (1997: 582)

The narrator's retelling of Fa Mu Lan's legend is a means for her to renegotiate her cultural affiliation, which is an important step in her self-creation. As Cheung puts it: 'Breaking the hold of a dominant tradition is a step toward self-deliverance for artists' (1988: 169). Referring to 'White Tigers', Kingston also says that it 'is not a Chinese myth but one transformed by America' (1998: 97). In this sense, the consequence of the narrator's response story-retelling is the reproduction of her own story.

Collaborative storytelling

The kind of Chinese cultural heritage with which the protagonist Maxine has to negotiate can be seen in the collaborative storytelling in *The Woman Warrior*. One example is the story that emerges in the exchange between Maxine's parents and the emigrant Chinese in 'White Tigers'. This episode begins with the parents and the emigrant Chinese repeating misogynist Chinese sayings, such as 'Feeding girls is feeding cowbirds' (48) and 'Better to raise geese than girls' (48). Upon hearing these proverbs, the young Maxine can only resort to screaming and crying, a reaction which not only fails to stop the adults talking, but encourages more criticism from them. At the core of this story is the traditional Chinese myth that girls have an outward tendency and that they will grow up leaving the family and becoming a member of their future husband's family, i.e. a member of a 'stranger' family.

The home Maxine has in America is dominated by sexist Chinese values. Through collaborative storytelling, the narrator presents members of the Chinese community in America as confederates who perpetuate the patriarchal myths and impose a wife-slave mentality onto daughters of Chinese emigrants like Maxine. The convergence of communal values and family values in this scene reminds us of the concerted effort of the villagers and the family of the no-name woman to annihilate her. The interaction between the listener (Maxine) and the storytellers (Maxine's parents and the emigrant Chinese) sheds light on the burden of Chinese culture that the young Maxine has to bear. Even when she has grown up and has a successful career in America, her family is still talking about the uselessness of daughters. These sexist collaborative stories create confusion for the young Maxine who, despite trying hard to prove her ability and move up the social ladder through studying, is stuck in a community whose regard for her is based solely on their gender-biased views.

How Maxine straddles Chinese and American cultures is illustrated by another example of collaborative storytelling in 'A Song for a Barbarian Reed Pipe', the conversation between young Maxine and the Chinese girl who does not speak. In this case, only Maxine is talking, while the Chinese girl only contributes to the collaborative storytelling by releasing such sounds as 'sobs, chokes, noises' (160). No matter how Maxine squeezes her face or honks her hair to force her to talk, she remains mute. Though she can 'yell in English and in Chinese' at home where no strangers are around and can read aloud in schools, she cannot produce speech in a public place. Her inability to co-narrate a story with Maxine is due to the tremendous cultural divide between

Chinese and American values. In this encounter with the Chinese girl, Maxine tries to assume an American identity and associates talking with being a 'cheerleader' (162) and being able to get dates and jobs, all of which are symbols of American success. The Chinese girl, on the other hand, is an embodiment of Chineseness and an outsider – having her 'China doll hair cut' (156) and being 'the last chosen for her team' (156) in sports activities. Her speechlessness, in contrast to Maxine's eloquence in that scene, tells the story of an individual from an ethnic minority who has lost her voice and whose identity is overwhelmed by the social environment she is in. This dilemma is aptly summarised by Maxine: 'If you don't talk, you can't have a personality' (162).

How Maxine tries to adopt an American voice can be reflected in the episodes about her own experience that are inserted into the collaborative storytelling between Maxine and the speechless Chinese girl. For example, the scene in which Maxine is forcing the Chinese girl to say her name is juxtaposed with another scene in which Maxine's teacher reprimands a Chinese boy for not knowing the name of his father. Through the juxtaposition of the two scenes, Maxine is shown to be behaving like the teacher, who takes for granted one's ability to self-identify. Towards the end of the encounter between Maxine and the Chinese girl, Maxine even adopts an authoritative tone by advising the Chinese girl's sister, 'I was only trying to teach her to talk. She wouldn't cooperate, though … Your family really ought to force her to speak … You mustn't pamper her' (163). This scene about the Chinese girl being bullied brings to mind Maxine's experience of being treated as intellectually inferior in the kindergarten, where her teacher equates her silence with stupidity, that is, possessing a zero IQ. In her collaborative storytelling with the Chinese girl, Maxine assumes the role of a teacher who uses the ability to talk as the only yardstick with which to measure one's intelligence. In so doing, Maxine expresses her aspiration to assimilate into American society.

The collaborative storytelling between Maxine and the speechless Chinese girl can be interpreted as an internal dialogue between Maxine's conflicting selves. While she yearns for American values, she is, like the Chinese girl, saddled with her Chinese identity, which makes her tongue-tied. A Chinese identity is not only about a difference in ethnicity, but involves family secrets. In Maxine's case, for example, she cannot tell the American teacher that her father is a gambler, not a farmer. Her mother keeps insisting 'Don't tell' (164) and reminding her not to expose their family's 'immigration secrets' (164) to avoid being deported back to China. Apart from her ethnic identity, her female identity also poses a constraint on Maxine's use of voice. This is explained by the narrator: 'American-Chinese girls had to whisper to make ourselves American-feminine' (155). As Ling observes, Maxine is 'forced by American social pressures to assume an 'invented' personality and voice' (1998: 177). After her encounter with the Chinese girl, Maxine's confinement to bed due to a mysterious and prolonged illness, is the price she has to pay for adopting an American voice that does not belong to her. Considering the two storytelling voices (Maxine's voice that is present and the Chinese girl's that is absent) in this (unsuccessful) collaborative storytelling, there emerges a story about Maxine, a Chinese American girl who is undergoing the complex process of untying the cruel knot created by the conflicting Chinese and American cultures.

Performative storytelling

The ability to talk-story is an indication of how well the characters can utter their identities in *The Woman Warrior*. This is particularly true for performative storytellers who need to capture their audience's attention and justify that their stories are worth listening to. An example of a performative storyteller is Brave Orchid. In 'Shaman', the medical student, Brave Orchid, appears as a performative storyteller with her classmates forming her audience. After spending a night in the haunting room in To Keung School, Brave Orchid recounts how she bravely fought against the monstrous ghosts and survived their attack. Throughout the process of the performative storytelling, Brave Orchid's audience is completely absorbed, believing all the details of her story. She has proved that she is qualified as a primary storyteller. When she asks her classmates if they have heard 'a sound like mountain wind' (71) and the sound of 'babies crying … tortured people screaming' (71) the night before, they all say yes. As evidenced by her classmates being convinced by her story, she has become a brave exorcist in their minds. After listening to her story, her classmates even follow her lead in exorcising the ghosts she claims to have confronted in the haunting room. Brave Orchid's performative storytelling in To Keung School testifies to her self-assuredness. Unlike Maxine, who is confused by the tension between Chinese and Western cultures, Brave Orchid enjoys a more stable self and is able to make use of the seemingly incompatible knowledge of science and magic to produce a boastful story.

Having been a successful performative storyteller in her home country in China, Brave Orchid continues to speak loudly after her emigration to America. Her voice, however, loses strength along with her cultural dislocation. This can be reflected in the different response of the audience to her performative storytelling in the two countries. Brave Orchid's classmates in To Keung School have no doubt about her ghost exorcism story. They even help her exorcise the ghosts after listening to her story. Yet, when the same story is told to her daughter many years later in America, Brave Orchid's story has lost its credibility. The narrator shows reservation towards the truthfulness of her mother's exorcism story. When the narrator recalls the conclusion of that story, she says with hesitation:

> When the smoke cleared, *I think* my mother said that under the foot of the bed the students found a piece of wood dripping with blood. They burned it in one of the pots, and the stench was like a corpse exhumed for its bones too soon. (*The Woman Warrior*: 72 [emphasis added])

By using the tentative expression 'I think', the narrator distinguishes herself from Brave Orchid's classmates who believe in the magical tale. The narrator also regards other Chinese stories told by her mother as 'impossible stories' (82), which she leaves in her dreams so that she can 'make [her] waking life American-normal' (82). After leaving her home in China, Brave Orchid has lost much of her power as a performative storyteller. Rather than leading to raised stature, her stories invite raised eyebrows in America, where her social status has declined. She has to reposition herself from being a professional doctor to a laundry worker, as she laments to her daughter: 'You have no idea how much I have fallen coming to America' (74). In the middle of the narrator's recalling of Brave Orchid's exorcism story, a comment is interjected. Referring to her mother, the narrator says: 'Her soul returned fully to her and nestled happily inside her skin [after the exorcism] not traveling in the past where her children were nor to American to be with my father' (70). This reflects Brave Orchid's sense of cultural dislocation after moving to America.

Another example of performative storyteller is Moon Orchid in 'At the Western Palace'. However, this is an example of unsuccessful performative storyteller. One of Moon Orchid's favourite activities is to tell the stories of Brave Orchid's children by describing aloud what they are doing. For example, observing her sister's children, Moon Orchid comments: 'Now they're studying again. They read so much' (127). In another instance, she says of her niece: 'Now she's shutting the gate' (128). Her storytelling runs contrary to what performative storytelling should be. Since she makes no effort in the selection and sequencing of content, her descriptive stories are akin to what Fludernik terms 'reports' (1996: 71) which, as opposed to a narrative, mainly 'consist of a series of actions or events' (1996: 71) and 'do not have to perform aesthetic gymnastics, balancing tellability with narrative point' (1996: 71). It seems only natural that Moon Orchid fails to hold her audience's attention. She receives almost no response from Brave Orchid's children except retorts and protests. They find her speaking aloud annoying and, in the end, they even have to resort to locking themselves up in their rooms to keep her at a distance.

The failure of Moon Orchid to engage her listeners with her storytelling underscores her failure to reach out of herself. Her world views and language are so different from the others that there is no room for a dialogue between them. America is no home for her. Once she has left China, she does not belong anywhere. As her husband ruthlessly but rightly asserts: 'You can't belong [to America]' (138). The faith that Moon Orchid has held on to throughout her life – that her husband cares for her because he has been sending her money – shatters once she meets him face to face in Los Angeles. Rejected by her husband, she loses her most important identity as a wife. Moon Orchid, an abandoned wife who cannot speak English and has no working ability, can but remain stranded in a precarious and marginalised position in America. As the narrator sympathetically recollects: 'Moon Orchid had misplaced herself, her spirit (her 'attention', Brave Orchid called it) scattered all over the world' (141).

Having failed in her attempt to communicate with people in America, Moon Orchid can only converse with some imaginary voices and keep repeating a hallucinatory story about her being hunted by 'Mexican ghosts' (140). This is the only story that she is left with – a story about the threat of annihilation. It is not until she is sent to the asylum that she can tell a new story about her happy life with other female inmates whom she calls 'daughters' (144). It is as if the asylum has become her new home. In the asylum, a space isolated from the real world of America, she has found a foothold to articulate a new identity for herself as a mother. Living among women, she no longer feels threatened by men. She also need not bother with a foreign language, English. Talking about herself and other inmates in the asylum, Moon Orchid tells Brave Orchid: '[W]e understand one another here. We speak the same language, the very same' (144). It is a tragedy that her new identity is only recognised by the insane, and the asylum is the only stage for her storytelling.

The example of Moon Orchid as a performative storyteller reflects the destructive impact of cultural displacement on one's identity. The one who can escape this fate is Ts'ai Yen, who is a performative storyteller in the legendary story, 'A Song for a Barbarian Reed Pipe'. In the story, Ts'ai Yen, a poetess in ancient China, is abducted from her homeland by the tribes of Southern Hsiung-nu, who speak a barbarian language. During her twelve years' stay in an alien land, Ts'ai Yen gives birth to two children who cannot comprehend Chinese and can only imitate her with 'senseless singsong words' (185). The breakdown of communication is finally brought to an end through performative storytelling. In the performance, Ts'ai Yen's song comes to a harmony with the barbarians' flutes:

> Ts'ai Yen sang about China and her family there. Her words seemed to be Chinese, but the barbarians understood their sadness and anger. Sometimes they thought they could catch barbarian phrases about forever wandering. Her children did not laugh, but eventually sang along when she left her tent to sit by the winter campfires, ringed by barbarians. (*The Woman Warrior*: 186)

In this scene, both Ts'ai Yen and the barbarians have become performers and audience for one another. Through a collaborative performance, music has become a common language to foster mutual understanding. Upon returning home after being ransomed, Ts'ai Yen has brought back to China three songs. She has titled one of them 'Eighteen Stanzas for a Barbarian Reed Pipe' (186) to pay tribute to the barbarians. This song, bearing the name of the barbarians, is played by the Chinese descendents with Chinese instruments. This piece of art, then, as a production of cross-cultural collaborative performance, manifests a harmonious union of two different cultural heritages. It displays Ts'ai Yen's ability to translate a foreign culture and appropriate it without having her self destabilised. Without denying her life experience of staying with the barbarians, she can still assert herself as a Han and leave behind a bicultural legacy.

Conclusion

Similar to Ts'ai Yen, the narrator is finally able to bring the two contradicting cultural heritages into harmony through storytelling. By telling and retelling the stories of the no-name aunt, Brave Orchid, Moon Orchid, the emigrant Chinese, the legendary and historical stories of Fa Mu Lan and Ts'ai Yen, the narrator affirms her affinity to her ancestral culture, while presenting a critique of its patriarchal ideology and practices. The inclusion of the varieties of storytelling and the appropriation of the myriad of voices in her life story reveal that the traditional Chinese narratives, while creating a labyrinth for her, can also be signposts in her process of identity formation. Having those stories told, retold and revised, she reinscribes them as ingredients for her own life story and translates them into the setting of America.

Through storytelling, she has learned to break silence, to stop quacking 'like a pressed duck' (172). She has acquired a voice of her own and can finally announce: 'I also am a story-talker' (184). Her adeptness in articulating her own self in the form of a polyphonic story testifies to her ability to find her own voice amidst the conflicting narratives of Chinese and American cultures and claim a space, which is both alien and home, in which to stage her story.

References

Brockmeier, J. & Carbaugh, D. (2001). Introduction. In J. Brockmeier & D. Carbaugh (eds), *Narrative and Identity: Studies in Autobiography, Self and Culture*. Amsterdam, Philadelphia: John Benjamins Publishing Company, 1–22.

Bruner, J. (2001). Self-making and world-making. In J. Brockmeier & D. Carbaugh (eds), *Narrative and Identity: Studies in Autobiography, Self and Culture*. Amsterdam, Philadelphia: John Benjamins Publishing Company, 25–37.

Cheung, K. (1988). 'Don't tell': Imposed silences in *The Color Purple* and *The Woman Warrior*. *PMLA* 103, 2: 162–174.

Cheung, K. (1993). *Articulate Silences: Hisaye Yamamoto, Maxine Hong Kingston, Joy Kogawa*. Ithaca: Cornell University Press.

Cutter, M. J. (1997). An impossible necessity: Translation and the recreation of linguistic and cultural identities in contemporary Chinese American literature. *Criticism* 39, 4: 581–612.

Fludernik, M. (1996). *Towards a 'Natural' Narratology*. London: Routledge.

Hall, S. (1996). Cultural identity and diaspora. In P. Mongia (ed.), *Contemporary Postcolonial Theory: A Reader*. London: Arnold, 110–121.

Huntley, E. D. (2001). *Maxine Hong Kingston: A Critical Companion*. Westport, Connecticut: Greenwood Press.

Kingston, M. H. (1981). *The Woman Warrior: Memoirs of a Girlhood Among Ghosts*. London: Picador.

Kingston, M. H. (1998). Cultural mis-readings by American reviewers. In L. E. Skandera-Trombley (ed.), *Critical Essays on Maxine Hong Kingston*. New York: G. K. Hall & Co., 95–103.

Lan, F. (2003). The female individual and the empire: A historicist approach to Mulan and Kingston's woman warrior. *Comparative Literature* 55, 3: 229–245.

Ling, A. (1998). Maxine Hong Kingston and the Dialogic Dilemma of Asian American Writers. In L. E. Skandera-Trombley (ed.), *Critical Essays on Maxine Hong Kingston*. New York: G. K. Hall & Co., 168–181.

Norrick, N. R. (2000). *Conversational Narrative: Storytelling in Everyday Talk*. Amsterdam, Philadelphia: John Benjamins Publishing Company.

Rushdie, S. (1991). *Imaginary Homelands: Essays and Criticism 1981–91*. London: Granta Books.

Smith, S. (1999). Filiality and woman's autobiographical storytelling. In S. L. C. Wong (ed.), *Maxine Hong Kingston's The Woman Warrior: A Casebook*. New York: Oxford University Press, 57–83.

Locations: The situated influences of Deepa Mehta's film trilogy

Sukhmani Khorana

UNIVERSITY OF QUEENSLAND

Introduction

This chapter locates Indo-Canadian filmmaker Deepa Mehta, the director of the elements film trilogy, in relation to the various cinematic traditions that have influenced her personally, culturally, as well as creatively.[1] Mehta may be considered representative of a growing breed of privileged South Asian intellectuals and artists in the diaspora whose lives and work are receiving increasing coverage in the home countries, in the diaspora, and in the 'liberal' west. While the complex location of such individuals and of their creative and critical work may at first seem difficult to theorise, they have been preceded by other 'ethnics' (diasporic and non-diasporic) who appear to disturb the east-west binary and cross over in terms of the content and form of their cultural products. For example, Chinese cinema in the mid-1990s is symbolic of such a disturbance, as it was considered to be 'undergoing a tension in redefining nationalisation and internationalisation' (Lau 1995: 22). The same may be said of recent Indian and Indian diasporic cinema, even though there are differences in the respective cinematic forms.

The Chinese precedent makes it imperative to inspect the local and global contexts that have produced, and are continuing to produce, cinema like Mehta's. She is directly comparable to a director like China's Chen Kaige for an investigation of whose work Lau considers it 'necessary to consult, rather than conceal, the different tropes, both cultural and cross-cultural' (1995: 22). Moreover, due to the social and political critique embodied in their films, both practitioners are considered controversial in their home countries, while being applauded at international festivals and independent film circuits. The specific cultural and cross-cultural tropes evident in Mehta's elements film trilogy are not within the scope of this chapter. My aim here is to demonstrate that these crossover tropes have been conceived as a result of the situated contexts of her filmmaking influences and therefore merit more attention. The contexts considered herein are broadly: transnational commercial cinemas represented by Hollywood and Bollywood, the national cinema of the host society that is Canada, South Asian diasporic film practice, as well as the category of transnational (albeit independent) world cinema.

Towards a situated reading of diasporic practice

> The Bemba of Africa have a ritual for when a girl comes of age. It's called the Chisungu, and they talk of it as 'growing the girls'. I mulled over the Bemba, and a famous anthropologist's argument that all rites of passage involve three stages: separation from one's old state, a liminal period where one is without definition, and a reincorporation into society in a new form. (Devyani Saltzman, 2006: 142)

The aforementioned rites of passage applicable to womanhood can also be used to describe the various stages of the creative process, as well as the states that one experiences as a migrant. The located becoming of this female-creative-diasporic rite of passage (which incorporates the personal, the poetic and the political) is useful in examining Mehta's influences as a diasporic creative practitioner. Deepa Mehta, the daughter of a film distributor and a Philosophy graduate from the University of Delhi married Canadian filmmaker Paul Saltzman and migrated to Canada when she was 23 years old. In an interview, Mehta speaks of growing up watching Hindi films, viewing a Satyajit Ray film at the age of 16, and falling into filmmaking by chance (Nadkarni 2007). In my own interview with her, she mentioned that as her father was a film distributor and cinema-owner, she grew up with a very healthy dose of Indian commercial cinema, but was exposed to non-Hindi and non-Hollywood cinema at university (Khorana 2009).

Mehta's first feature-length directorial venture was *Sam & Me* (1991); followed by two episodes of *The Young Indiana Jones Chronicles*; a Canadian-UK feature film called *Camilla* (1993); *Fire* (the first film of the elements trilogy) in 1996; *Earth* (1998); *Bollywood/Hollywood* (2002); *Republic of Love* (2003); *Water* (the film that completes the trilogy) in 2005; and the Toronto-based *Heaven on Earth* (2008). While the trilogy is her most acclaimed set of films to date, with *Fire* winning several international film festival awards, *Earth* being selected as India's nomination for the Academy Awards, and *Water* making the cut at the Oscars as a Canadian entry in the Best Foreign Film category, it also undoubtedly represents her most controversial body of work (in addition to being the work with which she is most identified). The opposition of the Hindu religious right in India to all three films, but *Fire* and *Water* in particular, caused Mehta to remark in an interview, 'I really felt hurt by what had happened to me in a country that I considered my own' (Thandi 2006).[2] In this sense, Mehta faces a burden of representation that, according to Kobena Mercer, is ever present 'whether one is making a film, writing a book, organising a conference or curating an exhibition, this 'sense of urgency' arises because the cultural reproduction of a certain racism structurally depends on the regulation of Black visibility in the public sphere' (Audrey-Foster 1997: 235). It is with this in mind that I explore Deepa Mehta's film-making location in relation to the two film traditions that hold the most sway in the public spheres of her home and host societies – that is, Bollywood and Hollywood.

Mehta and B/Hollywood

Mehta's complex relationships with the two major commercial cinematic traditions, broadly classified as the Bollywood and Hollywood film industries, is evident on a personal performative level, as well as in Mehta's discomfort with the political ideologies and the often essentialist cultural poetics embodied in these hegemonic film industries. One cannot ignore Mehta's association with Bollywood and Hollywood, as well as her use and appropriation of particular commercial devices in order to enhance the crossover appeal of her films.

Commenting on the fiery response to *Fire* from orthodox Hindu elements in India, Moorti (2000) reasons: 'Mehta's status as a Canadian resident and the film's disavowal of traditional norms were used to mark the product as 'western''. While Mehta may not construe her films as 'western', she nonetheless appears to be distinguishing herself from Indian popular cinema, or Bollywood, as she remarks in an interview after the stalling of *Water*: 'The situation in India at the moment is that if you produce films with song and dance routines or unserious films, you are fine. It doesn't matter how violent and vulgar they are.

But if you want to make something even slightly introspective it is a no-no' (Phillips 2000).

The recently instituted IIFA (Indian International Film Academy) Awards take place outside India, and are especially targeted at the vast Indian diaspora who are regular patrons of Bollywood. Despite Bollywood's nonchalance towards expatriate directors like Mehta, she received the award for the brightest Indian director abroad at the 2007 IIFA awards held in Yorkshire (Jha 2007). Ghosh mentions that although Mehta's father had just passed away, she came out of her seclusion to receive the award on the insistence of Amitabh Bachchan, a Bollywood stalwart (and the brand ambassador for IIFA) whom she could not refuse (2007).

Jha notes that winning the award made Mehta lose her discomfort with Bollywood, especially after her experience of being hounded out of Varanasi during the shooting of *Water* as she mentioned, 'This was my first award from home, the first bona fide Indian award. And I'm very happy. Sure beats burning my effigies' (Jha 2007). However, despite Mehta's acceptance within Bollywood, her work practices seem different from the more lackadaisical attitude of the subcontinental film industry. For instance, Saltzman notes in *Shooting Water* that John Abraham, the Bollywood actor who plays the character of Narayan in the film, reduced his rehearsal days and explains that this was the Bollywood system at work (2006: 220). At the same time, when I probed Mehta regarding her claim not to be a Bollywood director, yet continuing to use Indian actors, she replied:

> The talent of Indian actors in the west will grow with time, but is sadly very limited. One is stuck with Navin Andrews and Jimi Mistry, and that's it. There aren't many roles, so the opportunities are extremely scarce. There is an incredible pool of talent in India, so I feel fortunate to be able to tap into that. (Khorana 2009)

Therefore, it appears that Mehta's decision to use Bollywood talent in her films is driven by circumstance, as well as a possible strategy to raise the profile of her films amongst mainstream Indian and diasporic audiences, thereby facilitating the crossover.

Mehta's attempt at appealing to a wider audience is most evident in the second film of her trilogy, *Earth,* which 'spoke the languages of India ... and seems to be primarily directed to an Indian audience because of its choice of well known actors and a popular composer and lyricist as well as its use of unexplained visual clues' (Levitin 2003: 279). Commenting on the rather mainstream trope of melodrama in the film that is based on a literary work, Levitin adds: 'Partition becomes both backdrop to and catalyst for the love triangle's tragic outcome, an emotional narrative that, in contrast to Sidhwa's understated novel, is reminiscent of popular Hindi cinema's sensationalism' (2003: 279). Despite Mehta's disavowal of certain ideologies, practices and styles characteristic of commercial Bollywood, she is both influenced by a certain era of Indian cinema, and is willing to use Bollywood talent and tropes in her films.

Casting a glance at Mehta's filmography outside the elements trilogy, what emerges is an equally, if not more fraught, relationship with the dominant film industry-institution of the world: or Hollywood. Using provocative descriptives for her 'Indian' films, Majumder contrasts them with her 'white' films, namely, *The Republic of Love* and *Tuscan Soup*:

> After a lesbian bombshell, a smouldering partition saga and a stormy confrontation with India's political masters over filming the story of Benares widows, Ms Mehta seems to be in no hurry to pick up another Indian theme. Her two forthcoming films are entirely on 'white' subjects and targeted mainly at a Western audience. (2003)

Associating Mehta with a Hollywood/western sensibility rather than a hybrid cinematic discourse, Majumder adds that according to Mehta, 'she had lived in the West long enough to handle a 'white film'' (2003). At the same time, it is noteworthy that the one-time documentary maker's first foray into Hollywood, *Camilla*, occurred before she conceived the trilogy, and it proved disastrous for her career.

Soon after its failure, Mehta commented: 'Hollywood's so seductive. Before you know it, you're sucked in. Hollywood is not called the kingdom of smoke and mirrors for nothing' (Randoja 1996). Cormier seems to have foreseen Mehta's independent streak, as during the filming of *Camilla*, he noted: 'With her plainspoken style and her passion for character and dialogue, Mehta is unlikely to convert to the kind of frothy star vehicles that power the Hollywood glamour machine' (1993: 62). In other words, it is clear that despite Mehta's geographic location in the west, she does not associate herself, her politics, or her poetics with the practices of Hollywood.

Mehta's incomplete seduction by Hollywood, or rather her appropriation of multiple film traditions, is evidenced by the romantic comedy titled *Bollywood Hollywood* that she wrote and directed while taking a break from the *Water* controversy. According to Kapoor, the former film 'tackles the influence of both Hollywood and Bollywood on the lives of Indians living abroad' (2003). Musing over the 'nationality' of the film, Kapoor asks, 'Is *Bollywood Hollywood* an Indian film directed by an Indian or a Canadian film made by a director who is settled in Canada?' (2003). Mehta seems dismissive of critics' and reviewers' traditional adherence to nation-bound film categories as she remarks that when *Earth* won an award, both Indian and Canadian convoys were present and there was confusion over who should have collected the award (Kapoor 2003). She adds that she considers her films to be universal entities that belong to everyone (Kapoor 2003). At this juncture, it becomes crucial to inquire into Mehta's location in the national cinema of her host country and examine whether her ambivalent relationship with both Bollywood and Hollywood is echoed in her association with Canadian national cinema.

Mehta and Canadian cinema

Mehta's relationship with Canadian cinema reveals an evolution from a stage of considering her work as 'ethnic' to a more open approach in terms of funding and ownership. However, such a change does not mean that Mehta's films have necessarily become more 'Canadian' in content and form and hence she is more suitably located within the national film canon. On the contrary, it shows a re-definition of the national cinema itself which is now more accommodating of films with proven cultural capital and crossover appeal.

When *Fire*, the first film of Mehta's elements trilogy about the relationship between two sisters-in-law in a joint middle-class family in India, opened the Perspective Canada program at the 1996 Toronto International Film Festival, eyebrows were raised in India and overseas as contrary responses abounded. The most resonant question being asked was: if *Fire* neither conforms to the tenets of Canadian Cinema nor to that of Hollywood, why was it selected for a program like Perspective Canada? According to Liz Czach, the program traditionally includes films 'because they are 'representative' and adhere to a political agenda of what is good for the nation and good for Canadian film – not necessarily driven by quality, value, or good taste' (2004: 84). She adds: 'the film's Canadianness was called into question by numerous institutional bodies, including the media, which questioned the 'ethnic' slant of the programming choice' (Czach 2004: 86).

If *Fire's* rootedness or lack thereof in what is officially defined as 'Canadian national cinema' remains under a cloud, it is not the same with *Water*. While the latter film is also based in India, as it centres on the plight of widows during the pre-independence era and uses Indian actors, it was nominated by Canada as the country's official entry in the Best Foreign Film category of the 2006 Academy Awards. The recognition can be attributed to both an expanding definition of what constitutes Canadian cinema, as well as recent changes in Academy Award rules. Commenting on the huge success of *Water* at the Canadian box-office compared to domestic English-language films, Vlessing points out that in order to resuscitate the native film industry, 'the Canadian government is financing more home-grown movies that are 'Canadian' without being about Canada' (2006: 15). At the same time, while '[i]n the past, the Academy only allowed a country to submit a film in one of its national languages; this year, that rule has been waived, paving the way for Canada to submit Fox Searchlight's Hindi-language *Water*' (Galloway 2007: 8). Mehta herself seems to view the film as Canadian, as she says, regarding the film's surprise Oscar nomination, '*Water* changed the way Canadians looked at their own films' (Khorana 2009). At the same time, in the opinion of Mehta's partner and the producer of her films, David Hamilton, Telefilm Canada's decision to consider non-English and non-French films is not just an economic decision, but reflective of the changing attitude of Canada, which is finally living up to its multicultural nature (Hamilton 2007).

It is worth noting that prior to the acceptance of *Water* as a Canadian film, Mehta felt as rejected by Canada as she did by India:

> I find that I don't know what defines Canadian film anymore. Because I think that the definition is difficult as far as a person like me is concerned, a hybrid person who can move from continent to continent … make those films – whether it's *Fire*, *Earth*, or *Water*, and they are not considered Canadian films. So what am I? I feel like I've been really rejected and marginalized by Canada because I don't fit into any of

> the categories that are laid out by the government that defines what a Canadian film is. (Levitin 2003: 277–78)

The overlooking of ethnic filmmakers in the Canadian film canon is reflected in George Melynk's book titled, *One Hundred Years of Canadian Cinema* which, despite being published in 2004, divides the nation's cinema into the English-Canadian and the Quebec traditions and devotes only a few pages to Mehta's work. In a statement that possibly indicates that Melynk perceives Mehta's 'real' cinema as more Indian than Canadian, he says: 'Her films about Canada are a Mehta 'lite' version of her vision, while India gets the full brunt of her personal crusade' (2004: 180). However, in spite of the dismissal of her Canadian-themed films, Mehta is recognised by the author as 'English-Canada's pre-eminent immigrant female director, just as Lea Pool is Quebec's pre-eminent immigrant female director' (Melynk 2004: 180). Notwithstanding the recent eminence bestowed upon Mehta by Canada through the nation's Academy Award nomination, she is still regarded by a renowned film historian like Melynk as an 'immigrant female director', and not as a Canadian filmmaker. An examination of her work in relation to diasporic filmmaking will seek to establish whether that element takes precedence over descriptions of her cinema as either Indian or Canadian.

Mehta and diasporic/exilic cinema

Mehta's trilogy is part of a recent spate of Indian diasporic cultural productions, both in the cinematic and literary fields. While comparisons by postcolonial theorists and South Asian studies scholars to other expatriate Indian creative practitioners like Mira Nair and Salman Rushdie are inevitable, it is important to remember that unlike most diasporic film/literature that reflects on the diasporic condition alone, Mehta's trilogy is a return to the homeland. One of these returns, *Earth*, is the result of the inter-diasporic relations between filmmaker Mehta and writer Bapsi Sidhwa (author of the novel *Cracking India* on which *Earth* is based). Therefore, members of the South Asian diaspora are capitalising on their location for creative collaborations.

While Herman (2005) and others have examined the diasporic element of Mehta's filmmaking position as contributing to the sense of loss in her narratives, her cinema also exhibits exilic, and hence inevitably political and poetic (in addition to personal), attributes that have been largely overlooked. According to Naficy:

> Exilic filmmakers are not so much marginal or subaltern as they are interstitial, partial and multiple. And they are interstitial, partial, and multiple not only in terms of their identity and subjectivity but also in terms of the various roles they are forced to play, or choose to play, in every aspect of their films – from inception to consumption. (1999: 133)

Not only did Mehta conceive the trilogy when she returned to the homeland and was moved by the plight of widows in Varanasi (Nadkarni 2007), she also arguably 'wrestled to occupy the position of authority in relation to the Shiv Sena's Bal Thackeray' (Desai 2004: 185), thus making her akin to an exilic director. In *Film and Politics in the Third World*, Downing points out a dilemma that is unique to filmmakers in exile: 'How should they function in relation to their native lands?' (1987: 69). Given Mehta's rejection by her homeland, her location in diasporic/exilic cinema is not as unproblematic as might first appear to be the case.

To understand Mehta's positioning in diasporic and exilic filmmaking, it is important to examine the perception of these kinds of cinema, especially in the homeland. How are Mehta and her India-based cinema received in the public sphere in India? A detailed analysis of the reception of Mehta's trilogy is outside the scope of this chapter. However, it is important to point out that despite the growing transnational acceptance of Indian expatriate writers and filmmakers, they are often viewed suspiciously in the homeland. This is especially so if their texts reflect critically on the historical or contemporary conditions prevalent in the country they are presumed to have voluntarily forsaken over the more liberal west. Such association with western practices and values creates hostility and prevents an effective crossover.

When *Water* was an Academy Award nominee in 2006 and competed with *Rang De Basanti*, a new-age Indian film in the Foreign Film category, many India-based filmmakers did not hesitate to back the latter over the former on the grounds that it was a truer representation of their nation. Among these was Kunal Kohli, a successful Bollywood director who opined, 'I would rather an *RDB* wins over a *Water*. *RDB* deals with India and its problems and not with something that happened a hundred years ago' (2007: 'Why water finally went down the Oscar drain'). Even Naseeruddin Shah, an exponent of alternative cinema within India, is critical of diasporic practitioners like Mehta, as he comments that they lack intimacy in terms of both distance and time (Ansari, 1998).

In spite of the hostility in the homeland due to her association with diasporic cinema, Mehta appears to enjoy the privilege bestowed upon her through her position outside the creative and legal restraints of the Indian body-politic. Notwithstanding her run-in with a Hindu fundamentalist mob during the making of *Water*, which is most likely attributable to her perception as an 'inauthentic' Indian, it is this very lack of authenticity or hybridity that allows her an unprecedented degree of artistic freedom. Apparently conscious of this privilege, she remarks: 'I can be uninhibited about subject. Whether it is about choices for women (*Fire*) or Partition (*Earth*) I did not have to think about the repercussions as I would have in India. Nor did I have to wonder about the censor board' (Ansari 1998).

Therefore, it appears that in the absence of whole-hearted support from either their homelands or their adopted homes, filmmakers like Mehta must find their home in a community of fellow diasporic creative practitioners and help to sustain the other members of this location that is privileged and privileging in its own right. It is the situated becomings of this location that lend Mehta's work a crossover dimension and that justify an examination of her personal-political-poetic location in world cinema.

Mehta and world cinema

To prevent the diasporic label from hindering her crossover potential, I consider Mehta's location within the broad category of world cinema, and recognise the influence of other situated yet internationally renowned filmmakers on her work. In *Shooting Water*, Saltzman comments on the eastern and western cinematic influences on her mother's work:

> The actors didn't lip-sync to the songs in *Water*. It was a creative choice of Mom's, and one that reflected the influence of both East and West on her work. Bollywood had influenced her enough to insert six song situations in the film, but a love of Japanese director Yasujiro Ozu's restraint and Ingmar Bergman's meditations on psychology had made

> her leave room for silence. She chose to let the characters experience their songs, not sing them. (2006: 231)

Since there is no secondary literature directly comparing Mehta's trilogy to the works of any major international director-auteurs, I will attempt to both evoke the similarities in content and technique between her films and the films of those whom she cites as her influences, as well as employing the filmographies of these directors to locate Mehta's place in the annals of world cinema.

While both Yasujiro Ozu and Mehta may be put within the boundaries of world cinema due to the independent transnational distribution of their films (in addition to the hybrid content and form), it is worth noting that they are often associated in critical and mainstream western film discourse with 'Japanese' and 'Indian' cinema, respectively. Is this then, not only a similarity between the two filmmakers, but also a contradiction in the terms that define their work? Commenting on the style of Ozu's body of work, consisting of about 55 films over more than three decades, Richie comments:

> Ozu's method, like all poetic methods, is oblique. He does not confront emotion, he surprises it. Precisely, he restricts his vision in order to see more; he limits his world in order to transcend these limitations. His cinema is formal and the formality is that of poetry, the creation of an ordered context that destroys habit and familiarity, returning to each word, to each image, its original freshness and urgency. In all of this Ozu is close to the *sumi-e* ink drawing masters of Japan, to the masters of the haiku and the *waka*. It is this quality to which the Japanese refer when they speak of Ozu as being 'most Japanese', when they speak of his 'real Japanese flavour'. (1974: xiii)

At the same time, Russell writes that Ozu's association with a distinctively Japanese filmmaking sensibility ignores 'his appropriation of the breezy style of Hollywood comedy and the dramatic realism of American melodrama' (2004: 50). She particularly notes the amalgamation of cross-cultural and local themes and styles in one of Ozu's most celebrated films, *Tokyo Story*, opining that, 'On many levels this is a 'universal' story with deep currents of humanist emotion ... *Tokyo Story* is also very much about one city at one moment in time, and dwells on a level of historical specificity that is equally crucial to its lasting effects' (2004: 51). Despite being specific to Indian conditions, Mehta's trilogy, like Ozu's films, appeals to worldwide audiences as she comments: '*Fire* is about particular individuals, but it is also a universal question, not unlike *Earth*' (Phillips 1999). Mehta adds that she believes in the ideology put forth in filmmaker Luis Bunuel's autobiography, *My Last Sigh*, where he 'talks about the importance of characters being rooted to a place. He says that any character that is honest and rooted to a place immediately becomes universal because human emotions are universal' (Phillips 1999).

Besides intertwining crossover and situated elements in their films, both Ozu and Mehta meditate on the modernising aspects of their respective home countries through the use of water and train imagery, as well as the formal appropriation of natural settings. Reflecting on the national allegory that is *Tokyo Story*, Russell comments: 'This is not just a story set in Tokyo; it is the story of postwar Tokyo, a tale of the family of Japan trying to find the way forward after the twenty-year turmoil of war and occupation' (2004: 51). One could argue that Mehta's elements films, if considered chronologically (from the period when the stories are set rather than the order of their release dates), move from the 'foetal modernity' symbolised by Gandhian ideals in *Water*, to the 'infant modernity' of a partitioning sub-continent in *Earth*, and finally to the 'adolescent modernity' depicted by an identity crisis-ridden middle-class India in *Fire*. Not unlike Ozu, Mehta personalises, politicises and renders poetic the wider socio-political context, as she says of *Earth*: 'I wanted to tell this really large story from the standpoint of an intimate group of friends from different ethnic groups and trace out the process of partition through them' (Phillips 1999). Both directors juxtapose the material austerity of their characters' lives with a visual acuity that is at odds with the aesthetics of contemporary Indian and Japanese cinema.

Modernity and poetic austerity are themes evident in the faith trilogy by Ingmar Bergman, another world cinema director whose work Mehta claims to be influenced by. Although the dark and colour-deprived films of Ingmar Bergman may not, at first glance, appear to have anything in common with the 'exotic' fare that is Mehta's elements trilogy, a closer examination reveals several similarities in terms of dominant visual and thematic motifs. One of these is the recurrence of the train/journeying myth in Bergman films, a symbol that has great significance in both *Earth* and *Water*. Commenting on the importance of this metaphor in *The Silence,* as well as other Bergman films, Brightman argues that we cannot lose the thematic unity provided by Bergman's favoured myth of the journey because 'although it proves elliptical in *The Silence*, in many of his earlier films it serves to draw character along an arduous path of discovery and development, for better or worse' (1964: 7).

Despite the overpowering presence of despair over hope in Bergman's films, especially the faith trilogy, several critics have recognised the catharsis provided by the presence of children. Alexander, for instance, notes of *Winter Light* and *The Silence* that although the major characters are adults, 'the ethical base and much of the limited hope derives from the children' (1974: 25). He further reasons why Bergman's children (and by implication, the children of this world) are not necessarily doomed:

> In *Through a Glass Darkly* shimmering water was often seen through windows; in *Winter Light* one sees only fog and isolated barren branches, chillingly adequate symbols for the central figures. There are three exceptions, however, and in two of them children appear beyond the glass…some relation to these children is suggested as a substitute for the fog and barren thoughts of [Tomas's] soul. (1974: 26)

Similarly, the characters of Lenny in *Earth* and Chuyia in *Water* embody hope in a world torn apart by patriarchal and self-serving interpretations of religion. Both question the cruelty of their changed surroundings and represent the possibility of a less oppressive future for their generation.

Bergman and Mehta are also preoccupied with the themes of religion, the conflict of faith with knowledge, and the relevance of tradition in modern society. Phillips argues that partly due to Bergman's early upbringing as the son of an Evangelical Lutheran pastor, he 'used his camera to compose a continuing essay on man's relationship to God in the context of the problem of evil' (1975: 45). While it has been observed that *Fire*, *Earth* and *Water* concern the politics of patriarchy, nationalism and religion, respectively, the boundaries are arguably less distinct in that the religion-nationalism-patriarchy nexus infiltrates all three films and the politics depicted within them. The anti-conservative (yet not irreligious) ideology portrayed in the films seems to reflect

Mehta's own views on the subject of religion. While neither an atheist nor agnostic, she believes in the liberal Hindu philosophy of Vedanta 'which means the end of knowledge or the ultimate knowledge' and does not follow any rituals (Mehta 2007).

Bergman's cinema reflects his own ambiguity about faith and Phillips concludes that when we look at his body of work, he seems to be saying 'that the coexistence of good and evil is all that we can hope for from our fragmented existence' and indicating that: 'One cannot hope to establish a relationship with God by bypassing fellow human beings' (1975: 54). Mehta's trilogy seems to gesture towards the greater morality in community spirit and justice for marginal groups than in devotion to deities. At this juncture, it becomes imperative to view Mehta's trilogy alongside the work (especially the well-known *Apu Trilogy*) of fellow Indian and renowned humanist filmmaker Satyajit Ray, who is also noted as an influence.

In *Shooting Water*, Devyani Saltzman compares the mob faced by Mehta during the filming of *Water* in India to the criticism confronting Satyajit Ray in his own country:

> When Satyajit Ray made *Pather Panchali (Song of the Little Road)* in 1955, depicting life in a rural Bengali village, a famous Bollywood actress criticized him for glorifying India's poverty ... It seemed to me that India under the BJP was in the midst of a similar purification campaign. Pavan K. Varma, writer and member of the Indian Foreign Service, said 'all nations indulge in a bit of myth-making to bind their people together'. *Water* was one of the casualties of maintaining that myth. (2006: 85)

It is noteworthy that Saltzman uses the term 'myth' to describe the mainstream (and uncritical) representations of India because Heifetz, referring to Ray as a meditative lyricist rather than a realist, points out that his films move toward myth, albeit of a special kind (Heifetz 1985). He adds that these are

> myths of the supreme value of individual and limited moral choice, of women as charged poles of influence on weaker or tradition-bound men, of sexual desire outside marriage as emblematic of corruption, of the exaltation of childhood, all of these conditioned by the fact that he remained till the end an 'aristocrat' but not in the usual sense of the term. (Heifetz 1985: 72)

At the same time, Rex Roberts, a film reviewer, notes of Mehta's *Water* that its 'social realism works against its romanticism, the movie unable to decide whether it wants to be a historical epic or a Hallmark tear-jerker' (2005). Even if the moral compass of Ray's world was not as wide as Mehta's is now, it appears that both filmmakers, while dealing with confronting content, use a film grammar that is poetic and are often rebuked for doing so. There are, however, others like Salman Rushdie who commend such a combination of austerity and aesthetics as he observes of *Water* that: 'The fluid lyricism of the camera provides an unsettling contrast to the arid difficulties of the characters' lives' (Mongrel Media 2005).

While the glorification of poverty in Ray's cinema is debatable, a number of critics in India and overseas have applauded him for the humanitarianism and accessibility of his stories and characters, a quality that arguably won him an Academy Award for Lifetime Achievement at the tail end of his career. According to Sengoopta, the crossover quality of his films derives from their particularity, adding that Ray maintained that

> a truthful portrait of any human group would ultimately demonstrate the fundamental humanity of the subjects, a humanity that would bear some meaning for all human beings, across national and cultural boundaries. (1993: 249)

In Mehta's comparison to Ozu, her own films attempt to showcase cross-cultural themes through local tales. Mehta often lists Ray as a key influence on her work and is particularly moved by the deceptive simplicity of his cinema as she comments: 'He's the greatest humanist filmmaker that I've ever known. His work is simple, very complex yet uncomplicated. That is the beauty of it. I do not wish to emulate it, but I wish at some point I could reach his vision on some level' (McGowan 2003: 284). Besides the similarities in the stylistic features of their films, in her elements trilogy Mehta seems to be concerned with the same socio-cultural issues as Ray. During the course of his filmmaking, spanning four decades, he covered themes such as 'conflicts between tradition and modernity, the position of women, the nature of religious superstition' (Sengoopta 1993: 248).

Ray's cinema had a worldwide reach, not just due to its humanitarian themes and accessible content, but also because he told his stories in a way that might be considered 'western' in that it appropriated Italian neo-realism and American melodrama, rather than following the conventions of mainstream Indian (Bollywood) cinema. Sengoopta attributes this to the fusion of eastern and western traditions in Ray's own education and upbringing:

> Much of the appeal of Ray's work for Westerners stems from his deep familiarity with Western artistic conventions … Ray was as familiar with Shakespeare as with Tagore, had as much admiration for Tintin and Buster Keaton as for nonsense characters created by his father, was as conversant with Beethoven as with Indian classical music, and as fond of Piero della Francesca as of the murals of Ajanta. (1993:252)

Conclusion: towards a crossover location

While Mehta belongs to a generation that came after the Bengali Renaissance that influenced Ray, she is also a hybrid product of the east and the west, and this is not just due to her stint in Canada. Her upper middle-class upbringing helps justify the use of the English language in her films, even though it is not usually associated with world cinema or foreign films in the arthouse genre. Therefore, the use of English in Mehta's film trilogy renders it a crossover rather than symbolic of the world cinema tradition.

Given Mehta's various allegiances with and alienation from Bollywood, Hollywood, Canadian cinema and diasporic/exilic cinema, the question remains as how best to locate her in contemporary discourse on cinema. Levitin comes closest to providing an answer about her identity when she refers to Mehta as a transnational, feminist and independent filmmaker:

> The ability to manipulate content, aesthetics, and perhaps, controversy defines Mehta's special talent as an independent filmmaker competing in the global market. A more precise description of Mehta, then, might be as a transnational filmmaker attuned to the cinematic traditions of two very dissimilar societies, a feminist with a distaste for rigid nationalisms and oppressive power relations, and an independent filmmaker with an early-honed instinct for the art of film exhibition. (2003: 274)

Keeping in mind Mehta's allegiances with the cinema categories examined in this chapter, as well as those suggested by Levitin, it appears most appropriate to locate her work in the broad category of world cinema. However, given the association of this kind of filmmaking with the arthouse genre, even this label seems inadequate. In considering Mehta's own perspectives on home and identity, one can conclude that the use of 'crossover cinema' best describes her personal-political-poetic filmmaking location.

Notes

1 For this, I draw on primary and secondary sources that reference Mehta's own voice to locate her and her work, but do not always reflect on how their own locations affect the readings they produce. These include *Shooting Water*, the memoir about the making of *Water*; filmed interviews that I conducted with Mehta and her partner and producer, David Hamilton, on a film set in Toronto in December 2007; as well as secondary material on Mehta and other filmmakers in the popular press and in refereed publications.

2 While I was still in *my* country in 1996, I wasn't legally allowed to watch *Fire* because of its adult rating, but heard rumours of its taboo-breaking content from older friends and cousins who had managed to get hold of the pirated version after the film was prematurely taken off cinema screens in India. *Earth*, released in 1999, seemed more accessible and real as it appeared to be a cinematic rendition of our history chapters on the partition of the subcontinent. I had also, by that time, entered adolescence and was moving away from commercial Bollywood and Hollywood fare. I saw *Water* on DVD in my suburban Adelaide home in 2005, and was moved in an entirely different way – as a young diasporic Indian woman, I was viewing a story based in India, and written and directed by a woman who lived in Canada, but from a position that is geographically outside of both India and Canada. Although the film was eventually released in India in March 2007, it never reached my hometown of Jammu in the terrorism-torn state of Jammu and Kashmir.

References

Alexander, W. (1974). Devils in the Cathedral: Bergman's Trilogy. *Cinema Journal* 13, 2 (Spring, 1974), 23–33.

Ansari, R. (1998). Interviews with Deepa Mehta and Naseeruddin Shah. http://www.himalmag.com/read.php?id=1613 [online, accessed 8 May 2007]

Audrey-Foster, G. (1997). *Women Filmmakers of the African and Asian Diaspora: Decolonising the Gaze, Locating Subjectivity*. Carbondale and Edwardsville: Southern Illinois University Press.

Brightman, C. (1964). The Word, The Image, and 'The Silence'. *Film Quarterly* 17, 4 (Summer), 3–11.

Cormier, J. (1993). Mehta Morphosis. *Chatelaine* 66, 11 (November), 58–62.

Czach, L. (2004). Film Festivals, Programming, and the Building of a National Cinema. *The Moving Image* 4, 1: 76–88.

Desai, J. (2004). Home on the Range: Queering Postcoloniality and Globalization. In Deepa Mehta's *Fire* in *Beyond Bollywood: The Cultural Politics of South Asian Diasporic Film*. New York and London: Routledge, 159–191.

Downing, J. D. H. (1987). *Film and Politics in the Third World*. New York: Praeger.

Ezra, E. & Rowden, T. (2006). *Transnational Cinema: The Film Reader*. London and New York: Routledge.

Galloway, S. (2007). Passages from India. *Hollywood Reporter* 397, 33: 8–10.

Ghosh, A. (2007). Amitabh Bachchan writes a letter to Deepa Mehta. http://www.apunkachoice.com/scoop/bollywood/20070516-3.html [online, accessed 28 June 2007]

Hamilton, D. (2007). Interview with David Hamilton, Part I (Personal communication. Transcript available on request).

Heifetz, H. (1985). Mixed Music: In memory of Satyajit Ray. *Cineaste* 19, 4: 72–73.

Herman, J. (2005). Memory and Melodrama: The Transnational Politics of Deepa Mehta's *Earth*. *Camera Obscura* 20, 1: 107–147.

Jha, S. K. (2007). IIFA is my first Indian award: Deepa Mehta. *Hindustan Times*. http://www.hindustantimes.com/StoryPage/Print.aspx?Id=927f7ddf-fd7e-4f88–8afd-be5b0a06a1e2 [online, accessed 28 June 2007]

Kapoor, P. (2003). A matter of humour. *The Times of India*. http://timesofindia.indiatimes.com/articleshow/msid-33214051,prtpage-1.cms [online, accessed 14 September 2007]

Khorana, S. (2009). Maps and Movies: Talking with Deepa Mehta. *Bright Lights Film Journal*. http://www.brightlightsfilm.com/63/63mehtaiv.html [online, accessed 27 July 2009]

Lau, J. K. W. (1995). 'Farewell My Concubine': History, Melodrama, and Ideology in Contemporary Pan-Chinese Cinema. *Film Quarterly* 49. 1: 16–27.

Levitin, J. (2003). An Introduction to Deepa Mehta: Making Films in Canada and India. In J. Levitin, J. Plessis & V. Raoul (eds), *Women Filmmakers: Refocusing*. New York and London: Routledge, 273–283.

Majumder, A. (2003). Stop seeing red: Deepa shifts to 'white films'. *The Times of India*. http://timesofindia.indiatimes.com/articleshow/msid-43460,prtpage-1.cms [online, accessed 14 September 2007]

Mankekar, P. (2003). Off-centre: Feminism and South Asian Studies in the Diaspora. In J. Assayag & V. Benie (ed.), *At Home in Diaspora: South Asian Scholars and the West*. Delhi: Permanent Black, 52–65.

McGowan, S. (2003). Excerpts from a Master Class with Deepa Mehta. In J. Levitin, J. Plessis & V. Raoul (eds), *Women Filmmakers: Refocusing*. New York and London: Routledge, 284–291.

Mehta, D. (2007). I am: Deepa Mehta. *The Times of India*. http://timesofindia.indiatimes.com/articleshow/msid-1746537,prtpage-1.cms [online, accessed 14 September 2007]

Melynk, G. (2004). *One Hundred Years of Canadian Cinema*. Toronto, Buffalo, London: University of Toronto Press.

Mongrel Media (2005). *Water*: A David Hamilton Production of a film by Deepa Mehta. http://www.mongrelmedia.com/data/ftp/Water/Water%20-%20Press%20kit.pdf [online, accessed 20 March 2007]

Moorti, S. (2000). Inflamed Passions: *Fire*, the Woman Question and the Policing of Cultural Borders. http://www.genders.org/g32/g32_moorti.html [online, accessed 20 June 2006]

Nadkarni, G. (2007). Elements of Enlightenment. http://www.ascentmagazine.com/articles.aspx?articleID=186&page=read&subpage=past&issueID=29 [online, accessed 4 April 2007]

Naficy, H. (1996). Phobic Spaces and Liminal Panics: Independent Transnational Film Genre. In R. Wilson & W. Dissanayake (eds), *Global Local: Cultural Production and the Transnational Imaginary*. Durham and London: Duke University Press, 119–144.

Naficy, H. (1999). Between rocks and hard places: the interstitial mode of production in exilic cinema. In H. Naficy (ed.), *Home, Exile, Homeland: Film, Media and the Politics of Place*. New York and London: Routledge, 125–147.

Phillips, G. D. (1975). Ingmar Bergman and God. In S. M. Kaminsky & J. F. Hill (eds), *Ingmar Bergman: Essays in Criticism*. London, Oxford, New York: Oxford University Press, 45–54.

Phillips, R. (1999). An interview with Deepa Mehta, director of *Earth*. World Socialist website. http://www.wsws.org/articles/1999/aug1999/meh-a06.shtml [online, accessed 15 May 2007]

Phillips, R. (2000). Deepa Mehta speaks out. World Socialist website. http://www.wsws.org/articles/2000/feb2000/meht-f15.shtml [online, accessed 5 June 2007]

Randoja, I. (1996). Deepa Mehta. Heat rises as resilient director sets Fire to film fest's Canadian slate. *NOW* 16, 1.

Richardson, L. & St. Pierre, E. A. (2005). Writing: A Method of Inquiry. In N. K. Denzin & Y. S. Lincoln (eds), *The Sage Handbook of Qualitative Research* (Third Edition). London and New Delhi: Sage, 959–978.

Richie, D. (1974). *Ozu*. Berkeley, Los Angeles, London: University of California Press.

Roberts, R. (2005). Water. *Film Journal International*. http://www.filmjournal.com/filmjournal/reviews/article_display.jsp?vnu_content_id=1002425100 [online, accessed 8 May 2007]

Russell, C. (2004) Tokyo Story. *Cineaste* 29, 3: 50–51.

Saltzman, D. (2006). *Shooting Water: A Mother-Daughter Journey and the Making of a Film*. New Delhi: Penguin Books.

Sengoopta, C. (1993). Satyajit Ray: The Plight of the Third-World Artist. *American Scholar* 62, 2.

Thandi, P. (2006). Tumultuous Water. http://www.preetithandi.com/images/Published_Work/Films/Celebritiy_Interviews/DeepaMehta.pdf [online, accessed 4 April 2007]

Vlessing, E. (2006). Definition of indigenous expands in search for next local hit. *Hollywood Reporter* 394, 6: 15–16.

References with no author identified:

Anon. Satyajit Ray. *Wikipedia*. http://en.wikipedia.org/wiki/Satyajit_Ray [online, accessed 19 2007]

Anon. (2007). Why water finally went down the Oscar drain. *The Times of India*. http://timesofindia.indiatimes.com/articleshow/msid-1703103,prtpage-1.cms [online, accessed 8 March 2007]

Films:

Aparajito. 1956. Directed by Satyajit Ray. Artificial Eye. DVD.

Apur Sansar. 1958. Directed by Satyajit Ray. Artificial Eye. DVD.

Earth. 1999. Directed by Deepa Mehta. DVD.

Fire. 1996. Directed by Deepa Mehta. DVD.

Pather Panchali. 1955. Directed by Satyajit Ray. Artificial Eye. DVD.

The Silence. 1963. Directed by Ingmar Bergman. Criterion. DVD.

Through a Glass Darkly. 1961. Directed by Ingmar Bergman. Criterion. DVD.

Tokyo Story. 1953. Directed by Yasujiro Ozu. Criterion. DVD.

Water. 2005. Directed by Deepa Mehta. Mongrel Media. DVD.

Winter Light. 1962. Directed by Ingmar Bergman. Criterion. DVD.

On the radio program: *Die Sprachen Moabits*, Offener Kanal, Berlin

Bruna Emanuela Manai
BERLIN

Franco Manai
UNIVERSITY OF AUCKLAND

Introduction

The radio feature, *Die Sprachen Moabits* (The Languages of Moabit), authored by Bruna Emanuela Manai in collaboration with Vilma Cerón Palomino, Haydée Winkler and Mario Müller, was broadcast on Berlin's Offener Kanal in July 2007 and the recording is now available on line (Manai 2007). The hour-long program is the result of a field trip during which the authors recorded the voices and sounds of Moabit in an attempt to represent, if not all, at least most of the languages, cultures and social conditions of the neighbourhood. The urban area of Moabit takes its name from its first inhabitants, French Huguenots who had escaped from the Catholic pogroms of the seventeenth century. The Huguenots were granted rights in their new home, but their sense of exile never faded. They referred to themselves as Moabiter, inhabitants of the biblical region of Moab, a place of exile for the Jews. More than 300 years later, the neighbourhood is still a place for migrants, but they now come from all over the world. The radio program gives an acoustic image of the neighbourhood through the languages and voices of its current inhabitants and their guests. This chapter will consider the program's relevance not only as a documentary of the linguistic and cultural situation of a contemporary, large, densely populated and multi-multiethnic urban neighbourhood, but also as a work of aesthetic power and cognitive value.

A neighbourhood in Berlin becomes a culture medium for creolisation

The acoustic recording *Die Sprachen Moabits* documents the linguistic world of the neighbourhood of Moabit in Berlin. Fifty languages are represented, some by more than one dialect. They were all recorded in the naturalistic settings of everyday life, which, given the high concentration of cultures in Moabit, is extremely rich and varied. The order in which the language fragments are presented in the program is artificial and is the result of the author's editing, based on aesthetic criteria aimed at condensing, in the limited time available, the linguistic and social diversity of the neighbourhood.

The 200 million people who every year abandon their homes to live more or less temporarily in a foreign country (United Nations 2009) deeply transform not only the cultures from which they come and those with which they come into contact, but also, and especially, the very idea of culture. This phenomenon is of such magnitude that no one is immune: even those peoples who, like the Germans, are most strongly rooted in their land, history and blood community, and have been *de facto* caught up in the accelerated disassembling and reassembling of their social spaces as a result of migration flows. All the while, the debate continues over whether theirs should be called a country of immigration or not.

The floodtide of drifting cultures is moving at such a speed that even the 'process of creolization', as defined by the theoretician of complex cultures Édouard Glissant, cannot pause long enough to recognise itself (Glissant 1996: 11–16). The clash or co-penetration of two or more foreign cultures may be likened to elements forced into a reactive chamber, where neither can annihilate the other. At the same time the hard core of their structures creaks and ruptures under the strain of accommodating heterogeneous elements. Therefore, this fusion of cultures needs time. Such a co-penetration of cultures needs more time than we can afford to give it in the nerve centres of the planet, where the concentration of cultures is at its highest and in a state of accelerated fluidity.

The neighbourhood of Moabit, in Berlin's heart, may represent an example of a 'no-place' (Foucault 2005) in continuous movement. A marginal zone in the centre of the city, the neighbourhood is geographically an island, completely surrounded by waterways, rivers and channels, linked to *terra firma* by 21 bridges. The area was first settled in 1716, when 24 sections of uncultivated and swampy land were distributed to a group of Huguenots (French religious refugees), so that they could establish their homes and grow mulberry trees for breeding silkworms. The name Moabiter Land first appeared in official records in 1738: it was the name the Huguenots gave the land of their exile, after the biblical land of Moab, a place of exile for Jewish refugees.

There followed an accelerated process of industrialisation. In the second half of the nineteenth century, the quiet town of a few houses surrounded by green land was transformed into one of the densest and most emblematic urban conglomerations of the city. In the western part, some of the biggest European factories of the time (such as Royal Porcelain, The Bolle Dairy Company, the machinery factory of the Royal Navy and the factories of arms and weapons) were founded, while in the eastern part, there were huge barracks and prisons. Between 1910 and 1929, Moabit, being a highly populated working-class neighbourhood, was the theatre of bloody social struggles; it gave birth to a strong working-class movement and to the German Socialist Party.

In 1941, the Nazis built in Moabit the first temporary concentration camp of Berlin. From that camp, 35,000 people were sent to the death camps. In the 1960s and 1970s, huge numbers of foreign workers – Turks, in particular, but also Italians, Spaniards, Portuguese and Greeks – were encouraged to go to Berlin. Moabit welcomed a large percentage of them. Today the third generation of those guest workers (*Gastarbeiter*) accounts for 30% of its population. These Germans, with a history of migration (*mit Migrationshintergrund*, as they are defined by a bureaucratic neologism), might be the subjects of a process of creolisation, in Glissant's sense, because they are now the bearers of two foreign cultures, neither capable of overcoming the other.

However, in the last 15 years, the neighbourhood has been invaded by a vibrant mass of foreigners of the most diverse origins. Arabs (Palestinians and Lebanese), Slavs (Russians, Polish, Serbs and Croatians), Asians (Chinese, Korean, Vietnamese and Thai), Central Africans (from Ghana, Cameroun, Congo and Uganda) and Indo-Pakistani make up the largest ethnic groupings. Many others are represented in smaller numbers. Thus, after playing host to the whole gamut of migration, marginalisation, deportation and exile found in Western European history, the neighbourhood of Moabit finds itself on the frontline again, facing a new manifestation of the migrant story, one which is now destroying and redefining the social, legal and psychological bases of the modern State.

To that 30% of old-time foreigners, more or less integrated and known as 'Germans with a migration background', is added a further 35% of recent migrants, whose make-up is continuously growing and changing. These figures, taken from the Berlin-Brandenburg Office of Statistics (Berlin-Brandenburg 2007), do not include illegal immigrants, or those foreigners who are legally entitled to German citizenship because their ancestors abandoned Germany three centuries ago, such as the so-called Sudetenland Germans, many of whom retain no memory of German language or traditions. The arrival of these newcomers, who almost always belong to the socially disadvantaged classes, has prompted the flight of the middle classes, comprising not only the old-timers but also those more recent migrants who have prospered in their chosen land.

Languages in transit

In this sense Moabit is a 'no-place', a transit area, like a railway station or an airport, a place with which people do not identify and which arouses neither a sense of belonging nor of community among its inhabitants. Moabit does not fit comfortably with the image of Berlin constructed by the city for internal use and for tourists. It has no monuments or museums to visit, there are no clubs or venues à la mode to attract young people and, in spite of its central position, it shows all the social and urban traits of a suburb. Individuals seeking short-term accommodation in Berlin and who advertise in the papers or real estate agencies, would specify any central neighbourhood other than Moabit as their preferred location. Maybe it is precisely because it is far away from the spotlight that more and more obsessively highlights the city centre for international events, festivals, parades and large-scale media-intensive exhibitions, that the inhabitants of this neighbourhood can live on a small scale and without the tension that arises from living under scrutiny.

On the streets of Moabit, the German-Turkish pidgin Kanaksprak is also widely spoken as it is now almost a creole, that is, a distinct language with native speakers. This sociolect, or ethnolect to be more precise, is widespread in all the major German cities and has been the object of academic interest for many years. It has already gone through the process of mediatisation (re-elaboration and diffusion through, among other things, the mass media, theatre and books) to return to the streets legitimised, homogenised and enriched (Zaimoglu 1995; Tertilt 1996; Androutsopoulos 2001).

However, more recent than Turkish immigration is that coming from Arab countries, especially Lebanon, Syria, Iraq and Palestine, and North Africa. *Die Sprachen Moabits* documents the birth of a new German-Arabic pidgin, spoken by young and very young Moabitians, as can be heard in the classroom of an Arab school in the segment 'Religion, Alltag, Philosophie'. The young Arabic teacher, who belongs to the generation born or at least raised in Germany, uses a language that combines Arabic and German. The languages alternate in dominance, but on the whole the discourse is equally shared between the two. The children appear to be completely at ease in this linguistic mix and their responses betray neither uncertainty nor confusion. When, for example, the teacher says: 'Mariam hat geboren حيسم آل.عيسئ. Ohne Vater! Ohne يأش?' ('Mariam bore Jesus, the Messiah, without a father. Without what?'), the children immediately respond in unison: 'Ohne Vater!' ('Without a father!'). Neither the German nor the Arabic used in this pidgin are the standard varieties (assuming that such standards exist). The Arabic used is that spoken in the countries of the Fertile Crescent; the German is that spoken by immigrants with little schooling who have been exposed to the Berlin dialect and the German-Turkish pidgin mentioned above. The syntactic structure of this German-Arabic pidgin is not fixed and can be modified to allow the transition from one language to the other. It is a *status nascendi* pidgin which has not yet reached the point where it bestows an identifying charisma on its speakers, as the near-creole spoken by the young Turks does. However, it works perfectly well for the transcultural communication of this generation.

It is not only the language that is in transit. The organisation of the classroom, too, shows all the traits of spontaneous cultural contamination, as inevitably happens in contact zones. At the beginning of the lesson, the teacher adopts the age-old approach of teacher-centred instruction delivered from the front of the class, complete with an emphasis on mnemonics, continual checking and choral confirmation. This is a methodology that leaves little room for the children to develop individual attitudes and stances. Nevertheless, the atmosphere is not exclusively old-school, where authority was maintained through the stick and other terrors. The children are very attentive but also relaxed, as if passionately involved in a game. They show no fear of speaking out, as one child did after hearing the story of Jesus being conceived without a father. The child reacted with astonishment, exclaiming (perhaps influenced in his thinking by biology classes at his German school): 'Aber das ist gar nicht möglich!' ('But this is impossible!').

This teacher-centred instruction is then followed by a segment more in tune with the child-centred style of German classrooms, that is, where the children are encouraged to ask questions, to find answers to their classmates' queries, to make observations and express their own opinions. This time, too, the children participate with seeming unselfconsciousness, and with the spontaneity of those who expect to have the opportunity to express personal opinions, to question the world around them, and to seek explanations in order to better understand. In the final segment of the class, the children abandon themselves happily to the world of Islamic religious formulas and recite the 99 names of Allah with great gusto. This is a world that in a sense is depersonalising, but in another is intensely identifying.

Is there a contradiction between these styles of interaction? Or, to put it better, who perceives these styles as contradictory? According to Maffesoli: 'one of the most resistant and long-lived prejudices of our epoch is without a doubt individualism' (2003: 95). If, on the one hand, Western culture, and German culture in particular, finds its distinction in a uniquely individualist ideology (which goes hand-in-hand with the sovereignty of reason) and considers this to be the gaping chasm that separates Western and non-Western cultures, then the reality of everyday life apparently ignores such a philosophical hiatus. In this evening class, which undoubtedly takes place on the edge of the chasm, nobody feels dizzy. This place of transit between two cultures is experienced without conflict, partly because both the children and the teacher belong to generations that have known nothing else, that have never experienced integration within a 'pure' culture (assuming a culture can ever be pure, since a culture by definition is a historical and synthetic construction of different contributions). Essentially, these young people have never known spiritual union with that community which they imagine to be authentic and homogeneous. They have never experienced that mystical state of belonging to a culture which is in direct contact with its own roots and origins (Anderson 1984). If it is true, as Mary Louise Pratt supposes, commenting on the 'imagined communities' as defined by Anderson (Pratt 1991: 36), that an imagined community is reflected in the way in which people represent to themselves the language and the linguistic community, then in our case linguistic homogeneity is something that children born in migration have never experienced. The language these children use with such confidence is a hybrid language that has not yet lost its fragmentary character, has not yet found its own structure and cannot be considered a new language or even slang: it is still flagrantly heterogeneous.

The official discourse and the perception of people in the street

According to official institutions (Moabit West 2007), one of the neighbourhood's most pressing problems is the difficulty of communication between the different linguistic and ethnic groups, and the sense of alienation this brings. However, this does not correspond with the subjective perception of the inhabitants who blame their dissatisfaction on other causes that are all manifestations of the precariousness of their existence and social marginalisation, for example, issues like youth violence, child abuse, racism, unemployment, the lack of cultural centres, cinemas and meeting points. As can be partially understood by the listeners from the recording, all the people interviewed spoke positively about the diversity of languages and accents that resound in the neighbourhood's streets. They were not worried or disturbed by the fact that they do not understand everything and everybody; rather, they consider this variation a positive aspect of the neighbourhood.

In order to ride the tiger of the population's heterogeneity safely, the official discourse of social and cultural policies put in place by the different administrations of the city-state of Berlin, but also by the federal government, is framed by the concept of 'interculturality'; translated into the languages of the masses, this becomes 'multikulti'. A manifestation of such policy is the radio program appropriately named 'Radio Multikulti', which aired on the state radio station DeutchlandRadio until 2008, broadcasting in 24 languages and trying to cover as many 'multicultural' events as possible. The Karnaval der Kulturen ('The Carnival of Cultures') is yet another product of the same policy: a publicly-funded event held on Whitsundays comprising a carnival parade of floats which each year become more sumptuous, more commercial and more pretentious. The floats are decked out according to the taste or symbolism of each culture and are followed or preceded by representatives of that culture (and their German friends) dressed up in folkloric costumes, executing improbable imitations of popular dances typical of their region (Knecht and Levent 2007).

The city-state of Berlin has other institutions and public places dedicated to ennobling other cultures, such as the Haus der Kulturen der Welt ('The House of the Cultures of the World'), the futuristic former centre for international fairs that perches like an extraterrestrial spaceship in the green heart of the city. Today this place is dedicated to exhibiting the plastic arts, theatre, music, literature and the philosophy of non-European cultures, onto which is thus conferred a dignity comparable to that normally reserved for (European) 'high culture'.

At the neighbourhood level, there are numerous public initiatives intended to promote community life and tolerance between ethnic groups. These are, of course, on a small scale, but they are not so dissimilar to those at the state level. Examples of institutions of this kind are the Quartier Management, Nachbarschftshaus, Jugendzentrum and the like, which organise meetings, provide venues, organisational structures, technical tools, computers, acoustic systems and other equipment and amenities.

In Berlin all that is multicultural is welcome and popular. The broadcasting of *Die Sprachen Moabits* is an example of the type of initiative promoted by public policy through local institutions. The intention behind these policies is certainly laudable. However, according to the German philosopher, Wolfgang Welsch, the conceptual basis underlying them is theoretically obsolete (Welsch 1999). Welsch maintains that the traditional concept of culture, as elaborated by Johan Gottfried Herder at the end of the eighteenth century, is implicit in interculturality and multiculturalism (Herder 1967). Herder regarded cultures as closed spheres, totalitarian and self-referential systems capable only of differentiating between the internal (culture) and the external (non-culture, nature, barbarism). Such a model 'is not only descriptively unserviceable, but also normatively dangerous and untenable. What is called for today is a departure from this concept and to think of cultures beyond the contraposition of ownness and foreignness' (Welsch 1999: 194). In order to understand what happens in today's cities it is necessary, according to Welsch, to keep in mind the concept of transculturality, that is, to accept that cultures are permeable and tend to enrich themselves by appropriating more or less structured fragments of the cultures with which they come into contact:

> Cultures today are in general characterized by hybridization. For every culture, all other cultures have tendentially come to be inner-content or satellites. This applies on the levels of population, merchandise and information. (1999: 201)

Such a development makes it impossible or illusory to think of multi-culturalism as the alignment of cultures foreign to one another:

> Henceforward there is no longer anything absolutely foreign. Everything is within reach. Accordingly, there is no longer anything exclusively 'own' either. Authenticity has become folklore, it is ownness simulated for others – to whom the indigene himself belongs. To be sure, there is still a regional-culture rhetoric, but it is largely simulatory and aesthetic; in substance everything is transculturally determined. (1999: 201)

This normative and a priori discourse is a rap on the knuckles for social policy (which it accuses of being philosophically backward), as well as the protagonists of current social processes (whom it accuses of adhering to a folkloristic fallacy). It makes pronouncements from high up in the echelons of academia, but does not linger long enough to observe and understand the object of its own disquisition and ends up missing it altogether. Indeed, transculturality is not something that one can establish by decree, any more than one can abolish by decree the implicit folklorism in multikulti events, that are now highly valued by the public and have become an integral part of metropolitan life, proliferating spontaneously in every corner of the city. In order to get an idea of the vitality of this formula, one need only glance at the program of activities offered by an openly multikulti association located in one of the most forlorn corners of the city: the outskirts of Moabit. The association is called 'Internationaler Dodoverein e.V., Kunst – und Kulturtreff in Moabit – Art Kunst', also known as Dodo. It owns a tiny house on the banks of one of the two canals that separate the island of Moabit from the rest of Berlin and owes its name to an extinct species of bird indigenous to the island of Mauritius. The dodo bird has long been the object of artistic attention, from literature to painting and plastic arts. Through these representations is kept alive the memory of this clumsy, flightless and defenceless bird that ended its days on the plates of the colonisers. On any given night of the week, the visitor to the (always overcrowded) Dodo might encounter a conference on the Islamic mysticism of the Sufi with dancing and psalm-singing dervishes, a rock band, a concert of classical Indian music, a meeting of the Berlin Mauritians, Mexican dancers trying out their zapateo, African percussionists, a musician playing the Irish harpsichord, a quiz in the Berlin dialect or any number of other activities of the most diverse cultural origins. It was here at the Dodo that some of the languages of Moabit were recorded for the radio program *Die Sprachen Moabits*. It certainly is one of those places where multiculturalism is generated from below, in a playful way and without coercion.

The practice of representing oneself to oneself, as someone belonging to an anchored past and a unique culture, assumes an intensity which is all the more heartbreaking the further hybridisation advances. In this case, the participant observation of Pratt offers epistemological tools that are certainly more finely grained than abstract attempts at theoretical systematisation. In order to describe the self-representations aspiring to authenticity, Pratt talks of 'autoethnographic texts' by which she means:

> a text in which people undertake to describe themselves in ways that engage with representations others have made of them. Thus if ethnographic texts are those in which European metropolitan subjects represent to themselves their others (usually their conquered others), autoethnographic texts are representations that the so-defined others construct in response to or in dialogue with those texts. Autoethnographic texts are not, then, what are usually thought of as autochthonous forms of expression or self-representation (as the Andean quipus were). (1991: 35)

These are texts, literary works in a wider sense, but also drawings (for example, those used by the mixed-blood Inca-Spanish Guaman Poma to represent life in the kingdom of the Incas), and certainly Pratt's description applies also to practices of a diverse textuality, such as theatre, dance, musical compositions and other mixed types of expression. These are the texts that we more often find in the urban cultural life of neighbourhoods where multiethnicity is at its highest density.

The sharing of the sensible

The segment in *Die Sprachen Moabits* entitled 'Fado y muerte' records a scene in which Mexicans celebrate, with reinvented and reinterpreted rites, the Day of the Dead, one of the most important ceremonies in the Mexican religious and civil calendar. The rite takes place in the small and congested premises of a Spanish language association, El Patio – der Innenhof e.V. – and lies somewhere between a theatrical work for a foreign (and non-paying) public and a ceremony for the initiates of a religious shamanic sect, based on beliefs and ideas common to Mesoamerican pre-Hispanic peoples, mainly Mayas and Aztecs. These conceptions of the world and many of the ancient religious beliefs survive today in folklore and in the languages, but also in the recent literary works produced by the various native peoples of Central America. The Day of the Dead celebrated by the Mexican and Guatemalan immigrants in Moabit draws together cultural elements transmitted through the generations via oral traditions, sacred texts preserved on parchments or in the testimonies of the Spanish monks who followed the early colonisers, Western expressive forms (theatre and literature) and media *mise-en-scène*.

The seriousness and solemnity with which the diverse moments of the representation were executed, the use of incense and the music produced with instruments of supposedly pre-Columbian origin (large shells, cane flutes, leather drums), together with the poetic beauty of the recited texts transmitted a desire for authenticity, which was in itself extremely authentic. At the same time, the desire of the performers to display themselves, to let themselves be known and recognised, to feel that they are understood by, and united in fraternity with, their companions in global emigration.

The environment is charged with suggestion and suspense. During a pause in the ceremony, a Northern American guest, perhaps lulled by the dreamlike atmosphere of the recitation and the incense, recounts one of his dreams to a total stranger, unconcerned by the presence of the microphone. This genre of production can be compared to the autoethnographic representations that, as Pratt puts it:

> involve a selective collaboration with and appropriation of idioms of the metropolis or the conqueror. These are merged or infiltrated to varying degrees with indigenous idioms to create self-representa-

> tions intended to intervene in metropolitan modes of understanding. Autoethnographic works are often addressed to both metropolitan audiences and the speaker's own community. (1991: 35)

There is a different feeling to living in common in a city or in a neighbourhood, or generally in an extended community, a feeling that belongs to the non-rationalised common perception. It is what the French philosopher, Jacques Rancière, calls 'the sharing of the sensible' (Rancière 2006), that is, the aesthetic dimension of communal life, that does not necessarily imply either sharing a common system of values, reciprocal comprehension, or even rational communication. Glissant writes:

> For me it is not necessary any longer to understand the other, that is to find a place for him/her in my rational world, in order to live together with him/her or build something together. (1996: 54)

Cultures actually co-exist without the creation of a melting pot; they accept neighbours as strangers and others. The duty of transparency and communication is an artifice of the modern illusion that everything can be reduced to the common denominator of rationality. As Jacques Derrida writes: 'Isn't this the first violence: to force a foreigner to ask for hospitality in the language of the host?' (2000: 46). Do we have to force the foreigner to speak our language, in its widest meaning, before we welcome him/her into our home? True hospitality consists of dismissing the temptation to ask questions:

> Come in, stay in my house, I do not ask you either what your name is, or to take on a responsibility, or where you come from or where you are going. (Derrida 2000: 119–120)

The German government imposed the way of forced integration, asking the (by now) old guest workers (*Gastarbeiter*) to pass a German language test in order to obtain a passport for the country where they had worked all their lives, raised their children and their grandchildren. From the ground, especially where cultural co-existence is denser, a different indication of how to live together is suggested.

A series of imperceptible 'aesthetic changes', as Pierre Ouellet calls them (Ouellet 2003: 170), ends up by radically transforming the perceptive experience we have of ourselves and others, the relationship between individual and community. The Other is no longer a presence that must be faced and conceptually resolved, understood and absorbed or refused. The Other is rather a primary perception:

> The sense of the Other refers to the sensation of co-presence or co-existence, a sensation that is deeper than self-perception and perception of one's own body, whence Kant and Merleau-Ponty get their intuition of personal identity. (Ouellet 2003: 170)

The new 'aesthetic dimension' of living in common is this 'feeling of being' in the middle of perceptible diversity, before the moral imperatives that institute the other as *socius*. In this new dimension, perhaps it is not appropriate anymore to speak of society, as Maffesoli suspects (Maffesoli 2003: 53), and '[t]he uncertainty about one's own identity and the experience of alterity, which results above all from the intercultural character of social life' (Ouellet 2003: 14) are the bases for the development of living together in a way that is more felt than conceptualised.

It is the aesthetic world that above all reveals this new sensitivity. Its task is to let the new *polis* appear on the surface, a *polis* where there is no common property, spiritual or material, as the case may be, to administer, but there is a being-together to invent from scratch, a being-together that is always being-together in the language, or rather in the languages, because languages are no longer autonomous systems.

'I speak and especially write in the presence of all the languages in the world,' writes Glissant. He states: 'This does not mean that I know them all' (1996: 55). Those who speak and write today feel that their language or their languages are in a process of rapid transformation, influenced, enriched, and sometimes threatened by bordering or parallel languages. They speak in reaction to the presence of the other languages, starting a dialogue or fighting with them, or switching from one to another, but they cannot ignore or forget them.

The 50 languages of Moabit collected in *Die Sprachen Moabits* are intertwined, superimposed and entangled. They might detach themselves from the other's clasp, as it were, and for a moment resound in isolation, with their own melodies, characteristic sounds, accents, souls that inhabit them, then they immerse themselves again in the jungle of languages that all seem to throw light upon each other. The recordings were not made in a studio but in real life situations, captured in the streets, at private or public festivals, in the headquarters of the many associations that dot the neighbourhood, in restaurants, bars, places of worship, supermarkets, parks and shops.

The density of languages in Moabit is such that no language can create a vacuum around itself. It is always spoken over a background of noise, an accompaniment that, even if not consciously caught, or the object of consideration, cannot pass completely unnoticed. In Moabit, all larger ethnic groups nurture their languages, teach them to their youngsters, occupy spaces and create situations in which to speak them and encourage groups who can develop their literary and artistic potential, for example, through theatre or music. It is quite evident that everybody puts a great deal of effort into maintaining the prominence of their languages amid the choir of voices, in order to prevent them from being obliterated or overwhelmed by the other languages, whose presence is, however, also a stimulus for this drive and a support. This is what prevents minority languages from having to withstand alone the dominant language of the host and atrophying themselves in the process.

Amidst the neighbourhood's anonymous and colourful throng, special places are created: associations, salons, sports fields, public venues like restaurants, bars or shops, that become meeting points, churches and chapels, 'marked places ... where people inscribe their own presence', as Maffesoli writes (2003: 80–82), 'places which are lived emotionally, spaces of celebration' that mark the territory, drawing for everybody the personal map of their habitat.

These small *haut-lieux* (high places), as the French religious tradition designates the holy places that maintain a relationship with heaven (Maffesoli 2003: 79n), are characterised in Moabit above all by the languages spoken. These are the places that, once again according to Maffesoli, 'allow the explorer of sociality to decode a given symbolic order (crystallization of a space-time) that is already constituted or in gestation' (2003: 82).

Today the high places that delineate the mobile spaces and allow the post-modern urban tribes to wander (in the biblical tradition), are not, at least in Moabit, places of political debate and organisation. They are mostly places of religious or para-religious cults, meeting places with a playful or celebratory character, and all strongly characterised linguistically and ethnically. In those cases where the characterisation is not inherent in the place, such as at the Dodo, it is bestowed by the different groups and communities making use of the space on the day.

In some cases these groups' activities vary between the show and the collective action, that is, their language (musical, literary, figurative, gestural, ritual) has a dual recipient/interlocutor: the external one, the public, and the internal one, the 'us', the community that is representing itself. In other cases the events are 'internal', ceremonies mainly intended to create or maintain community cohesion, to reinforce the identifying symbolism of an ethnic, national or religious group. This is the case, for example, with the annual meeting of the Mauritians in Berlin which takes place at the Dodo. During this meeting, the heterogeneous Mauritian community, who through their clothing, their religions, their skin colours and the iridescent facets of their creole language exhibit vestiges of the many cultures and ethnicities that formed them, curiously celebrate the unity of their own dislocated existence.

This is also the case in the small Portuguese restaurant where it is mostly the regular customers who linger after midnight. This is when the owner, after a hard day's work in the kitchen, at the counter, and at the tables, dons her black lace hat-veil and, in the dim candlelight, transforms herself into a 'fadist' fatale. She sings accompanied by the guitar and vocals of an equally nostalgic fellow countryman. They abandon themselves to their homemade versions of the most renowned *fado* songs, while the Portuguese regulars join in with heavy hearts as they end yet another evening in their migrant story, clustered around the few tables, to the astonishment of any 'outsider' customers, who start to feel out of place.

The so-called 'Henna Parties' in the Turkish community are another example. These are celebrations that take place on the eve of every important occasion in an individual's life, such as circumcision and marriage, and it is the women who are responsible for organising them. In Moabit they take place in the premises of small associations and are almost invariably private events, since they concern only one or two families along with their intimate friends and neighbours. Nonetheless, a good number of people are gathered. The ceremony of the distribution of henna to women, who use it to colour the palms of their hands, and the picturesque *mise-en-scène* of the breaking with their previous life, all the colours' symbolism, the white roses, the red flowers, the veils and the dances, all of this is exclusively for 'internal' perusal, as it were, a re-immersion in the original community, 'doing it as it has always been done' without asking questions, in the reassuring cycle of tradition. However, the reality is not quite like this: the family, the small community might be located anywhere in a foreign metropolis and no action can be without conscious thought. It is the result of a decision; a choice that has become compulsory because it is possible. The choice in favour of tradition is thus free and deliberate. This adds a wealth of meaning to the ceremony.

In the segment 'Fado y muerte' (Fado and Death), the climax to one of the henna ceremonies can be heard. It is the future bride's farewell to her mother and sisters, a farewell that is expressed by a third party. A friend sings of the pain of separation, while both mother and daughter weep and the other women perform the dances and steps of the ritual, following the prescribed order. The betrothed, covered by a veil, are sitting in the middle of the room and everything revolves in a circle around them. All of a sudden something happens that is neither expected nor allowed in the original protocol: the room is raided by the bridegroom's brothers and friends who join in the ceremony by circling, together with the women, around the veiled couple. Is it impertinence, a provocation? It should be considered as such, but here they are immigrants, in the big city, a place where gender separation is not even contemplated, so the women accept the intrusion, amused and smiling at this innovation.

Conclusion

The high places of the amorphous city are points charged with a strong symbolic power; places that allow communities to reunite in ecstatic moments, to leave behind the grey, everyday life of the urban individual, stopping time with an ecstasy that transforms it into a small eternity. The bond between the group members becomes tangible, real, as in the ancient natural tribes. Maffesoli (2003) talks about urban tribes, but these ecstatic moments of self-representation cannot keep at bay the signs and influences of the surrounding cultural space and constitute extremely complex conglomerations of meaning. Everyday life is, in a sense, designed by the geography of the high places and derives its sense and form from them. However, both sense and form are fluctuating, mobile, comprised of the disparate journeys of the individuals who migrate from one language to the other, from one community to the other.

Post-modern art shows a particular interest in everyday life. However, in representation, which is mimetic, the mover is subjective: it is a matter of reproducing an internal image of the Other, an image that was first created in the artist's mind. Everyday life 'omnipresent and elusive, without either a beginning or an end, escapes every attempt that tries either to catch it or theorize it' (Huglo 2007). The changing and polymorphic nature of the background noise of our lives appears in an elementary way in the voices of the Moabiters, in the languages that overlap like waves on the shore. Maffesoli writes:

> life that flows in our roads, markets, what structures that life without quality and, so far, too often considered as 'insignificant' is where we can catch a glimpse of the most indicative signals of the 'contemporary being-together'. (2003: 65)

The fragmentation of social life into infinite groupings, each of them centred on a language, a jargon, a dialect, a meeting place, marks the perhaps irreversible demise of the twentieth-century social Utopia. At the same time, it creates a new constellation, 'a concatenation of marginality, where none of them is more important than the others' (Maffesoli 2003: 53), that could result in a grass-roots and organic restructuring of being-together.

All English translations in the text are by the authors.

References

Androutsopoulos, J. K. (2001). *From the Streets to the Screens and Back Again. On the Mediated Diffusion of Ethnolectal Patterns in Contemporary German.* Essen: LAUD.

Anderson, B. (1984). *Imagined Communities: Reflection on the Origins and Spread of Nationalism.* London: Verso.

Berlin-Brandenburg, Amt für Statistik. (2007). Statistik 2007. http://www.statistik-berlin-brandenburg.de/ [online, accessed 17 November 2007]

Derrida, J. (2000). *Sull'ospitalità.* Milano: Baldini & Castoldi.

Foucault, M. (2005) (1994 1st ed.). *Eterotopia. Luoghi e non luoghi metropolitani.* Sesto San Giovanni (MI): Mimesis Edizioni.

Glissant, E. (1996). *Introduction à une poétique du divers.* Paris: Gallimard.

Herder, J. G. (1967). *Auch eine Philosophie der Geschichte zur Bildung der Menschheit.* Frankfurt: Suhrkamp.

Huglo, M.-P. (2007). Présentation à *Raconter le quotidien aujourd'hui. Temps zéro. Revue d'étude des écritures contemporaines* 1,1. http://tempszero.contemporain.info/document71 [online, accessed 20 November 2009]

Knecht, M. & Levent S. (2007). *Plausible Vielfalt. Wie der Karneval der Kulturen denkt, lernt und Kultur macht.* Berlin: Panama-Verlag.

Maffesoli, M. (2003). *Notes sur la postmodernité.* Paris: Editions du Félin.

Manai, B. E. (2007). *Die Sprachen Moabits*, Radio Program. Offener Kanal: Berlin. Available at http://www.arteleggenda.de/moabit/index.htm.

Moabit West, Q. (2007). Das Geiet Moabit West. http://www.moabitwest.de/Das-Gebiet-Moabit-West-Charakteristik-Besonderheiten-Probleme.162.0.html [online, accessed 20 November 2007]

Ouellet, P. (2003). *L'esprit migrateur. Essai sur le non-sens commun.* Montréal: Trait d'Union.

Pratt, M. L. (1991). Arts of the Contact Zone. *Profession* 91: 33–40.

Rancière, J. (2006). *The Politics of Aesthetics: The Distribution of the Sensible.* London: Continuum International Publishing Group.

Tertilt, H. (1996). *Turkish Power Boys. Ethnographie einer Jugendbande.* Frankfurt: Suhrkamp.

United Nations Human Development Report (2009). *Overcoming Barriers: Human Mobility and Development.* http://hdr.undp.org/en/media/HDR_2009_EN_Complete.pdf, p.2 [online, accessed 13 August 2010]

Welsch, W. (1999). Transculturality – The Puzzling Form of Cultures Today. In F. Mike & S. Lash (eds). *Spaces of Culture: City, Nation, World.* London: Sage, 194–213.

Zaimoglu, F. (1995). *Kanak Sprak. 24 Misstöne vom Rande der Gesellschaft.* Hamburg: Rotbuch Verlag.

Notes on the Contributors

Michelle Barrett is a PhD candidate at Curtin University. Her thesis examines the lived experience of people who identify as 'Eurasian' in Australia. Having lived in Malaysia, Brunei and England as a child, and having a Scottish father and a Sri Lankan Burgher mother who identifies as Eurasian, she is interested in the complexities of self-identification and understandings about 'race' and ethnicity. Her research is informed by hybridity theory, border studies and critical whiteness studies. She has also worked as a research associate on a number of research projects and is currently coordinating a first year unit in Social Sciences at Curtin University.

Andreas Boldt, originally from Germany, has recently finished his PhD in History at the National University of Ireland, Maynooth. His research interests lie in historiography, environmental history and European history. He currently lectures in German and History in Maynooth. Among his publications is the volume *The role of Ireland in the Life of Leopold von Ranke (1795–1886): The historian and historical truth* (2007).

Eric Bouvet is a Senior Lecturer in French and currently Head of the Department of Language Studies at Flinders University (Australia). His main research interests lie in Applied Linguistics (reading in a foreign language) and in migration studies with a focus on the French in Australia. Eric is currently researching the specificities of post-World War II French migration to Australia, an area in which he has published several articles. He is the co-editor of the academic ejournal *FULGOR* (Flinders University Languages Group Online Review).

Wayde Brown is an Associate Professor in the College of Environment and Design, University of Georgia (USA), and a member of the Royal Architectural Institute of Canada. He holds degrees in architecture (Dalhousie University, Canada) and architectural conservation (University of York, UK). He is currently completing work on a PhD dissertation at the Welsh School of Architecture, Cardiff. His research focus is the history of the heritage conservation movement in North America, especially the role of 'historic re-constructions'. He is the author of several articles.

Sonia Floriani is Assistant Professor at the University of Calabria (Italy), where she teaches 'Sociology of Culture' and 'Comparative Cultures'. She is a member of the Doctoral School *A.G. Frank* in 'Knowledge and Innovations for Development' and has carried out research in the United States, Canada and Great Britain. Her present interests of study are in the sociology of migration and sociology of literature. Her publications on the topics of this volume include: *Incontri fra le righe. Letterature e scienze sociali* (2010, edited with R. Siebert); *Identità di Frontiera. Migrazione, biografie, vita quotidiana* (2004) and *Appartenenza, multiculturalismo e globalizzazione* (2003, edited with C. De Rose).

Diana Glenn is Associate Professor in Italian and Deputy Dean of the School of Humanities at Flinders University (Australia). Her principal research interest is in Dante Studies and she is the author of *Dante's Reforming Mission and Women in the Comedy* (2008), and co-editor of *Dante Colloquia in Australia 1982–1999* (2000) and *Flinders Dante Conferences 2002 & 2004* (2005). She is currently completing an oral history project on cultural dislocation in connection with Italian migration to Australia, and has published various articles connected to this project.

Maria Holt is a Senior Lecturer in the Department of Politics and International Relations at the University of Westminster (UK). She has carried out considerable research on Muslim women and violent conflict in the Middle East and has published a book and several chapters on this topic. Her work includes research into the lives of Palestinian refugees in Lebanon and an oral history project on the final years of

British colonial rule in Aden. She is currently working on a project about women and Islamic resistance in the Arab world.

Keith Jacobs has published widely on housing and urban policy issues and is the author of *Dynamics of Local Housing Policy* (1999) and co-editor, with Jim Kemeny and Tony Manzi, of *Social Constructionism in Housing Research* (2004). Since moving to Australia in 2002, he has established the Housing and Community Research Unit at the University of Tasmania. He is currently an Associate Professor in the School of Sociology and Social Work and the Associate Dean in the Faculty of Arts with responsibility for research. He has recently published *Experience and Representation: Contemporary Perspectives on Migration in Australia* (Ashgate Press, 2011) and co-edited, with Jeff Malpas, *Between the Outback and the Sea: Cosmopolitanism and Anti Cosmopolitanism in Contemporary Australia* (UWA Press, forthcoming).

Sukhmani Khorana is a Research Fellow in the Centre for Critical and Cultural Studies at the University of Queensland. Her current research project examines the discourses of India's television news media. Sukhmani recently completed a critical-creative PhD in diasporic cinema at the University of Adelaide. The documentary component of her doctoral project, titled 'I Journey Like a Paisley' can be viewed online at: http://vimeo.com/9520203. Sukhmani's work has appeared in high-ranked media and film journals, and she also writes for community and independent online publications.

Bruna Emanuela Manai was born in Oristano, Italy, and studied philosophy at the University of Pisa. She taught at the Department of Philosophy at the National Autonomous University of Honduras in Tegucigalpa, the Institutes of Romance Languages at the Universities of Greifswald and Dresden in Germany and also at the Technical University of Brandenburg in Cottbus. She now works as an artist in Berlin.

Franco Manai studied at the University of Pisa and Brown University in Providence (R. I.) and has taught Italian language and culture in the USA at various colleges such as Vassar, Wellesley and Smith. He joined the Department of Italian at the University of Auckland in 1993. He has published *Capuana e la letteratura campagnola*, which examines the contribution of Luigi Capuana to the representation of rural life in Italian fiction till the 1920s, and *Cosa succede a Fraus? Sardegna e mondo nel racconto di Giulio Angioni*, a study of the fiction of contemporary anthropologist, Giulio Angioni. In addition, he has published on Pietro Bembo, Niccolò Machiavelli, Carlo Goldoni, as well as on modern and contemporary Italian and New Zealand writers such as Carlo Levi, Witi Ihimaera and Hone Tuwhare.

Colette Mrowa-Hopkins holds a PhD from the University of Adelaide (Australia). She is a Senior Lecturer in French and Coordinator of the Applied Linguistics major in the Department of Language Studies at Flinders University (Australia). Her current research interests include cross-cultural pragmatics and emotion communication, and its implications for language learning and teaching. She is the co-editor with Jean Fornasiero of a volume of selected essays from the inaugural conference of the Federation of Associations of Teachers of French in Australia, entitled *Explorations and Encounters in French* (2010).

Venus Tsang received her BA and MA from the University of Hong Kong. She subsequently obtained her MSc from the London School of Economics and is currently a doctoral student at the University of Oxford. Her dissertation considers the representation of transgenerational transmission of memory in ethnic American literature, with a particular focus on the literary works of Maxine Hong Kingston, Toni Morrison and Leslie Silko. Her research interests include cultural theories, women's writing and life writing.

Editors' Note

The concept for this interdisciplinary volume arose from a vibrant international conference held at Flinders University, 3–6 December 2007, entitled *Moving Cultures, Shifting Identities: Migration, Connection, Heritage and Cultural Memory.*

Acknowledgements

The Editors are grateful to the Faculty of Education, Humanities and Law at Flinders University and the Flinders Institute for Research in the Humanities for publication grants towards the production of this volume, and extend special thanks to Richard Maltby, Graham Tulloch and Robert Phiddian.

Lyn Leader-Elliott provided precious help and inspiration, while Rebecca Vaughan contributed enormously with timely and valuable editorial support and advice.

We wish to express our sincerest thanks to the anonymous referees who generously gave of their time and expertise to read and evaluate the authorial submissions.

Our warm thanks to Michael Bollen at Wakefield Press for helping us to realise our project. A special debt of gratitude is owed to Michael Deves for his expert advice, unfailing patience and invaluable assistance during the preparation of this volume.

Wakefield Press is an independent publishing and
distribution company based in Adelaide, South Australia.
We love good stories and publish beautiful books.
To see our full range of titles, please visit our website at
www.wakefieldpress.com.au.